THE LAWYER
AND HIS COMMUNITY

THE PRACTICING BAR
IN A
MIDDLE-SIZED CITY

THE LAWYER
AND HIS COMMUNITY

THE PRACTICING BAR
IN A
MIDDLE-SIZED CITY

Joel F. Handler

THE UNIVERSITY OF WISCONSIN PRESS

Madison, Milwaukee, and London, 1967

Published by the University of Wisconsin Press
Madison, Milwaukee, and London

U.S.A.: Box 1379, Madison, Wisconsin 53701
U.K.: 26–28 Hallam Street, London, W.1

Printed in the United States of America by
The Colonial Press Inc., Clinton, Massachusetts

Library of Congress Catalog Card Number 67–20759

to Audrey

Acknowledgments

A person who engages in interdisciplinary studies runs up more than the usual number of debts; this study is no exception. Dr. Jerome E. Carlin first interested me in the idea of comparing the results of his research on big city lawyers with a study of the bar in the smaller community, and his assistance extended throughout the study. He helped me with methodology, organization, and conceptualization, gave sympathetic encouragement, and read the entire manuscript. I owe him a great debt.

During the period of gathering data, Dr. George A. Pownall, of the Department of Sociology, University of Maryland, was of great help in constructing the final questionnaire, in arranging for the interviews, and in conducting several of them. He helped process the data to make it intelligible to a law professor and was both patient and persistent during this phase of the work.

Two of my colleagues at the University of Wisconsin, Lawrence M. Friedman of the Law School and Robert R. Alford of the Department of Sociology, spent countless hours on successive drafts of the manuscript. Their criticisms were rigorous (if not ruthless), invariably constructive, and represented the highest traditions of colleagueship. They have made unique contributions to this study. It is difficult for me to express adequately my gratitude to them.

I also wish to thank other colleagues and friends who read the manuscript and offered constructive criticism: J. Willard Hurst of the Wisconsin Law School, Jack Ladinsky of the Wisconsin Department of Sociology, Herbert Jacob of the Wisconsin Department of Political Science, J. Rogers Hollingsworth of the Wisconsin Department of History, Geoffrey Hazard of the Chicago Law School and the American Bar Foundation, and Rita James Simon of the University of Illinois

Department of Sociology. Gilbert Steiner of the Brookings Institution gave assistance during the formative period of the study. My colleagues at the Wisconsin Law School, Ted Finman and Stewart Macaulay, helped me solve particular problems.

The study was financed primarily by a grant from the Walter E. Meyer Research Institute of Law, Inc. The foundation was generous in its support and very sympathetic to the inevitable delays. I particularly want to thank Ralph Brown, Jr., of the Yale Law School, Director of the Institute during most of the period of my research. The very early stages of the study were financed by the University Research Board of the University of Illinois.

The data for the study are primarily interviews of lawyers in a middle-sized city in the Midwest. With very few exceptions, these lawyers were cooperative, generous of their time, and genuinely interested in the study. I gratefully acknowledge the information they gave me and their willingness to let me interrupt their busy schedules.

Those who have been fortunate enough to have spent some time at the University of Wisconsin know of the intellectual excitement and the emphasis on interdisciplinary exchange at that institution. I would be remiss, therefore, in not acknowledging my debt to the Sociology and Law Program financed and nurtured by the Russell Sage Foundation, which has fostered, between the Law School and the Departments of Sociology and Political Science, a true community of scholars; this environment has been of great value to me in this work and otherwise.

My appreciation also goes to Nancy Williamson, who typed successive drafts and caught several errors in style and statistical tabulations, and to Leah Friedman, who devoted many hours to checking and editing the final draft, including the statistics. Mary Grossman prepared the Index.

JOEL F. HANDLER

Madison, Wisconsin
March, 1967

Contents

Tables

THE LAWYER
AND HIS COMMUNITY

THE PRACTICING BAR
IN A
MIDDLE-SIZED CITY

Chapter 1

INTRODUCTION

Professions have been called "communities within communities." [1] Members of a profession share a common training, they have a sense of identity, and they tend to define roles, values, and interests similarly. Professions have codes of ethics and private trade languages. The solidarity and homogeneity of the professional community separate it from the larger society. But the concept of a profession refers to a job —a function—and the job of the professional binds him functionally to his society. The profession must adapt to economic and social changes or lose its claim to distinctiveness and its right to exclusive use of its skill. The legal profession has these problems of adaptation just as any other profession does. Indeed, the literature on the legal profession is largely concerned with conflict between traditional professional values and societal pressures. Perhaps these conflicts always existed. Yet some scholars believe that they have become more intense in recent generations. "The profession's golden age of public leadership," in the words of J. Willard Hurst, was "the years from 1765 to 1830"; the bar was then characterized by "qualities of independence of judgment, and pride in the responsibility and dignity of legal counseling and the shaping of social institutions. . . . [The men of that age] had neither the over-belligerent nor the anxiety-tinged dogmatism of men who feel themselves only the agents of a situation to whose fortunes their own are committed." [2] Many studies dwell on the change in the profession since the "golden age" of professional pride and responsibility. Stressing social change and its impact on the profession—how the real or mythological elements of the legal profession have been altered—these studies have pointed to the decline of the generalist (the individual practitioner), the rise of giant law firms, the increase in specialization, the struggle of the organized bar to protect lawyers from lay competition, and the

3

failure of the profession to maintain high ethical standards in modern society.[3]

The image of the early lawyer and the foil for the portrait of the mid-twentieth-century lawyer is the general practitioner. He practiced alone, or with a single partner, or perhaps with a younger man "reading law," and was a litigating lawyer. In his office he prepared deeds and mortgages, drafted contracts and notes; but his practice centered upon courtroom work. His fame depended upon public participation in litigation. He served his established clients but remained aloof and exercised independent judgment on the justice of the claim of prospective clients. He was a leader in social and political affairs. The model is Abraham Lincoln.

But great changes in the urban practice of law began to take place by the 1870's. In the late nineteenth century the large law firm developed. Leading members of the bar were no longer courtroom advocates; they became advisers and counselors to great business and financial interests. Several studies claimed that leading lawyers traded their concern for public affairs for nonpartisan business security. The generalist gave way to the specialist. While small firm lawyers and individual practitioners handled personal injury, small real estate transactions, criminal and family law, the large firm lawyers captured the significant business practice, and the bar split along economic and social lines. Lawyers at the top were recruited from older, well-to-do American families and attended prestigious colleges and law schools. Those at the bottom had less privileged backgrounds; immigrants or sons of immigrants, many had little or no college training and had been graduated from night law schools.

"History had no record of the minds and hearts of the hundreds of thousands of men who practiced law in the United States; we must not forget this in generalizing about attitudes of 'the bar,' "[4] cautions J. Willard Hurst. History also has no record on other questions concerning the hundreds of thousands: their daily tasks, divisions of labor, economic organization, professional integration and responsibility. Biographies of famous lawyers and large law firms provide most of the accessible information on nineteenth-century lawyers; information on the mass of lawyers below the heights comes from scattered sources and inferences. This remains largely true today. But recently, rigorous empirical studies have begun to appear. These studies have confirmed the standard portrait of the bar in major metropolitan centers.[5] Elite lawyers are still drawn from the privileged classes and trained in the best universities and law schools; they become counselors to the great corporations. Those at the bottom—small firm lawyers and individual practitioners—come from a different world and toil in a different world: a world of small claims, collections, divorce, crime, and personal injury. In the lower reaches of the bar, anxieties, tensions, and corrupting pressures are prevalent. Patterns in the middle-sized firms are mixed. Most big city lawyers are specialists. Large firm lawyers work in teams on the problems of their corporate clients; small firm lawyers and individual practitioners specialize by areas of practice. The big city bar has split into groups with little contact with each other; and differences in class background, training, clients, economic organization, and style of practice all serve to raise near impenetrable barriers between the groups.

In the 1960's, according to these studies, a unified legal profession in the major metropolitan centers existed in name only. Type and quality of training varied widely; definitions of role and values conflicted; and a sense of identity had given way to jealousies and antagonisms. Patterns of ethical behavior applied within, but not between, strata. Separate bar associations served the small firm lawyer and the individual practitioner. In short, the bar was highly stratified.

Information on the American legal profession, in the main, has come from the big city bars; scientific study of the bar has been almost wholly confined to big-city practice. This study, however, deals with practicing lawyers in a middle-sized community in the Midwest. It concerns itself with many of the same questions asked by the urban studies: the type of legal services performed by lawyers, the division of labor, the economic position of lawyers, the organization of lawyers, the professional and ethical problems of the bar, and the role played by lawyers, both as a group and individually, in the civic life of the community. What has happened to the profession outside of the major metropolitan centers? To what extent do lawyers in the smaller communities resemble their colleagues in larger cities? Answers to these questions for a middle-sized bar may in turn shed light on the bar as a whole and perhaps even on the theory of the professions.

METHODOLOGY

The study is based primarily on information obtained from interviews of lawyers in private practice in a middle-sized Midwestern city, which we shall call Prairie City, during the first three months of 1964. The term "private practice" is used to refer to the practice of those members of the legal profession who earn their living as independent practitioners or who are employed by independent practitioners. Included are practicing lawyers who may from time to time represent a government body as a client (e.g., a part-time township attorney) along with their other clients, and, of course, lawyers who represent corporations as clients;[6] but judges, prosecutors, and other full-time salaried lawyers employed by the government or by corporations are excluded, as well as lawyers who have retired or for whom the practice of law provided less than 25 per cent of their income. As near as can be determined, ninety-one lawyers were engaged in the private practice of law in this community at the time that the interviews were conducted.[7] Interviews were obtained with eighty-three of these lawyers.

We have used the same basic interview schedule that was employed in a study of the New York City bar conducted by Dr. Jerome E. Carlin,[8] although changes were made in those parts of the New York schedule which were inadequate or inappropriate. We have also used, where appropriate, Dr. Carlin's mode of analysis. This study, then, is both a replication and comparative study.

PRAIRIE CITY

Prairie City is located in the central part of the state. At the time of this study, it had a city population of about 80,000 and a metropolitan area population of about 120,000. Approximately fifty miles to the east of Prairie City and forty miles to the west were cities of comparable size.

More than a third of the population of the state lived in one major metropolitan city. In states with one or two major metropolitan areas, lawyers make a conscious choice whether to practice in the large urban center or in the "country." There are, to be sure, gradations of "country" practice; the practice in Prairie City will not be the same as practice in the small farming towns. But the sharpest difference in community and work life is between the large urban center and the rest of the state. Some lawyers may perhaps try to achieve what they consider the best of both possible worlds by locating in a satellite city in the state's big metropolitan area, but most lawyers in the state (including the Prairie City lawyers) had to choose one or the other. In subsequent chapters we will try to learn why the lawyers studied selected Prairie City and whether their expectations were realized. Here we are concerned with what they selected.

ECONOMIC DEVELOPMENT[9]

In 1829 Prairie City was platted and designated the county seat. The arrival of the railroads in 1854 linked the city with the major Midwestern water systems. Stimulated by the Civil War industrial boom, Prairie City developed several large farm equipment companies; wagon, carriage, and buggy manufacture; iron and nonferrous metal establishments; lumber, furniture, and planing mill industries; breweries; oil refineries; cigar factories; woolen mills; box factories; and harness factories. In 1874 coal mines were opened nearby. By the end of the century metal working had been expanded, and, in addition, ladies' garments, plumbing parts, machine parts, the first automotive parts, and household appliances were manufactured locally.

Between 1900 and 1929 Prairie City continued to prosper and expand. A large locomotive repair shop was established, and grain processing became a major industry. The development of automobile traffic greatly enlarged the retail trade and commercial base of the city. During this period, an association of commerce was formed, and a city planning commission began attempts to control the physical growth of the city.

The local economy was severely hurt by the Depression. Prosperity and population growth resumed only during the war years, when several local industries adapted to war production and expanded, and new war industries located in Prairie City, including an important military depot and a munitions factory. After the war, the city prospered along with the rest of the nation. The war industries were converted to consumer production, and the city acquired the manufacture of specialized automobile hardware, air conditioning equipment, and heavy construction equipment. By 1950 more than two-thirds of the county population lived in the city, and more than three-quarters worked there. The city was the main retail center serving a population of 277,000 within a radius of seventy miles.

At the time of the study, the city had a diversified commercial and industrial economy. Wholesale and retail trade employed 20 per cent of the working population and were a major source of wealth. Almost 30 per cent of the working population was employed in manufacturing, both durable and nondurable. Products produced in Prairie City included construction equipment, machine parts, plumbing, electronics, glass, iron, brass, chemicals and pharmaceuticals, meat, grain, plastics, and garments. Over thirty firms served international markets, and many more served nationwide markets. No single industry dominated the manufacturing sector of the economy; the largest industry—food and kindred products—employed 31 per cent of the manufacturing workers. The other larger industries were machinery, except electrical (22 per cent of the manufacturing workers), metal industrials (18 per cent), transportation equipment (8 per cent), and printing, publishing, and allied industries (6 per cent).[10] Only four companies employed more than 1,000 workers, accounting for about 10 per cent of a working population of over 44,000.[11] A grain processing plant was the largest employer in the community, with over 3,000 employees.[12]

POPULATION AND SOCIAL CHARACTERISTICS

Before the advent of the railroads, most residents of the Prairie City area came from the border states; much smaller numbers came from New England and the Deep South. After 1870 a foreign-born population developed, the largest groups coming from Germany, Ireland, and Great Britain, in that order. The British, and to a lesser extent, the Irish, were easily assimilated. Although the Germans established themselves quickly in the local economy, for several decades they maintained their social and cultural distinctiveness through a German language newspaper and through clubs, societies, and associations. The newspaper and most of these ethnic organizations have since disappeared.

The highest absolute number of foreign stock[13] was reached in 1920 even though the proportion of foreign stock had declined steadily from its high in 1870. Heavy immigration of native Americans from surrounding rural areas and the border states perhaps served to reduce immigration from eastern and southern Europe. In 1960 only 5 per cent of the population were children of foreign or mixed parentage.[14]

The lack of significant recent immigration from Europe and the relative homogeneity of the community was reflected in the church membership. Less than 1 per cent of the population was Jewish, and less than 20 per cent was Roman Catholic.[15] Most of the Catholics, moreover, were of either German or Irish origin and had been in the city for at least two generations. The Greek Orthodox church had about five hundred members. The nonwhite population (basically Negro) was the only segment of the community that could be accurately described as a minority, constituting slightly more than 5 per cent of the city population.

Despite ethnic homogeneity, a city of this size and economic diversity may produce a rather complex system of social stratification. A study of Prairie City, based on data up to 1950, explored class distinctions.[16] Although a core of old families existed, the local "aristocracy" was not clearly separated from the newer business class. Through the years the core group of older landed, industrial, and commercial families added new members. The solidarity of the business class was strengthened by their concentration in one section of town. The sharpest differences in the social structure were between the business class and the rest of the community; below this line, gradations were gentle. Differences in house type, organized social life, and voting behavior existed in the working and middle classes, but these differences were "matters of degree and do not indicate gaps as deep as those which mark off the business class." Many members of the middle class belonged to unions and were thus affiliated with semiskilled and unskilled workers. Since these members of the middle class were wage earners, they had different social contacts and orientations from the small businessmen, white collar workers, and minor professionals. The study argued that this employer-employee division in the middle class tended to blur distinctions between the middle and lower classes.

POLITICAL BEHAVIOR

The election of 1928 was the last time that the Republican Party completely dominated the city. The development of a fairly evenly divided two-party system has been a continuous trend since that time. In 1932 there was a general shift to the Democratic Party, and in 1936 the Democrats overwhelmed the city much as the Republicans had done in 1928. Thereafter, the Republicans continued to gain in strength until there was a fairly even division.

At the time of this study, the city manager, a man of administrative ability, imagination, and political skill, was the dominant political force in the community. The local Association of Commerce had been important politically but by the 1950's had declined in influence. The business organization that had taken over part of the functions of the Association was the Downtown Council, a body composed primarily of those who had a significant economic stake in the downtown area— retailers, property owners, and service (insurance, banks, realtors).[17]

Businessmen in the largest businesses were not very active or influential in local political issues.[18] Banfield and Wilson point out that the businessmen who are most active in civic affairs are those with significant economic stakes in the affairs of local government.[19] (In Prairie City, this group was represented in the Downtown Council.) Since the plants of big business, with national or international markets, are usually located on the outskirts of the city, officials of these companies are primarily interested in maintaining good public relations. Downtown parking, intown transportation, and the economics of the central business district are not their major concerns. The social and economic elite discharge their public responsibilities through civic affairs that are politically neutral—as trustees of colleges, hospitals, and museums, officers of charities, and members of consultative or advisory boards. All cities, of course, do not fit this picture, but apparently Prairie City does.[20]

Thus, in the 1960's Prairie City was well diversified. There were several major industrial organizations, but small and medium-sized establishments predominated. Wholesale and retail trade were an important source of wealth. Class lines, at least below the business class, were blurred. For a long time the Association of Commerce had cooperated with the labor unions, and in the 1960's labor people secured appointments to the Planning Commission and other public agencies. No single religious group dominated the community. The city had enjoyed competitive two-party politics for many years.[21]

Part I

The Social Structure

CHAPTER 2

A PROFILE OF THE PRAIRIE CITY BAR

The distinctive characteristic of the Prairie City bar was its homogeneity. This chapter describes the general features of the bar and compares these features with the New York City bar. Chapter 3 examines the differences among the Prairie City lawyers.

JOB DISTRIBUTION

There were approximately 118 employed lawyers in Prairie City. Of this number, four were judges, seven worked for some agency of government, sixteen were employed by corporations, and ninety-one were in the private practice of law.

As one might suspect, there were no large firms in Prairie City, at least as that term is applied in the major metropolitan centers.[1] In fact, judged by those standards, it might be argued that there were not even any middle-sized firms. In Prairie City there were only three firms with more than five lawyers (eight, six, and six respectively). There were eighteen firms with five or fewer lawyers; twenty-four lawyers were individual practitioners; and there were only five associates (*i.e.,* lawyers who were full-time employees of private practitioners).[2] Most of the private practitioners in Prairie City practiced either alone or in two- and three-man firms; the distribution of the ninety-one lawyers, including the eight who were not interviewed, by size of firm was as follows:

Size of firm by number of lawyers	Percentage of lawyers in each firm size
1	26
2	15
3	19
4	13
5	5
6	13
7	0
8	9

Prairie City appeared to have a disproportionately small number of individual practitioners and a disproportionately large number of firm lawyers. In both the United States as a whole and in cities of between 50,000 and 200,000, the proportion of individual practitioners was about 44 per cent of all lawyers; the proportion of firm lawyers (both partners and associates) was about 34 per cent. In Prairie City, only 19 per cent of all the lawyers were individual practitioners and 58 per cent were firm lawyers.[3] It will be pointed out in Chapter 3, however, that the distribution of Prairie City lawyers by size of firm was not very significant since all of the lawyers studied were essentially general practitioners. Although there were differences among the lawyers, on the whole, these differences were not related to firm size.

THE LAWYERS' CLIENTS

Practically all of the lawyers in Prairie City did at least some work for business clients, and 57 per cent reported that half or more of their income was derived from work on business matters. Although the business clients presented a very wide spectrum of enterprises, ranging from the smallest retail stores to utilities, the principal businesses were retail trade, manufacturing, real estate, banking, and insurance, in that order. Publicly held corporations constituted half or more of the business clients for only about five lawyers (6 per cent of the bar). Less than 15 per cent worked mainly for businesses with gross incomes of $1,000,000 or more per year. For almost half of the bar (45 per cent) "business clients" meant small retail and service enterprises with gross incomes under $50,000.

Lawyers in Prairie City tended to draw their individual clients from the upper and middle income groups of the population. Forty-five per cent of the lawyers estimated that the median incomes of their individual clients was $10,000 or more per year, which meant that these lawyers dealt with families and individuals whose incomes were in the top 15 per cent of the Prairie City population. Twenty-one per cent of the lawyers estimated the median income of their individual clients to be over $20,000 per year, which was the top 4 per cent of the population. In spite of the fact that 42 per cent of the population earned less than $5,000, less than 10 per cent of the lawyers had individual clients with median incomes of that amount.

On the other hand, practically all of the lawyers did have some individual clients in every income bracket. For 87 per cent of the lawyers, 10 per cent of their individual clients earned less than $5,000 per year, and for almost 90 per cent, at least the same number of clients earned more than $20,000 per year. No lawyer served only "poor" clients (families and individuals earning less than $5,000 per year).

There was very little specialization along ethnic or religious lines. Less than 10 per cent of the bar could identify a particular ethnic or religious group as comprising a sizeable proportion of their clients. Over 80 per cent of the bar had Negro clients. Sixty-five per cent said that the proportion of their Negro clients ranged up to 7 per cent; four lawyers (5 per cent) reported that 13 per cent, or more, of their clients were Negro.

AREAS OF PRACTICE AND SPECIALIZATION

In order of importance, the five leading areas of practice for the Prairie City bar were (1) business, corporate, and commercial; (2) real estate; (3) wills, probate, and trusts and estates; (4) personal injury for the defense; and (5) personal injury for the plaintiff; some of the lawyers listed more than one of these as their main area of practice. Thirty-three per cent of the lawyers did more business, corporate, and commercial work than any other kind of practice. Business practice was general: articles of incorporation, preparation of minutes of directors' meetings, negotiation and preparation of contracts, handling personal matters for officers, advice on general business policy, and, less frequently, the handling of routine filings, licenses, permits, franchises (building, zoning, liquor, etc.), minor work for employees, and personnel work. Less than 10 per cent of these lawyers worked "often" (as distinguished from "occasionally") in the corporate specialties— labor relations, securities and credit financing, patent-trademark, antitrust, and unfair competition.

Seventeen per cent of the lawyers spent more time in real estate transactions than in any other area, chiefly in residential and mortgage closings. Sixteen per cent of the lawyers did more work in wills, probate, and trusts and estates (including business problems arising out of problems of succession) than in any other area. The same proportion also listed defense work for insurance companies as the main area of practice; 13 per cent represented plaintiffs in personal injury suits as their principal area of work.

The main area of practice for the remaining 23 per cent of the bar was scattered: collections, domestic relations (mostly divorce), federal income tax, criminal, and municipal.

Lack of specialization (as measured by time devoted to the "main" area of practice) was startling. More than half (57 per cent) of the lawyers in Prairie City considered themselves specialists, but only 17 per cent spent at least half of their time in their main area of practice; only four lawyers (5 per cent) spent three-quarters or more of their time in only one area. Eighty-nine per cent of the bar devoted about one-third or less of their time to the area listed as the main area of practice. The small amount of time spent in a main area accounted for the fact that 20 per cent of the lawyers said that most of their time was divided between two or more main areas of practice.

ACTIVITIES: OFFICE WORK AND CONTACTS WITH COURTS, AGENCIES, AND OFFICIALS

Almost 70 per cent of the lawyers said that they spent most of their office time conferring with and advising clients, either in person or on the telephone; no lawyer said that he spent little or no time in this activity. Over half said that the next most time-consuming activity was either research on legal problems (briefs, memos, etc.) or negotiations on behalf of clients. Less time was spent on updating and working with case files, conferring with other lawyers in the firm, reading legal material to "keep up," preparing and drafting legal documents (including trial documents), or in developing clients and maintaining goodwill with clients.

Only one lawyer in Prairie City—a 69-year-old senior partner—never went to court. Over 80 per cent of the bar averaged two or more hours per week in court, almost half averaged an hour a day, and over 20 per cent averaged two or more hours per day. Inevitably, a certain amount of court time is spent waiting around, and most lawyers (63 per cent) reported that up to 30 per cent of their court time was spent in this way. Most court time, however, was working time, spent either filing papers, on court calls and motions, or in trial. Three-quarters of the lawyers did not spend any time in appellate work, and only eight lawyers (10 per cent) spent at least 10 per cent of their court time in this activity. Time spent in the judge's chambers—talking informally, trying to settle cases, and the like—did not account for much of the bar's court time, for over half of the lawyers spent less than 10 per cent of their time in this form of court work.

More than half of the lawyers reported that they had most contact with courts in the "middle" range of the judicial hierarchy—either in the Probate Court (jurisdiction over estates, guardians, conservators) or the Circuit Court (the trial court of general jurisdiction), or both, and, in the case of about a third, the County Court (minor civil and criminal jurisdiction). The bar as a whole spent less time in the highest and lowest courts. Only 12 per cent spent most of their court time in the Justice of the Peace court; and 42 per cent of the bar appeared in that court less than once a month or never.

Almost all of the lawyers in Prairie City (98 per cent) had at least some contact with administrative agencies, although the time spent there was considerably less than the time spent in the courts (Table B.2). About 80 per cent of the bar spent some professional time with taxing agencies, both federal and local (*e.g.,* the assessor, city treasurer, board of review). In fact, about half of the lawyers saw these agencies one or more times per month, on the average.[4]

About 70 per cent of the lawyers spent at least some professional time with agencies concerned with (1) planning and zoning (the local or county zoning board, the plan commission, the urban renewal board); (2) housing and building construction (the building inspector, the city engineer, the board of local improvement); (3) taxation and assessments; and (4) the Secretary of State's Office (either for motor vehicle violations or corporate problems). Almost half of the lawyers visited planning and zoning officials, taxation and assessments officials, and the Secretary of State's office one or more times per month; and 30 per cent saw housing and building agencies this often. In contrast, only about 10 per cent of the bar spent this much professional time (one or more times per month on the average) with state agencies regulating banks, savings and loan associations, and utilities. Three lawyers (4 per cent) spent this amount of time with the federal regulatory agencies, including the Antitrust Division of the Department of Justice.

Almost 60 per cent of the lawyers spent some professional time with the city manager; 21 per cent saw him one or more times per month, on the average. Of those who had spent time with this official, over 60 per cent saw him on property matters such as zoning and urban renewal.[5] On the other hand, over 60 per cent of the bar spent no professional time with the mayor or the council members, and more than 75 per cent never saw state legislators professionally. Those lawyers who did have occasion to deal with these officials reported that they saw them on matters concerning permits, assessments, and licenses (including Alcoholic Beverage Commission matters), condemnation and land purchases, and legislation, either in general or on behalf of clients (only ten lawyers, or 12 per cent, reported having spent any time on legislative matters).

PROFESSIONAL ASSOCIATIONS AND ATTITUDES

Membership in both the local bar association and the state bar association was very high among Prairie City lawyers. All the lawyers but one belonged to the former, and 90 per cent belonged to the latter. On the other hand, membership in the American Bar Association was only 56 per cent of the bar. Forty-two per cent of the lawyers, at one time or another, had held office in the local bar association and 35 per cent had served on committees. In the state bar association, 40 per cent belonged to sections, 12 per cent served on committees, and 6 per cent held office. But in the American Bar Association, only 14 per cent were members of a section, only 4 per cent were on committees, and only one lawyer in the community had ever been an A.B.A. officer. Thus, participation in bar activities varied directly with the geographical interests of the professional organizations, ranging from very high on the local levels to very low on the national level.

There appeared to be a high degree of satisfaction with the work of the local and state bar associations among the lawyers. Almost 95 per cent thought that either or both associations spoke for the average lawyer, and over 80 per cent did not believe that either association primarily represented any one group of lawyers. Three-quarters of the bar, on the average, thought that their professional organizations both should engage in and were doing a good job in the following activities: (1) in defining and clarifying ethical standards and giving guidance on ethical problems, (2) in improving the economic condition of the bar, (3) in helping lawyers to keep up on the law, (4) in working toward judicial reform, and (5) in working for improvements in local, state, and federal law. On the other hand, the percentages dropped rather sharply as to whether the bar associations had been doing a good job in disciplining lawyers, that is, in enforcing professional standards, and in helping to create a more favorable public image of the bar through public relations; for less than 50 per cent of the bar thought that the associations are performing well in these areas.

Judges in this state were elected, and only 38 per cent of the bar were in favor of changing to an appointive system. Almost 70 per cent of the lawyers, however, thought that the bar should make recommendations for the selection of judges; a majority of lawyers were thus in favor of the bar associations' taking a public stand on the candidates for the judicial offices. This opinion is subject to a number of interpretations. Some lawyers might have thought that the leaders of the bar were more competent than the general public to evaluate the qualifications of the candidates. Others might have been unhappy with the present judges and the selection process and might have thought that the bar, speaking as a group, would have more influence with the political parties than individual lawyers. On the other hand, the use of the bar associations might have served as a convenient escape from the dilemma that the election method of judicial selection can pose for the individual lawyer. A prudent lawyer might well prefer to remain passive or, if active, at least anonymous, rather than risk the consequences of a public commitment to a candidate who later was defeated. If the bar association took a public stand, the chances of notoriety might be less; in any event, the lawyer might feel safer as part of his professional group. Finally, this opinion could indicate an excuse for failure to assume professional responsibilities. A lawyer unwilling to spend the time, money, and effort in the campaigns might rationalize by adopting the attitude that judicial selection is the job of the bar associations anyway.

As will be seen, the bar as a whole was very inactive politically. Yet almost 60 per cent of the bar thought that their associations should participate in efforts at political reform. Though public commitment by individual lawyers on local public issues involved professional risks as well as the expenditure of time and money, organized group activity tended to avoid or lessen both of these inconveniences.

PARTICIPATION IN SOCIAL AND POLITICAL ACTIVITIES

Social Activities

Only about one-quarter of the practicing bar belonged to service clubs (*e.g.,* Lions, Rotary, Kiwanis, Jaycees), fraternal organizations (*e.g.,* Moose, Elks, Eagles, Masons), ethnic-religious organizations (Knights of Columbus, B'nai B'rith), or veterans' organizations. On the other hand, about 70 per cent participated in local civic organizations such as the Association of Commerce, the United Fund, or the Red Cross, and over 60 per cent participated in local social clubs—the country clubs and the Downtown Club.

Many people think of young professionals as "joiners" attempting to get clients through social activities, yet the lawyers' assertion that little time was spent in developing clients and maintaining their goodwill seemed borne out by their low level of participation in service clubs, ethnic-religious organizations, and veterans' organizations. The high level of participation in local civic associations might have reflected a high degree of civic mindedness on the part of the bar. On the other hand, perhaps the times had changed, and civic and social organizations had become more fruitful areas of gathering clients than service, fraternal, ethnic, and veterans' organizations. Certainly, high position in the local United Fund had public relations value, and a wide circle of wealthy friends at the country club might have done more for the rising lawyer than the Moose or the Elks. Whether or not there was a relationship between joining civic and social organizations and types of practice and clients will be explored in Chapter 3.

POLITICAL ACTIVITIES

Although the population of Prairie City as a whole was rather evenly divided between the two major political parties, the upper classes were heavily Republican,[6] as was the bar. Seventy per cent of the lawyers said that they were either Republican or "independent" Republicans.

All of the lawyers but two said that they had voted in the local election immediately preceding the study. Nevertheless, the lawyers in Prairie City were not very active politically. Sixty-five per cent stated that during the past three years they had not campaigned for or against a candidate for local public office. Seventeen per cent campaigned for or against more than one candidate, but almost half of this 17 per cent restricted their involvement to candidates for judicial office. Only ten lawyers (12 per cent) had campaigned for or against candidates running for offices not connected with judgeships. Furthermore, the participation of those who had engaged in these campaigns was not of major importance. Only two lawyers had held significant campaign offices. Over 60 per cent of those who claimed to have campaigned meant that they had either contributed money, talked to friends, or, to a lesser extent (4 lawyers), canvassed or telephoned. The others (5 per cent) had engaged in public speaking or social promotion and entertaining. Over 80 per cent had not done any campaigning for or against local political issues appearing on the ballot, such as bond referendums or statewide judicial reform, and almost 60 per cent did not belong to political clubs or partisan citizens' groups.

Sixty-six per cent of the lawyers had never been candidates for elective office. Added to this group should be the 14 per cent who had been candidates for only the lowest political office—the party precinct or ward representative, a position which usually was unopposed—and 16 per cent of the lawyers had run for political offices for which only lawyers were qualified (judgeships and prosecutors). Twelve lawyers, or 15 per cent, had sought nonlegal offices, but three persons in this group had ended their political activity by about the time of World War II. The offices that the remaining nine lawyers ran for were U.S. Congress (two), state executive (one), state legislative (two), local government (four), school board (two), and Democratic County Chairman (one). At the time of the study, one lawyer was a member of the city council, another was a member of the school board, and another was the Democratic County Chairman.

Over 90 per cent of the bar had never served on any public board of commission which had decision-making authority such as the planning commission, the housing authority, or the zoning board. At the time of the study, there were three lawyers on such bodies—one on the county zoning board, another on the traffic and parking commission, and a third the police pension fund. In the past, a few other lawyers had served on such bodies as the board of review, the post-World War II rent control authority, the urban renewal board, and in high state regulatory positions. Other committees or boards on which Prairie City lawyers served were advisory only, including the library board, the Mayor's Special Committee on Legal Questions, medical boards, and county memorial committees; and even the number participating in these activities was very small. Over half of the bar served public bodies in a professional capacity, as attorneys for school boards, cities, villages, special districts, and state agencies. But the great bulk of these jobs were nonpartisan positions; they were not regarded as payoffs for political debts.

The data on the political role of Prairie City lawyers qualify, at least for this community, the impressions generated by empirical studies of lawyers in politics. These studies, focusing on the prominence of lawyers as an occupational group in legislative and executive positions in state and national government, conclude that

No occupational group stands in more regular and intimate relation to American politics than the legal profession. Lawyers make up a large proportion of American politicians at all levels and in all branches of government, in the political parties, and in other political organizations. The affinity of law and politics as vocations is a matter of record. In the United States, probably more than in any other nation, lawyers are the "high priests of politics." . . .
That lawyers have an almost complete monopoly of public offices connected with law enforcement and with the administration of law in the courts is not surprising. But they are also prominent as an occupational group in the executive and legislative arenas of government. This has been true from the earliest days of the republic. . . .
There is no need to belabor further the fact of the lawyer's ubiquity in politics. It is surely an outstanding phenomenon of American political life.[7]

Since we have no data on the political activities of other occupational groups in Prairie City, it cannot be inferred that the political activities of the Prairie City lawyers were any more or less extensive than the activities of other occupational groups in the community. On the other hand, the very small number of lawyers in positions of authority indicated that the lawyers were not running Prairie City. A single lawyer on the city council, one or two on other public bodies of importance, the two or three participating importantly in political campaigns—these hardly warrant the characterization "high priests of politics." [8]

SOCIAL COMPOSITION OF THE BAR

All of the lawyers in Prairie City were native-born white males, practically all of whom had roots in or cultural ties to either the city or closely similar regions. Three-quarters of the lawyers had been born in the state, and thirty-three lawyers had been born in Prairie City. An additional eight lawyers (or 49 per cent total) had been raised in whole or in part in the community even though born outside of the state. Of the thirteen remaining lawyers, only one had not been born in a state immediately adjacent to the state, but this lawyer had been born in North Dakota. All of the lawyers, then, had spent part of their earlier years either in Prairie City or in the same geographical region.

Ninety-two per cent of the lawyers had been born and/or raised in middle-sized or smaller communities. Seven lawyers had been born in metropolitan centers very much larger than Prairie City, but two of these lawyers had been raised in Prairie City and had obtained at least part of their higher education in Prairie City or at the state university, located in another middle-sized city. Three others, although raised in a large urban center, had had a similar educational experience. In other words, only two lawyers in this community had an urban background unaffected by youthful years or a higher education in a middle-sized city.

Cultural homogeneity was indicated by other data. Seventy-three per cent of the Prairie City bar was Protestant, 17 per cent was Catholic, and 7 per cent was Jewish. The ancestors of 46 per cent of the lawyers came from the United Kingdom and Canada, 29 per cent from Northern and Western Europe, and 14 per cent from Ireland.

The legal profession was not used as an avenue of upward mobility in Prairie City. Almost 80 per cent of the Prairie City lawyers came from a business, professional, or managerial background. Eighteen per cent were the sons of lawyers, an additional 28 per cent had had a lawyer in their immediate family at the time that they entered practice, and almost 60 per cent had had at least one professional relative at that time.

All of the lawyers but one attended college. Ninety-three per cent attended college for three or more years, and 90 per cent had received degrees. The majority—70 per cent—had graduated from a college or university in the state: 17 per cent from the small, private college located in Prairie City and 40 per cent from the state university. Two lawyers had attended an Ivy League college, and one was graduated.

All of the lawyers but one had gone to law school and had received a degree. Forty-three per cent had received their legal education in the state university, and an additional 22 per cent had graduated from other law schools in the state. Twelve per cent had gone to other Big Ten law schools or to Notre Dame, and 5 per cent had gone to Ivy League law schools. Only 6 per cent of the lawyers, all of whom had been admitted to practice before World War II, had received their legal education at night. Less than 30 per cent had clerked in a law office either before or during law school.

Educationally, the bar was in the top 10 per cent of the city popula-tion. The bar ranked higher educationally than lawyers throughout the United States and in cities with populations between 50,000 and 200,000.[9]

AGE AND CAREER PATTERNS

The Prairie City bar was somewhat younger than lawyers throughout the United States and in cities of between 50,000 and 200,000 (Table 2.1). The median number of years in practice for this bar (at the time

TABLE 2.1—Distribution of Lawyers by Year of Birth: United States, Cities Between 50,000 and 200,000, and Prairie City

	% by years				
Locality	1904 or earlier	1905– 1914	1915– 1924	1925– 1934	1935 or later
United States*	23	22	24	26	5
Cities of 50,000–200,000*	22	20	25	27	5
Prairie City	18	14	35	29	4

* No data were available for 1 per cent of the lawyers.
Source: American Bar Foundation, *1964 Lawyer Statistical Report* (1965), pp. 27–28.

of the study) was nineteen. There appeared to have been no undue delay on the part of these lawyers in being admitted to practice; most of the lawyers were admitted at about age twenty-five (Table B.3).

Seventy per cent of the lawyers had started out immediately in private practice—either as associates (46 per cent), or as partners (12 per cent), or on their own as individual practitioners (12 per cent). An additional 11 per cent had started with legal jobs that were totally salaried: house counsel (2 per cent), or working for a judge (2 per cent) or for an agency of government (7 per cent). Eight per cent counted as their first job military service, and only 10 per cent had held nonlegal jobs, including work as claims adjustors or investigators for insurance companies or in banks and trust companies. In addition, some lawyers had held managerial positions, lower white collar jobs, or teaching positions. In any event, the tour of duty in all of the non-private practice positions was relatively brief. Excluding military service, the average time spent was three years, but the median was only one and a half years. With few exceptions, all of the lawyers were quickly engaged in the private practice of law.

At the time of the study, five lawyers held associate positions. Of the remaining seventy-eight lawyers in partnerships or individual practice, 62 per cent had been employed as associates by other private practitioners either as their first legal job or as their first job in private practice. For almost two-thirds of this group, the experience as an associate was for one job only; their next job in private practice was either as a partner (in the same or a different firm) or as an individual practitioner.

Of the present five associates, three had been employed for less than a year, one for two years, and one for four years. The average time spent as an associate for the other lawyers was about four and a half years.[10] In addition, although the numbers were small, it seemed that more younger lawyers had held associate positions than had older lawyers when they were young; on the other hand, these younger lawyers appeared to have spent less time as associates than the older lawyers. That is, fewer older lawyers had held these jobs, but when they did, they held them for longer periods of time (Table 2.2). This apparent shift in associate tenure could indicate a change in the conception of the associate's role in the bar, but we have no data on this question.

TABLE 2.2—Percentage of Lawyers Spending Time in Associate Positions by Age

Age of lawyers	% who had held assoc. positions*	Av. no. of yrs. in assoc. positions†	Total no. of lawyers
−30	67	1.5	(3)
30–39	71	3.6	(24)
40–49	62	5.6	(29)
50–59	42	6.2	(12)
60+	53	3.9	(15)

* This includes those who were associates at the time of the study.
† The average time spent as an associate for all age groups was 4.5 years.

Table 2.3 correlates the ages of lawyers by their first job in private practice and their position at the time of the study. Considerably more lawyers in their fifties had started their careers as individual practitioners than the lawyers in the other age brackets, apparently reflecting the fact that over 80 per cent of this group had been admitted during the

Depression (Table B.3). At the time of this study, individual practitioners tended to be older than partners; the average age of the former was fifty-three, as compared to forty-six for the latter. Of the sixteen lawyers who started private practice as individual practitioners, eight never changed. Seven remained individual practitioners for about seven years, on the average, before going into partnerships. Another lawyer had an interlude as a government lawyer and as a partner before returning to individual practice. The ranks of the remaining individual practitioners (ten out of nineteen at the time of the study) had been recruited, with one exception, from lawyers who had started out immediately as associates. Two had gone into partnerships and then to

TABLE 2.3—Job Distribution by Age: First Job in Private Practice and Position at the Time of the Study

Age of lawyers	First position (%)			Present position (%)		
	Assoc.	Partner	Indiv. prac.	Assoc.	Partner	Indiv. prac.
−30 (3)	100*	0	0	67*	33	0
30–39 (24)	83†	8	8	13†	75	13
40–49 (29)	62	21	17	0	72	28
50–59 (12)	42	17	42	0	58	42
60+ (15)	53	20	27	0	80	20

* Includes two of the present five associates.
† Includes three of the present five associates.

individual practice, four went directly from their associate position to individual practice, and the final four ranged from a second associate position to government legal work to nonlegal work before ending up as individual practitioners. The average time spent by this group of ten lawyers before they became individual practitioners was about six years. In sum, the individual practitioners had a history of low job mobility. The average number of jobs held by these lawyers (excluding military service but including their position at the time of the study) was 2.1 jobs per lawyer.

Thirteen lawyers started out in practice as partners. Nine of these lawyers never changed positions. The job histories of the other four show considerable mobility: the average was over five jobs per lawyer, including their position at the time of the study.

The eighty-three lawyers of the bar had a total of 245 jobs, or about three jobs per lawyer. Two hundred and sixteen jobs were legal jobs, nineteen were in the military, and ten were nonlegal. Fifty-two per cent had no more than two legal jobs, and 77 per cent had no more than three. Actually, despite the fact that these figures indicate a very low rate of job mobility, they are still on the high side, for we classified as job changes several situations which just as easily could have been considered the same job. Not infrequently lawyers returned to the same firm after military service, after a government legal job, or after a legal position with a corporation. In other situations, two firms would merge, or a firm would add new partners and thus become a large firm. Finally, in this bar it is even questionable whether a change in jobs has occurred when a partnership is formed. In Chapter 3 it will be shown that this bar was essentially composed of individual practitioners and that the fact of partnership was of relatively minor importance. Nevertheless, we classified all of the above situations as changes in jobs.

Table 2.4 tabulates by age the duration of the present job. We see that the amount of time spent in the present position had absorbed a substantial portion of the professional careers of this bar. Not deducted from the existing professional life span in Table 2.4 is military service,

TABLE 2.4—Duration of Present Position by Age of Lawyers

Age	No.	Prof. life span (yrs.)	Av. no. of yrs. in present position	% of lawyers holding present position						
				−1 yr.	1–2 yrs.	2–4 yrs.	4–5 yrs.	5–8 yrs.	8–11 yrs.	11+ yrs.
60+	(15)	40*	25	0	0	0	0	7	7	87
50–59	(12)	30	17.5	0	0	0	0	8	17	75
40–49	(29)	20	10.2	0	0	17	0	24	14	45
30–39	(24)	10	4.2	8	8	38	8	33	4	0
−30	(3)	...	0.6	67	33	0	0	0	0	0
ALL LAWYERS	(83)			5	4	17	2	21	10	42

* Assuming that the average age in this bracket is 65.

but if this period of time were subtracted, then the proportion of time spent in the present position would have been even greater. Also to be noted in Table 2.4 is that 73 per cent of the bar had been employed in their present position for more than five years, and 42 per cent for more than eleven years.

In short, this was a comparatively young bar; most of the lawyers had started out in private practice as associates but had moved rather quickly into partnerships or individual practice. There was some indication of more mobility among the younger members of the bar, but the dominant characteristic was one of great stability. The Prairie City lawyer, for the most part, got his position in private practice and stuck with it.

REWARDS AND ATTITUDES

The median figure for net income from all sources for Prairie City lawyers was $17,500 (this figure excludes the nine lawyers who gave no information on incomes), almost three times as great as the median family income in Prairie City (1960 figures). Nearly 70 per cent of the lawyers had incomes from all sources of $15,000 or more per year as compared to only 4 per cent of the families; only 1 per cent had less than $6,000 as compared to half of the families (Table 2.5).

TABLE 2.5—Distribution of All Prairie City Families and of Prairie City Lawyers by Net Income from All Sources

Net income	All families	Lawyers*
$15,000 or more	4%	69%
$14,999–8,000	22	23
$7,999–6,000	22	7
$5,999 or less	51	1
Median	$5,943	$17,500

* Excludes nine lawyers who gave no information.

Prairie City lawyers compared very favorably with other lawyers in the state, including the lawyers practicing in the major metropolitan city of the state.[11] Because comparable statistics were unavailable, precise comparisons between the incomes of Prairie City lawyers and lawyers in the rest of the country could not be made. However, it seemed clear that Prairie City lawyers were generally more prosperous than other lawyers outside the state (Tables 2.6, 2.7, and 2.8).

TABLE 2.6—Distribution of Self-Employed Lawyers in the United States and in Prairie City by Net Income from All Sources

Net income	All self-employed lawyers	Self-employed Prairie City lawyers*
$15,000 or more	40%	69%
$14,999–8,000	29	23
$7,999–6,000	11	7
$5,999–4,000	10	1
Under $4,000	10	0

* Excludes the nine lawyers who did not give any information as to incomes.

Source: U.S. Census, *Characteristics of Professional Workers*, 1960. "Self-employed lawyers" excludes women and associates. The figures are based on 1959 incomes.

TABLE 2.7—Distribution of Prairie City and New York City Lawyers by Net Income Before Taxes

Net income	From practice		From all sources	
	P.C.	N.Y.C.	P.C.	N.Y.C.
$50,000 or more	6%	6%	10%	10%
$49,999–35,000	4	5	6	8
$34,999–20,000	22	16	25	18
$19,999–15,000	23	11	20	12
Total	55%	38%	61%	48%
$14,999–11,000	13%	. . .	13%	. . .
$10,999–8,000	12	. . .	7	. . .
To $7,999	9*	. . .	7	. . .
Total	34%	49%†	27%	38%†
No answer	11%	13%	11%	13%

* This includes one respondent who was a senior partner in one of the large firms but who took a disproportionately small income from the practice of law.

† My categories for the groups below $15,000 do not coincide with those in the New York study. The New York figures are as follows:

	From practice	From all sources
To $6,999	15%	8%
$7,000–8,999	9	7
$9,000–11,999	13	12
$12,000–14,999	12	11
	49%	38%

The figures for New York City lawyers are 1960 data gathered by Jerome E. Carlin; see Carlin, *Lawyers' Ethics: A Survey of the New York City Bar* (New York, 1966).

TABLE 2.8—Income Distribution of Prairie City Lawyers by Age

Income	Age				
	−30	30–39	40–49	50–59	60+
From Practice					
Average	$6,300	$15,000	$21,600	$19,400	$27,300
Median	6,000	13,000	17,500	17,500	27,500
$50,000 or more	0%	0%	3%	8%	20%
$49,999–35,000	0	4	0	0	13
$34,999–20,000	0	8	42	8	20
$19,999–15,000	0	21	24	42	13
$14,999–11,000	0	29	10	8	0
$10,999–8,000	0	25	7	8	7
$7,999–6,000	67	0	0	8	7
$5,999–4,000	33	0	0	0	7
To $3,999	0	0	3	0	7
No answer	0	13	10	17	7
From All Sources					
Average	$7,000	$17,800	$22,800	$25,700	$30,500
Median	7,000	13,000	27,500	27,500	27,500
$50,000 or more	0%	0%	7%	17%	27%
$49,999–35,000	0	8	3	0	13
$34,999–20,000	0	8	42	33	20
$19,999–15,000	0	25	24	8	13
$14,999–11,000	0	29	10	8	7
$10,999–8,000	0	17	3	8	0
$7,999–6,000	100	0	0	8	7
$5,999–4,000	0	0	0	0	7
To $3,999	0	0	0	0	0
No answer	0	13	10	17	7

Most of the income of Prairie City lawyers was the result of legal fees paid directly by clients. For more than three-quarters of these lawyers, none of their net personal incomes was salaried.[12] Excluding the five associates, who were practically totally salaried, only five lawyers (6 per cent of the bar) reported a salaried income amounting to more than 8 per cent of their total net income. On the other hand, approximately 20 per cent of the lawyers had sources of income in addition to that earned from the practice of law.[13] Three-quarters of this group owned real estate properties, including farms, or other businesses. Only 11 per cent of the bar, however, reported that income from these outside sources amounted to 25 per cent or more of their total net income. Finally, only five lawyers (6 per cent) were either accountants, real estate brokers, or insurance brokers, but only two of these reported that income derived from these activities amounted to as much as 10 per cent of their net income; the others were "inactive." These lawyers, then, were well-off, and they made their living primarily from the practice of law.

The lawyers were satisfied with their community. Sixty-three per cent of the practitioners gave as the reason for deciding to practice law in Prairie City the fact that it was their hometown or that of their immediate family. Sixteen per cent said that they came because an opportunity arose there, and 17 per cent said that they liked the size and location of the city. One lawyer summed up the reasons for selecting this community given by those lawyers with no family ties to Prairie City: "I wanted a medium-sized city and a small firm with a general practice. This was the best offer."

Whatever the reason for coming, most of the lawyers were not sorry about the decision. Sixty-five per cent were quite sure that they would come to Prairie City if they had it to do all over again, 27 per cent probably would, and only 8 per cent definitely would not. Of those who had doubts about Prairie City, or definitely would not have come, the majority said that they did not care for the geography or the climate. Only three lawyers (4 per cent of the bar) gave economic reasons (e.g., too many old firms, too hard to get clients).

Although the lawyers as a whole did well financially, there was competition for legal business both among themselves and from non-lawyers. Almost 90 per cent of the bar recognized that there was at least some, if not a great deal, of competition among lawyers, and 22 per cent admitted that they had been hurt by it. Over 70 per cent thought that there was also competition from nonlawyers (mostly real estate brokers), and 22 per cent also admitted economic injury from this source. Despite the competition, however, the lawyers apparently liked what they were doing. Sixty-one per cent were very satisfied with their own field of practice, and 70 per cent were very satisfied with the practice of law in general. No one was very dissatisfied with either his own field of practice or the practice of law in general, although 4 per cent were somewhat dissatisfied with their own field and another 5 per cent with the practice in general. Only 6 per cent said that they would not be lawyers if they had to do it all over again. Seventy-seven per cent definitely would, and 17 per cent probably would. Almost 40 per cent said that their present earnings were more than they would have predicted three or four years before; 13 per cent said their earnings were less. The vast majority were optimistic as to their future, for over 70 per cent did not think that they had reached their maximum income from the practice of law, and almost half of the bar thought that they would eventually make more than $27,500 per year. Finally, 85 per cent thought that the prospect of getting to the top for a young man of modest means just starting out was either good (57 per cent) or excellent (28 per cent). No one thought that the chances were poor.

A COMPARISON WITH THE NEW YORK CITY BAR

The general features of the Prairie City bar stood in sharp contrast to those of the New York City bar.[14] Although practically all of the New York lawyers were native-born white males, their background and social characteristics were very different from those of the Prairie City lawyers. More than half of the New York City lawyers had at least one foreign-born parent. In contrast, almost 60 per cent of the Prairie City lawyers had both parents and all grandparents born in the United States; only 12 per cent had one or both parents born abroad. Forty-eight per cent of the New York lawyers were of eastern European descent; this was true for only 5 per cent of the Prairie City bar. Both bars had approximately the same proportion of Catholics. But slightly over 60 per cent of the New York lawyers were Jewish as compared to 7 per cent of the Prairie City bar, and only 18 per cent of the New York lawyers were Protestant as compared to 73 per cent of the Prairie City bar.[15]

Sixty-five per cent of the New York City lawyers had received college degrees as compared to 90 per cent of the Prairie City lawyers. Only a third of the New York lawyers received law degrees from a full-time university law school[16] as compared to 94 per cent of the Prairie City bar. Overall, there was probably considerably less variation in the quality and types of colleges and law schools that Prairie City lawyers attended than was found in the colleges and law schools attended by the New York City lawyers.[17]

High proportions of both bars worked for business clients, but about 70 per cent of the New York lawyers earned half or more of their income from this source as compared to 57 per cent of the Prairie City lawyers. More New York lawyers, of course, worked primarily for very large businesses than did Prairie City lawyers, and only 18 per cent of the New York lawyers, as compared to 45 per cent of the

Prairie City lawyers, worked primarily for the very small enterprises. And, as Table 2.9 indicates, there was much more of a spread of both rich and poor individual clients among the Prairie City bar than in the New York City bar.

TABLE 2.9—Distribution of New York City and Prairie City Lawyers by Income of Individual Clients

Client income	New York City lawyers*	Prairie City lawyers†
Proportion of individual clients earning less than $5,000 per year		
0%	52%	13%
1–19	18	45
20–39	8	22
40–79	5	8
80–100	3	0
Proportion of individual clients earning more than $20,000 per year		
0%	16%	11%
1–19	17	42
20–39	13	14
40–79	15	17
80–100	25	4

* Fourteen per cent of the New York City lawyers did not indicate incomes of individual clients.

† Six per cent of the Prairie City lawyers did not indicate incomes of individual clients.

The difference in the distribution of rich and poor clients within the two bars points to a more basic difference between New York City and Prairie City lawyers. Since lawyers perform services for clients, what lawyers do depends on the type of legal problems his clients bring to him. Clients in different income groups tend to have different types of legal problems; therefore, the distribution of clients by income groups is an indicant of differences in specialization. Thus, in New York City, over 70 per cent of the lawyers spent at least half or more of their time in one area of practice, as compared to only 17 per cent of the Prairie City lawyers. Almost 40 per cent of the New York lawyers spent three-quarters or more of their time in only one area, as compared to 5 per cent of the Prairie City lawyers.[18] Again, in New York only 5 per cent spent less than 30 per cent of their time in their main area, as compared to 89 per cent of the Prairie City lawyers.

Specialization among the New York lawyers was also reflected in professional contacts with courts and other government agencies. More New York lawyers spent time in higher courts and with federal regulatory agencies than Prairie City lawyers; lower proportions of New York lawyers dealt mainly with local agencies than of Prairie City lawyers.

All but one of the Prairie City lawyers belonged to the local bar association, and 42 per cent had held offices in the association. Membership of the New York bar was divided among several local bar associations.

The New York City bar was large and heterogeneous. In contrast, the central fact of the Prairie City bar was its homogeneity—in background, in education, and in professional life. The lawyers were born and raised in Prairie City or in similar communities. Ethnically, they mirrored the local population—native-born and Protestant, but educationally and financially they were at the top of their community. The practice of law was diversified in terms of clients, areas of practice, and contacts with courts and agencies. They liked their work and the community, and they were rewarded well for their labors. Similar backgrounds and education, both rich and poor clients, and lack of specialization meant that there was a large measure of shared experiences among all of the lawyers.

CHAPTER 3

STRATIFICATION IN THE BAR

In comparison with the variety of the New York City bar, all Prairie City lawyers looked alike. Of course, they were not all alike. The purpose of this chapter is to examine the differences among Prairie City lawyers—to identify strata in the bar. The conventional method of stratifying (classifying) lawyers is by size of firm, but size of firm, as we shall see, was a relatively unimportant indicator for this bar.

The basis of ranking used here combines professional income and wealth of clients. This stratification system will be called the income-client measure.[1] The lawyers in the "low" group had the lowest incomes and the least well-off clients; conversely, the lawyers in the "high" group had the highest incomes and the wealthiest clients. The "middle" group, as the name implies, were lawyers between the high and low groups both in terms of incomes and wealth of clients. A subgroup of the high group, the "elite," consisted of lawyers who represented the largest enterprises in town (businesses with gross incomes of $5,000,000 or more per year), excluding banks and insurance companies. In this subgroup were the principal business lawyers in the community; lawyers working for banks and insurance companies were excluded from the elite group since they often did routine tasks (*e.g.,* mortgage closings) or defense work in personal injury litigation. Excluded from the income-client measure were the five associates; they were all young lawyers in a unique status and will be discussed separately. Also excluded were three lawyers who could not be placed (see Appendix A). The distribution of the lawyers on the measure was as follows:

Elite	*High*	*Middle*	*Low*	*Total*
17%	27%	25%	31%	100%
(13)	(20)	(19)	(23)	(75)

DIFFERENCES IN CLIENTS

All of the lawyers on the income-client measure derived some portion of their income from work on business matters as distinguished from work on personal matters. Proportions of income from work for business clients were related to the income-client measure. All but two of the elite lawyers derived over 80 per cent of their income from this source, as compared to only 25 per cent of the high group and 11 and 4 per cent of the middle and low groups. None of the elite lawyers had less than 30 per cent of their income from this source, in comparison to 48 per cent of the low group (Table 3.1).

TABLE 3.1—Distribution of Lawyers by Income-Client Measure According to Income from Business Matters

Proportion of income	% of lawyers			
	Elite	High	Middle	Low
80% or more	85	25	11	4
50% or more	92	65	68	39
Less than 30%	0	25	21	48
	(13)	(20)	(19)	(23)

The elite lawyers were defined as those who had as business clients enterprises with gross incomes of $5,000,000 or more per year. Only 20 per cent of the high group, 16 per cent of the middle group, and 4 per cent of the low group had such clients, even when banks and insurance companies are included. More than half of the middle group and almost 80 per cent of the low group of lawyers indicated that 60 per cent or more of their business clients had gross incomes of less than $50,000 per year. On the other hand, this was also true for 31 per cent of the elite lawyers. In other words, even though the elite lawyers had the wealthiest business clients in town, they also represented the small businesses. The difference between the groups was not whether a lawyer represented very small businesses—practically all of them did—but whether he represented any of the wealthiest businesses and, if so, how many (Table 3.2).

The difference in the groups was also indicated by the types of businesses that the lawyers worked for. All of the elite lawyers listed manufacturing firms as one of their main types of business clients, whereas the highest proportions of the other three groups listed retail trade and

TABLE 3.2—Distribution of Lawyers by Income-Client Measure According to Wealth of Business Clients

Wealth of business clients	% of lawyers			
	Elite	High	Middle	Low
Business clients with gross incomes per year of*				
$5,000,000 or more	100	20	16	4
$1,000,000 or more	31	35	11	4
Proportion of business clients with gross incomes of less than $50,000 per year				
80% or more	8	15	26	65
60% or more	31	25	53	78
	(13)	(20)	(19)	(23)

* Including banks and insurance companies.

stores as constituting their primary business clientele. The high and middle groups had more real estate clients than did the other groups; the low group had more farmers. On the other hand, 31 per cent of the elite lawyers also listed retail trade and stores as a main type of business client (Table 3.3).

The distribution of individual clients by wealth was the same as the distribution of business clients. Three-quarters of the elite lawyers reported that the median incomes of their individual clients was $20,000 or more per year; whereas only 28 per cent of the high group, 16 per cent of the middle group, and none of the low group reported an equivalent median client income. Conversely, three-quarters of the low group reported 30 per cent or more of their individual clients earning less than $5,000 per year as compared to 37 per cent of the middle group, 6 per cent of the high group, and none of the elite group. On the other hand, half of the elite lawyers had at least 10 per cent of their individual clients in the lowest income category, and 62 per cent of the low group had at least that number in the highest income category.

Since the ranking on the income-client measure was related to wealth of clients, one would expect that the lawyers with the wealthier clients would have a smaller number of clients, less turnover, and more retainer clients, and that the fees from retainer clients should account for a higher proportion of professional income than would be the case among the lawyers with poorer clients. In general, this was true, although the dif-

TABLE 3.3—Distribution of Lawyers by Income-Client Measure According to Main Types of Business Clients

"What are the main kinds of businesses you have done work for in the past twelve months?"

	% of lawyers*			
Kinds of businesses	Elite	High	Middle	Low
Manufacturing	100	30	32	17
Transportation, communications, utilities	15	0	0	8
Banks, trust companies	23	25	21	13
Check cashing, loan companies	15	10	16	17
Brokerage	8	0	0	0
Insurance	31	30	11	9
Real estate	0	35	58	9
Construction	8	10	11	4
Wholesale	0	20	16	4
Retail trade and stores	31	55	63	48
Restaurants and bars	8	10	11	22
Farmers	8	10	11	39
Professional services	0	5	0	13
Small businesses (unspecified)	0	10	5	4
	(13)	(20)	(19)	(23)

* Percentages do not add to 100 because several lawyers listed more than one kind of business.

ferences between the elite and the high groups were small; the principal differences were between the high group and its subgroup, the elite, on the one hand, and the other two groups on the other (Table 3.4).

TABLE 3.4—Client Characteristics by Income-Client Measure

	% of lawyers			
Client characteristics	Elite	High	Middle	Low
Retainer clients				
Some, but less than 20%	77	75	53	33
20% or more of income from retainer clients	54	45	16	0
	(13)	(20)	(18)	(21)
Less than 200 clients for whom some work done during past year	77	85	53	39
	(13)	(20)	(19)	(23)
75% or more of clients previously worked for	85	70	53	36
	(13)	(20)	(19)	(22)

DIFFERENCES IN AREAS OF PRACTICE

Practically all of the elite, high, and middle groups spent some time working for business clients, as compared to 70 per cent of the low group. However, this area of practice was of far greater importance to the elite lawyers than to the other groups. The median amount of time spent in the area by the elite lawyers was 44 per cent, as compared to a median of only 10 per cent for the other three groups (Table B.4, Appendix B).[2] While 69 per cent of the elite lawyers listed this area as their main area of practice, only about 15 per cent of the others did so (Table B.5). Over half (54 per cent) of the elite derived the largest portion of their income from this area, but this was the case with only 9 per cent of the low group and with none of the other groups (Table B.6).

The business practice of the elite lawyers was concerned more with the corporate specialties (*e.g.,* patent-trademark, antitrust and unfair competition, personnel work such as pension planning) than that of the other groups, but these lawyers also handled a lot of other business matters, including routine matters (incorporation and preparation of minutes of directors' meetings; licenses, permits, and franchises; routine filings). Since these lawyers represented the largest enterprises, they also did more labor relations work than the other groups. All of the elite lawyers handled personal matters for the officers of their business clients, and three-quarters gave advice on general business matters, indicating perhaps a close connection between the elite lawyers and the biggest businessmen in town (Table 3.5).

All of the lawyers but one (a middle group lawyer) spent time on trusts and estates. This area was of least importance to the high lawyers; the median amount of time spent was 15 per cent, and only 20 per cent of this group listed it as their main area of practice or principal source of income. The median amount of time spent in this field for the elite and low groups was about 24 per cent. Sixty-three per cent of the middle group and 52 per cent of the low group derived the largest portion of their income from this source, as compared to 23 per cent of the elite lawyers and 20 per cent of the high lawyers. Trusts and estates, then, figured prominently for the middle and low groups. On the other hand, these lawyers had much poorer individual clients than the elite and high groups, and size of estates (and legal fees) were probably related to wealth of individual clients. Thus, although the middle and low groups

TABLE 3.5—Relation Between Income-Client Measure and Type of Business Practice
Engaged in Occasionally or Often

| | % of lawyers | | | |
Type of practice	Elite	High	Middle	Low
Incorporation, preparation of minutes	100	65	47	35
Routine filings	39	30	16	26
Building, zoning, liquor, etc. licenses, permits, franchises	39	45	32	17
Negotiations and drafting of leases, contracts, etc.	92	80	53	44
Minor work for employees	8	20	26	17
Personal matters for officers	100	70	53	30
Advice on general business policy	77	55	42	39
Labor relations	54	35	16	4
Personnel work (pension plans, etc.)	62	15	16	4
Securities and credit financing	54	20	11	26
Corporate tax advice	39	40	21	13
Patent-trademark	31	15	0	0
Antitrust, unfair competition	46	10	5	0
	(13)	(20)	(19)	(23)

did more trust and estate work than the other two groups, the high and elite lawyers had the richer clients and probably the bigger estates and fees (Table B.7).

Over half of the elite lawyers (54 per cent) represented plaintiffs in personal injury matters; proportions increased to 78 per cent for the low group. About 30 per cent of the elite, middle, and low groups also did defense work, as compared to 55 per cent of the high group. The personal injury area of practice figured most prominently for the high group, half of whom derived the largest portion of their income from this source and 40 per cent of whom listed it as their main area of practice; this area of practice was also prominent for the low group. The difference between the high and low groups was that the former did much more of the steady, lucrative defense work: 25 per cent more of the high group than the low group worked in this area, 30 per cent of the former listed it as their main area of practice in contrast to only 9 per cent of the latter, and the median time spent by the high group in this area was 23 per cent, as compared to 4 per cent by the low.

High proportions of all groups spent some time in real estate, but the median amount of time spent was less than 15 per cent for all groups.

More of the middle group (about a fifth) listed this as the main area of practice than of the others.

More lawyers in the middle and low groups did collections and matrimonial work than did the lawyers of the elite and high groups; however, the median amounts of time spent in these areas were small for all the groups, and few lawyers listed these areas as their main areas of practice or principal sources of income. None of the elite lawyers did any criminal work. Higher proportions of the high group (60 per cent) and of the low group (70 per cent) practiced criminal law than of the middle group (42 per cent), but the median time spent was small for the three groups. For Prairie City lawyers, then, criminal law was not important either in terms of time spent or as a principal source of income.

On the whole, principal areas of practice differed among the four groups of lawyers. The elite lawyers were the principal business lawyers. The high group was more heavily concentrated in personal injury and, in particular, defense work. The low group had a substantial practice in estates and personal injury, but these lawyers had the poor individual clients and more of the plaintiffs than the defendants. The middle group was also concerned with estates, plaintiff's personal injury, and real estate. But, in general, there were not great differences in areas of prac-

TABLE 3.6—Percentage of Lawyers Spending at Least Some Time in Any One Area of Practice by Income-Client Measure

Areas of practice	% of lawyers			
	Elite	High	Middle	Low
Business, corporate, commercial	100	95	90	70
Wills, probate, estates, trusts	100	100	95	100
Real estate	92	95	95	96
Collections	15	25	63	61
Personal injury: plaintiff	54	65	63	78
Personal injury: defendant	31	55	32	30
Matrimonial: divorce	39	60	84	80
Matrimonial: other	31	40	74	83
Federal tax	46	65	68	91
Criminal	0	60	42	70
State and local tax	39	35	37	39
Other	39	20	42	44
	(13)	(20)	(19)	(23)

tice. Even though the elite lawyers did little collection and no criminal work, many of these lawyers did personal injury and matrimonial work. Of the thirteen areas of practice considered, the elite group practiced in a median of six areas, the high in seven, the middle in nine, and the low in ten (Table 3.6).

DIFFERENCES IN CONTACTS WITH COURTS, AGENCIES, AND OFFICIALS

Differences in practice should be reflected in differences in contacts with courts. A business lawyer, for example, who does little or no matrimonial, personal injury, and criminal work will spend little time in court. In the Prairie City bar, however, differences in practice related not so much to areas of practice as to how much time was spent in a particular area. The elite lawyers spent more time with business law, but they also did other kinds of legal work. Thus, although contacts with courts reflected to some extent the differences in practice, the absence of major differences in court contacts also pointed to the general lack of specialization in the Prairie City bar.

By and large, the high and low groups spent more time in court than the other two groups. The median number of hours spent in court per week by the high and low was six, as compared to two hours for the elite and three and a half for the middle. About 60 per cent of the high and the low groups averaged five or more hours per week in court, as compared to about 40 per cent of the elite and the middle. The longer court hours of the high and low groups seemed to reflect the fact that higher percentages of these lawyers derived the largest portions of their income from personal injury than the other groups. Forty-six per cent of the elite lawyers spent less than two hours per week in court on the average, but only 16 per cent of the middle group spent this little time in court. The former were the principal business lawyers; trust and estate work, which involved court time, was of great importance to the latter.

The high and elite groups spent more court time in trial; the lower groups spent more court time in the routine tasks (filing papers, court calls, motions). More of the elite lawyers spent time in appellate argument than the other groups.

The particular courts in which the lawyers spent time reflected areas of practice and was also related to the income-client measure. Half of the low group appeared in the Justice of the Peace Court about once a week on the average, but most of the elite never appeared in this court at all. Practically all of the high, middle, and low groups appeared one or more times per month in the County Court, which handled criminal cases and smaller civil claims, in comparison to less than half of the elite lawyers. Almost 80 per cent of the lawyers in the middle group appeared an average of once a week in the Probate Court, reflecting their concentration in trusts and estates. Ninety per cent of the high and low lawyers averaged one or more appearances per month in the Circuit Court, the trial court of general jurisdiction; these lawyers were more heavily engaged in personal injury litigation than the others. The elite lawyers who spent much time in court were concerned primarily with trusts and estates and personal injury, usually representing the defendant (Table 3.7).

TABLE 3.7—Court Appearances by Type of Court

Av. no. of visits per mo. by type of court	% of lawyers			
	Elite	High	Middle	Low
Justice of the Peace				
0	69	20	21	9
Less than 1	31	20	5	14
1–3	0	40	47	27
4 or more	0	20	26	50
	100%	100%	100%	100%
County Court				
0	15	0	5	0
Less than 1	39	10	11	0
1–3	39	45	32	32
4 or more	8	45	53	68
	100%	100%	100%	100%
Probate Court				
0	0	0	0	5
Less than 1	15	15	0	5
1–3	46	30	21	27
4 or more	39	55	79	64
	100%	100%	100%	100%
Circuit Court				
0	8	5	11	0
Less than 1	23	5	5	5
1–3	23	15	37	36
4 or more	46	75	47	59
	100%	100%	100%	100%
	(13)	(20)	(19)	(22)*

* One lawyer gave no answer.

Prairie City lawyers spent less time with government agencies and officials than they spent in court. Generally, fewer elite lawyers than lawyers from the other groups devoted time to agencies dealing with planning, zoning, housing and building construction, taxation, and assessments. About 45 per cent of all groups dealt an average of one or more times per month with the Secretary of State's office, an agency which handled motor vehicle problems as well as corporate matters. The low group tended to deal more frequently with the Internal Revenue Service than the other groups, reflecting the fact that more of this group did federal tax work than the others. Comparatively few lawyers spent time with federal regulatory agencies, the highest proportions being among the elite lawyers. Not many of the lawyers had professional contact with state legislators, the mayor, or members of the city council, but higher proportions spent time with the city manager; of the four groups, the elite lawyers spent the least time with the city manager. The differences in contacts with the other officials were, on the whole, small and not related to the income-client measure. Prairie City lawyers most frequently consulted government officials about zoning and land use (Table B.8).

DIFFERENCES IN INCOME

Table 3.8 lists the incomes of the four groups according to the income-client measure. These income figures tell us something about the lucra-

TABLE 3.8—Income from the Practice of Law

	Income of all lawyers	Income of*			
		Elite	High	Middle	Low
Median	$17,500	$27,500	$27,500	$17,500	$11,200
Average	21,200	29,500	30,900	15,900	11,700

* One elite lawyer, three high lawyers, and one low lawyer gave no answer (see Appendix A).

tiveness of areas of practice. The elite and high groups earned about the same from the practice of law. The elite were the principal business lawyers and represented the largest businesses in town. Half of the high group derived the largest portion of their income from personal injury cases. But of the five lawyers who earned $50,000 or more per year from the practice of law, only one was an elite lawyer; the rest were high. Yet personal injury work was also an important area of practice for the low group. The differences in incomes between the high and low groups, however, probably reflected the fact that the former had more of the steady defense work while the latter had more of the plaintiff's work. Trusts and estates work was important for the middle and low groups. Their low professional income seems to support the suggestion made earlier that these lawyers had the poor individual clients and probably the smaller estates (and fees).

DIFFERENCES IN BACKGROUND

One might plausibly assume that success in practice could be correlated with lawyers' backgrounds—that the most successful lawyers would emerge from white Protestant families of English or northern and western European background, comfortable circumstances, and good education. In general, however, the Prairie City bar was very homogeneous. Over 70 per cent of the lawyers were Protestant; over 90 per cent had fathers who were businessmen, professionals, or semiprofessionals, or who had held higher white collar positions; almost 90 per cent of the lawyers had received college degrees; all but one graduated from law school; only 5 per cent went to law schools offering both day and evening divisions, and all of this group had been admitted to practice before World War II.

There were, however, some differences worth mentioning between elite lawyers and the rest of the bar. None of the elite lawyers were Catholic or Jewish; fewer elite lawyers than the rest of the bar were second generation (at least one grandparent born abroad); none of them were sons of fathers who worked in the lower white collar or manual occupations; more of the elite lawyers than the others had fathers who attended college or professional school. This would seem to indicate that there was some relationship between privileged background and what could be considered the most successful practice. On the other hand, some lawyers in the high group came from less privileged and minority group backgrounds. In Prairie City, then, the legal profession was apparently a means of income mobility, although a minority group background might still have barred access to the major business clients (Table B.9).[3]

PARTICIPATION IN AND ATTITUDES TOWARD
PROFESSIONAL ORGANIZATIONS

All of the lawyers but one belonged to the local bar association. Even
though higher proportions of the elite and high groups than of the
middle and low groups held offices or committee positions in the local
bar association, the differences in the proportions were quite small—
74 per cent of the low group as compared to 85 per cent of the elite.
Despite the differences in clients, incomes, and practice, the lawyers
in the four groups shared fairly evenly in the work of the local bar
association.

Membership in the state bar association was also widespread among
the four groups. Few lawyers in the community, however, had held a
state bar association office, and most of these were elite lawyers. Membership in the American Bar Association was related to the income-
client measure, for significantly higher proportions of the elite and high
lawyers belonged to the national organization than of the middle and
low (Table 3.9).

TABLE 3.9—Participation in Professional Organizations

	% of lawyers			
	Elite	High	Middle	Low
Local Bar Association				
Member	100	100	100	96
Officer	54	55	42	35
Committee member	31	30	37	39
State Bar Association				
Member	100	95	85	87
Officer	23	5	0	4
Committee member	8	15	16	13
Member of a section	54	45	32	48
American Bar Association				
Member	85	80	47	32
Officer	8	0	0	0
Committee member	8	0	5	5
Member of a section	31	15	11	14
	(13)	(20)	(19)	(23)*

* The number for the low group for the American Bar Association is 22.

The local bar association served to bridge whatever gaps existed between the four groups and to reinforce professional relationships among

the lawyers. Almost 20 per cent more of the elite lawyers had held office than the low group, but when asked whether the local bar "primarily represents any one group of lawyers," 87 per cent of the low group (and 77 per cent of the elite) said no. When asked whether the state bar association or the local bar association "speaks for the average lawyer," 74 per cent of the low group answered either that both did or that the local bar association did so more than the state bar association. Over 70 per cent of all of the lawyers and 78 per cent of the low thought that the local bar association was "doing a good job" in "improving the economic condition of the bar." Furthermore, 70 per cent of the lawyers and 74 per cent of the low group agreed with the local bar association's minimum fee schedule. Though less than half (47 per cent) of the lawyers thought that the bar association was "doing a good job" in "helping to create a more favorable public image of the bar," there were no differences in the rates of approval of this activity between the elite and the low. In general, not only was the work of the local association fairly evenly spread through the four groups, but there was also a high amount of satisfaction concerning most of the association's activities. Only in a very few instances was there much difference among the groups as to the work of the association.[4] Thus, there was a consensus among the lawyers that the local association represented the whole bar.

DIFFERENCES IN SOCIAL AND POLITICAL ACTIVITIES

SOCIAL

Few Prairie City lawyers participated in the local service clubs or in fraternal, ethnic-religious, or veterans' organizations. As Table 3.10 indicates, the level of participation was roughly the same for all four groups of lawyers. On the other hand, there was markedly more participation in local civic and charitable organizations such as the United Fund, the Red Cross, and the Association of Commerce, especially among the elite lawyers. For example, about 55 per cent more of the elite than of the other groups belonged to the Association of Commerce. These lawyers, whose practice was primarily in business, may have seen participation as important to their public relations, especially since local businessmen also participated in these same organizations. The comparatively low level of participation of the high group is explainable in terms of their practice. Many of these lawyers made their money by representing insurance companies in negligence cases; there would be little or no public relations gain from involvement in civic and charitable affairs.

TABLE 3.10—Participation in Local Civic and Social Organizations

Organization	% of lawyers			
	Elite	High	Middle	Low
Service clubs	31	15	42	22
Fraternal organizations	31	15	11	26
Ethnic-religious organizations	0	25	5	13
Veterans' organizations	23	20	16	26
Civic organizations				
Association of Commerce	85	30	37	30
Participation in at least				
one civic club	100	70	63	65
Participation in more than				
one civic club	77	35	42	35
Social clubs				
Downtown Club	85	60	47	22
Prestige country club	62	30	16	4
Participation in at least				
one social club	92	80	63	30
Participation in more than				
one social club	62	35	21	4
	(13)	(20)	(19)	(23)

Only one member of the bar was a member of the Downtown Council, a group of downtown businessmen and property owners concerned primarily with downtown problems. The biggest businessmen and their lawyers were not members although they belonged to the Association of Commerce as well as to the other civic and charitable organizations. At the time of the study, the Association of Commerce was no longer a political force in the community, but the Council was, and it dealt with politically sensitive problems. Membership in the Association of Commerce, the Red Cross, the United Fund, and the Boy Scouts served the public relations objectives of the elite lawyers without their running the risk of alienating groups with conflicting interests over downtown problems.

Participation in local social clubs was related to the income-client measure. Higher proportions of the elite and high groups belonged to the Downtown Club than the middle and low groups, and elite lawyers were more likely than the other groups to hold membership in the most prestigious country club. Religious affiliation may also have been a factor in membership in the country club; in this connection, it should be recalled that no Catholic or Jewish lawyer was an elite lawyer. Only two Catholics were members of this club, and at the time of this study, the club did not admit Jews.

POLITICAL

When a lawyer commits himself publicly on controversial issues, he runs the risk of displeasing clients. We would expect, then, that lawyers would reflect the political attitudes of their clients; but, in fact, no relationship was found between political behavior and the high, middle, and low groups. There was, however, a relationship between political behavior and the elite lawyers. The fact that all of the lawyers from the high, middle, and low groups had a wide range of clients was probably one of the reasons for the similarity in political behavior; if, as suggested, the political behavior of lawyers was related to their own economic well-being, then consciously or subconsciously, they had less reason (or were less able) to take account of the opinions of their clients. Wide ranges of clients would speak with muted, if not conflicting, voices.

The elite lawyers also had a diversified clientele, but they might well have been more responsive to the attitudes of their principal business and individual clients. These clients were clearly identifiable; their lawyers were in a continuing relationship with them and probably knew their political preferences well. The choices and risks of political behavior, then, were no doubt better defined for the elite lawyer than they were for the rest of the Prairie City bar. For example, the president of a major locally-owned industry would probably be more concerned about the political activities and attitudes of the company's lawyer (an elite lawyer) than would the branch office of an insurance company about its lawyer (a high group lawyer).

Although the bar as a whole was 70 per cent Republican and 30 per cent Democratic, all but one of the elite lawyers were Republican.[5] Higher proportions of the elite group than of the other groups had never campaigned for or against a candidate running for elective office and had never campaigned for or against local issues appearing on the ballot. For example, only two elite lawyers said that they had campaigned for or against candidates running for local public office. For one of these lawyers, "campaigning" meant mailing literature. The other elite lawyer had been very active, but the campaigns in which he participated were for offices for which only lawyers could qualify, such as prosecutor or a higher court judgeship. It would be unusual for offices of this type to arouse the interest, let alone the displeasure, of large business clients. This same elite lawyer had been heavily involved in a campaign for a sanitary district bond issue. Since he was the lawyer for the sanitary district, if this issue carried any political liability, he was already identified with his client. Another elite lawyer who said that he had campaigned for a local political issue appearing on the ballot meant by this that he spoke to a PTA meeting on behalf of a proposed judicial amendment to the state constitution.

None of the elite said that they were presently interested in running for political office. Only two elite lawyers, both of whom were Republicans, and two lawyers in the high group had done so, as compared to 39 per cent of the low group. One of the elite lawyers ran for a judgeship and the other for state-wide office. And it is of interest to note that although these two lawyers had large business clients, they did not have as many of these clients as most of the other elites. The two high lawyers ran for public offices which were not law-connected, but one of these lawyers had run in the early thirties. The other was presently very active in local politics, but, perhaps significantly, his most important area of practice was real estate.

None of the elite lawyers had served on a public board or commission that exercised governmental authority (*e.g.,* zoning board or school board) as distinguished from being advisory only (*e.g.,* Mayor's Special Committee on Legal Questions); none had held city or village attorney positions or had worked in local criminal law activities. Many of these lawyers, however, had served public bodies in a professional capacity. Usually these jobs were for school boards or in the state attorney general's office.

The elite lawyers seemed to differ from the rest of the bar in their attitudes towards politically sensitive issues. One of the most significant local issues that had faced Prairie City was the adoption of a city manager form of government. This form of government is usually supported by the upper business and commercial classes and by those residents who do not have strong loyalties to their local political districts. Since government by a city manager is nonpartisan, it had been opposed by the local political parties in Prairie City. The lawyers split fairly evenly on this issue. Almost two-thirds of the elite lawyers, however, said that they had favored the change. At the time of this study, the lawyers were asked whether or not they still favored the city manager form of government; 77 per cent of the elite said yes, as compared to about 50 per cent of the other groups.

More of the elite lawyers than those of the other groups were indifferent or uninformed about the state's new code of criminal procedure; none of these lawyers engaged in criminal work. The low group was the most informed, and higher proportions of this group did criminal work than of the other groups. Half of the elite lawyers opposed changes in the personal injury compensation system, and almost 70 per cent opposed changes in the method of selecting judges. These are not the attitudes normally to be expected from the leading business lawyers. It must be remembered, however, that in Prairie City, even though the elite lawyers were the principal business lawyers, over half of them spent at least some time in personal injury litigation, the median amount of time spent in this area being roughly comparable to the time spent by the high group, and that 15 per cent of the elite derived the largest portion of their income from personal injury. In other words, personal injury litigation was an important area of practice for these lawyers, they did well in it, and, not surprisingly, they tended to defend the *status quo*. The other groups, more extensively involved in personal injury work than the elites, were even more strongly opposed to changing the compensation system (about 75 per cent of these lawyers as compared to 54 per cent of the elite lawyers). On the other hand, about 20 per cent more of the middle and low groups than of the elite and high were in favor of changing the method of selecting judges to the appointive system. That is, the elite and high groups were more successful in personal injury, and they tended to support the *status quo*—both the compensation system and the method of judicial selection. The middle and low were less successful in personal injury; they were willing to maintain the compensation system, but they tended to favor a different method of judicial selection.

In regard to other issues, the elite lawyers again tended to advocate the *status quo*. Slightly more lawyers of the elite, high, and middle groups (about 55 per cent) were opposed to a "tax-supported program to provide free or low cost legal services to needy individuals in civil matters" than of the low group (39 per cent). Although the bar was about evenly split with no differences between the groups on whether "laws preventing racial discrimination in employment should be extended and strictly enforced," fewer elite lawyers (about 15 per cent) were in favor of enactment and strict enforcement of anti-discrimination laws for housing than the other groups, about 37 per cent of whom recommended these measures. Finally, more of the elite lawyers than the other groups did not think that "the bar should take a publicly active role in supporting civil rights legislation." [6]

In short, evidence suggests that the clients of the elite lawyers were more capable of making their political opinions known and respected than the more heterogeneous clients of lawyers in the other groups. The data on the social and political activities of the lawyers show that in general the elite lawyers were in the upper class social clubs, were careful about their civic involvements, avoided public commitments on issues that could become politically sensitive, were more conservative than the other groups, and tended to take positions on certain issues that were also taken by their business clients. The activities and positions of the other lawyers were not nearly so clear-cut.

DIFFERENCES IN PROFESSIONAL ATTITUDES

In Chapter 2, it was pointed out that Prairie City lawyers, on the whole, were very satisfied with the practice of law in general and with their own fields of practice. One would expect that the lawyers in the lower groups would be less satisfied than the elite and high lawyers. This was true only in part, for high proportions of all groups were very satisfied with the practice of law in general, with very small differences between the groups. However, less than half of the middle and low groups were "very satisfied" with their own fields of practice as compared to 85 per cent of the elite and high. In other words, lawyers liked being lawyers rather than something else, but among themselves, they were less satisfied with their relative position within the profession. Nevertheless, we must not exaggerate the differences: most of the middle and low groups were "moderately satisfied"; only three lawyers in the entire bar were even "somewhat dissatisfied."

The reasons for the comparative satisfaction, despite the differences in incomes, clients, and practice between the groups, are not very clear. More of the low group said that they had been hurt by competition from other lawyers (36 per cent) and from nonlawyers (44 per cent) than had the other groups, 15 per cent of whom had been hurt by competition from other lawyers and 12 per cent, from nonlawyers. So far as injurious rivalry from nonlawyers was concerned, the low group complained mostly about real estate brokers. About 20 per cent more of the low group than of the other groups thought that political connections were either "very important" or "somewhat important" in how a lawyer was treated in court, which perhaps explains why they tended to favor changing the method of judicial selection. The groups agreed on the importance of political connections when a lawyer dealt with government agencies or officials, or asked for court appointments (*e.g.,* guardianships *ad litem*). Yet only 48 per cent of the low group thought that such connections were important in "getting business, generally," in contrast to about 73 per cent of the elite, high, and middle group lawyers. In other words, even though the lawyers from the low group realized the importance of political contacts with regard to courts and agencies and were most active politically, their political connections had been of little consequence to the growth of their practices. Political connections, perhaps, were not important for the clients of these lawyers—the "walk-in" trade.

Regardless of these factors, overall satisfaction was apparent. Eighty-five per cent of the elite, high, and middle groups said that they definitely would be lawyers if they had to do it all over again; a smaller proportion—57 per cent—of the low group expressed this attitude. But only two lawyers in the low group would not be lawyers if they had to do it all over again; the others in the group (35 per cent) would still be lawyers but were not as emphatic as the elite, high, and middle lawyers. Finally, more than 80 per cent of the bar thought that "the chances of getting to the top for a young man of modest means just starting out in the practice of law" were either "good" or "excellent," and there were no real differences in proportions holding this opinion between the groups. The members of the low group were somewhat less satisfied with their careers than the others, but they were not discontent.

Prairie City lawyers may have been satisfied because of their prosperity. The median income for the lawyers in the low group was $11,200 —almost twice as much as the median income of Prairie City families.[7] Obviously, even lawyers low on the income-client measure were relatively well-off in Prairie City. While 35 per cent of the low group thought that they were earning less at the time of the study than they had predicted that they would be earning three or four years before, as compared to practically none of the other groups, yet 30 per cent of the low group thought that they were earning about the same and 35 per cent thought that they were earning more than what they predicted. In other words, their relatively low professional incomes did not represent disappointed expectations for two-thirds of this group. Eighty-six per cent of the low group did not think that they had reached their maximum income at the time of the study—a proportion only slightly higher than for the other groups. But half of these low group lawyers expected to earn, as a maximum income, $25,000—which was $2,500 less than the median incomes of the elite and high. Many of the low group, then, thought that they would improve their economic position, but their sights were relatively low, either because they simply had low expectations or because they were unaware of how much more money the other lawyers in the community were making. Either interpretation would explain the relatively slight degree of dissatisfaction on the part of the low group.

DIFFERENCES BY SIZE OF FIRMS

Of the eighty-three lawyers interviewed, twenty were in firms of more than five lawyers, forty-four were in firms of between two and five, and nineteen were individual practitioners. The distribution of the lawyers on the income-client measure by firm size, shown in Table 3.11, suggests

TABLE 3.11—Distribution of Lawyers by Size of Firm*

Firm size	% of lawyers			
	Elite	High	Middle	Low
Large firms (more than 5 lawyers)	54	20	16	4
Small firms (3–5 lawyers)	46	55	74	48
Individual practitioners	0	25	11	48
	100%	100%	100%	100%
	(13)	(20)	(19)	(23)

* The three lawyers who were excluded from the income-client measure were an individual practitioner, a small firm lawyer, and a large firm lawyer. Four of the associates were in large firms; one was in a small firm.

that size of firms was related to the stratification system of the Prairie City bar. None of the elite lawyers were individual practitioners, whereas almost half of the low group were; the proportions were about the reverse for the large firms. The stratification (classification) of lawyers by size of firms is the conventional method of description. In this bar, however, size of firms was not generally a significant indicator of differences among the lawyers. In many important respects there were no differences between the lawyers when classified by firm size; in others, the differences were greater when the lawyers were classified by the income-client measure than by firm size.

Large firm lawyers tended to have wealthier business and individual clients than either small firm lawyers or individual practitioners (Tables B.10 and B.11). But fewer than half of the large firm lawyers had as clients the largest businesses (gross incomes of $5,000,000 or more per year), and fewer than half (44 per cent) of the large firm lawyers reported that the median incomes of their individual clients were $20,000 or more per year, as compared to 75 per cent of the elite when the lawyers are classified by income-client measure.

More large firm lawyers had business practices than did the small firm lawyers and individual practitioners, but this area was not so much of a specialty for them as for the elite. More of the elite lawyers listed business as their main area of practice, derived the largest portion of their income from this source, spent time in the corporate specialties (e.g., antitrust, patents, trademarks, securities, labor relations), and gave advice on general business policy than of the large firm lawyers.

Generally, the income-client measure was related to the proportions of lawyers spending time in the "one-shot, trouble" areas of practice—personal injury plaintiffs and matrimonial and criminal cases (Table 3.6, above); the elite in particular spent less time in these areas than the middle and low groups. The distribution of lawyers by firm size, however, did not indicate differences in these areas of practice. In fact, about 20 per cent more large firm lawyers than small firm lawyers and individual practitioners spent some time representing plaintiffs in personal injury cases. The differences between the three firm sizes were small with regard to matrimonial (divorce and other) and criminal cases.

Since the Prairie City lawyers were not specialists, they spent comparatively little time in any one area of practice. But there were differences in time spent between the one-shot, trouble areas and those areas where the lawyers had continuing, long-term relationships with clients. In order to measure this difference, the proportion of time each lawyer devoted to personal injury plaintiffs, matrimonial cases, and criminal cases was subtracted from the proportion of time devoted to business, trusts and estates, real estate, and personal injury defendants. The lawyers were then divided into thirds; the upper third spent more time in business, trusts and estates, real estate, and personal injury defendants, and the lower third spent more time in the one-shot, trouble areas. The purpose of this scale was to indicate, in a rough way, which lawyers had continuing relationships with their clients and which lawyers had more of the walk-in trade. Table 3.12 indicates the relationship

TABLE 3.12—Relationship Between Stability of Clients and the Income-Client Measure and Size of Firm

	No. of lawyers	% of lawyers with		
		Stable clients	Mixed clients	Unstable clients
Income-client measure				
Elite	(13)	77	23	0
High	(20)	35	35	30
Middle	(19)	11	37	53
Low	(23)	17	44	39
Firm size				
Large	(20)	35	50	15
Small	(44)	34	32	34
Individual practitioners	(19)	26	32	42

between stability of clients and the income-client measure, as well as between client stability and firm size. The lawyers in the upper third (referred to as having a stable clientele) had fewer clients and higher proportions of business clients whom they represented for five or more years than did the lawyers in the bottom third (referred to as having an unstable clientele). The bottom third spent more time in court than the upper third (Tables B.12, B.13, and B.14). There were clear differences between the elite lawyers and the low group; 60 per cent more elite than low were in the upper third of the stability measure. Although there was also a relationship between the stability measure and firm size, this relationship was not nearly so pronounced as when the lawyers were classified in terms of incomes and wealth of clients. Again, firm size does not provide a clear index to the strata in the Prairie City bar.

Large firm lawyers spent about the same amount of time in the various courts as small firm lawyers and individual practitioners. In-

dividual practitioners, however, spent more time than large firm lawyers in the lower courts and in routine court tasks such as filing papers,
court calls, and motions. There were no important differences in terms
of firm size concerning contacts with government agencies and officials.
Since firm size did not indicate differences in areas of practice as well
as the income-client measure, neither did the size indicate as successfully
as the income-client measure differences in contacts with courts, agencies, and officials.

The average incomes of the large firm lawyers and the small firm
lawyers were about the same ($24,000) but considerably higher than
the individual practitioners' ($14,600). However, the median income
of the small firm lawyers was considerably less than the median income of the large firm lawyers ($17,500 as compared to $27,500).
The reason for the difference between the averages and the medians was
that there were a few small firm lawyers who did extremely well—in
fact, better than the large firm lawyers in the highest bracket: four
small firm lawyers reported earnings of $50,000 or more per year from
the practice of law, as compared to only one large firm lawyer.

There was not so clear-cut a relationship between firm size and
ethnic, religious, and economic backgrounds as there was between
income-client measure and background. No Catholic or Jewish lawyers
were in the elite group, but four Catholic lawyers and two Jewish lawyers were large firm lawyers. While no elite lawyers were of central,
eastern, or southern European descent, two large firm lawyers were.
None of the fathers of elite lawyers had held lower white collar or manual labor jobs, yet three fathers of large firm lawyers had. Fathers of
large and small firm lawyers were better educated than fathers of individual practitioners, but the incomes of the fathers of all three groups
at the time the respondents entered law school were roughly comparable. Finally, the quality of legal education of the lawyers was not related to firm size.

Participation in the local bar association was related neither to
the income-client measure nor to firm size; in fact, about 20 per cent
more individual practitioners than large firm lawyers held offices in
the local bar association. About the same proportion of large firm lawyers and individual practitioners participated in more than one civic
organization. About 20 per cent more large firm lawyers than small
firm lawyers or individual practitioners, however, were members of the
Association of Commerce, and more large firm lawyers than small firm

lawyers were members of the Downtown Club and the prestige country club.

There was no relationship between political activities and firm size; the proportion of Republicans, for example, in each firm size was about the same. The lawyers in one of the three large firms were almost totally inactive politically. Each of the other two large firms had two politically active senior partners, one a Republican and the other a Democrat. The inactive lawyers in the third firm represented far more large corporate enterprises than did the lawyers of the other two large firms, additional evidence that in Prairie City, political activity was related to clients. There was not much difference in the political activity between the small firm lawyers and the individual practitioners. About 35 per cent more large firm lawyers than elite lawyers were against changing the personal injury compensation system, but more large firm lawyers than elite were in personal injury. There were no significant differences of opinion between the lawyers, by firm size, concerning the new code of criminal procedure or the city manager form of government. Higher proportions of large firm lawyers than of individual practitioners favored stronger civil rights legislation in employment and housing.

GENERAL PRACTICE AND THE MEANING OF "PARTNERSHIP"

As we have seen, size of firms was not a particularly good indicator of other aspects of professional life in Prairie City. When lawyers were considered within such a context, similarities among the groups of lawyers were usually far more impressive than differences, primarily because all Prairie City lawyers, regardless of size of firm, were basically general practitioners. Even though some lawyers spent more time in one area of practice than in another and therefore considered themselves specialists, more often than not, the actual time spent in the specialty was only a small proportion of the total time devoted to the practice of law.

Prairie City lawyers performed a wide range of legal services. The lawyers who had the major business clients took care of all, or practically all, of the legal problems of those clients, including personal matters of corporate officers. In addition, these lawyers did real estate, probate, and personal injury work, and to a lesser extent, matrimonial work—types of practice shared with small firm lawyers and individual practitioners. The widespread general practice meant that all Prairie City lawyers appeared more or less in the same courts and before the same administrative agencies and government officials. Professional, civic, social, and political activities were related to work and also cut across classification lines. Indeed, differences among the large firm lawyers themselves were more pronounced than differences between large firm lawyers and members of the other two groups.

Implicit in attempts to classify lawyers by firm size are assumptions about the internal relationships of firm lawyers. It is assumed, for instance, that a law partnership is a group of lawyers in a joint venture, in which members share assets and liabilities. All receipts are paid to the firm, and after the payment of expenses, including salaries, the members of the firm distribute the profits among themselves according to a scale of percentages previously agreed upon. The members hold themselves out to the public as a firm: clients are clients of the firm, and these clients can hold each member of the firm or all of them for the mistakes of one. No one partner has a proprietary interest in a client. This, along with size, encourages the members of the firm to specialize. Each partner or associate handles the legal problems that he can do best, enabling the firm to offer legal services at a higher level of efficiency.

In an office-sharing arrangement, as contrasted to a partnership, a group of lawyers share the expense of running a suite of offices. Each lawyer has his own clients and keeps his own receipts. Two or more lawyers may work for a single client, or one lawyer may work for another lawyer, but the employing lawyer, or the lawyer who brought in the client, makes compensatory arrangements with the other lawyers for their services. In an office-sharing arrangement, the attorney-client relationship is more like that of individual practitioners. Specialization is discouraged: a lawyer runs the risk of losing a client if he has to refer the client to an outside specialist. Normally, the office-sharer, like the individual practitioner, does all or substantially all of the legal work of his clients.

If these are accurate descriptions of the internal relationships within groups of lawyers, then size of firm will indicate differences between types of lawyers and legal practice. The large unit will be better able to handle the wealthy client, the lawyers in the unit will be more specialized, and there will be more contact with higher level courts and officials than the individual practitioners or the lawyers in the smaller units have. The lawyers in different firm sizes will also differ in terms of professional, political, and social activities. In Prairie City, however, classification by firm size was not an accurate indicator of these differences. Even though, in the classification of the Prairie City bar, lawyers were counted as firm lawyers if two or more of them held themselves out as a partnership, the internal relationships among the firm lawyers did not conform to the ideal picture of a partnership.

Nineteen firms were included in this study, accounting for sixty-four lawyers (including five associates), or 77 per cent of the bar. Six of these firms (sixteen lawyers) held themselves out as partnerships, and were so classified in the principal legal directory, but were in fact closer in behavior to groups of office-sharing lawyers. The methods of computing the share of office expenses varied, ranging from each lawyer's paying a fixed percentage of his gross to a senior man who then paid all of the expenses, to complex formulae based on the gross receipts of the lawyers in the group. Some lawyers within these "firms" handled matters for the clients of another lawyer. But basically, each lawyer had his own clients, spent most of his time with these clients, did all or substantially all of the legal work for these clients, and took in his own receipts.

The other thirteen firms paid their expenses as a group, and the member lawyers received fixed percentages of the profits. In this respect, these firms conformed to the model of a partnership. There was, however, considerable variation in the extent to which these conformed to other conventional partnership features.

In order to determine what variations existed in the internal organization of these firms, lawyers were asked several questions: "Are any of the clients of the firm identified as clients of a particular partner, as distinguished from firm clients?" "What proportion of the clients of the firm are clients of a particular partner?" "What proportion of your time is given to your 'own' clients?" "Are there any clients of the firm who are considered to be your clients? (If yes) Are these clients you brought in or were assigned to?" "How important are the following in allocating work among the partners—Who is free? Specialty? Whose client it is? Client's wishes?" "In important matters that you handle, do you generally take full responsibility for setting the fee, or do you review it with your partner?" "In handling client matters, as a matter of practice, do you invariably review major issues with your partners?"

The data contained many surface contradictions. Quite often within a single firm two senior partners gave very different estimates as to the proportion of clients that could be identified as clients of a particular partner; one senior would say, for example, that all clients were the firm's clients, and another senior would say that all or substantially all of the clients were clients of a particular partner. It was our impression that much of this contradiction arose from the fact that several of the firm lawyers when asked this question (which was the first of this series) resisted the notion of conceiving of their firms as groups of office sharers. They often had been working together for a long time, had a partnership basis for compensation, had held themselves out as a partnership, and had thought of themselves as a team. Sometimes inconsistent answers were gestures of generosity on the part of seniors who really did "own" the clients. On the other hand, lesser partners might have been unwilling to confess to an inferior position within the firm. For example, in some firms where the line between senior and junior partners was quite clear, senior partners said that all or substantially all of the clients could be identified as clients of a particular partner; whereas junior partners in the same firm said that none of the clients, or only a small proportion of the clients, could be so identified. The juniors' answers were understandable even though inaccurate. In most instances where senior partners denied that clients could be identified as clients of a particular partner, they contradicted themselves by saying that "whose client it is" was very important or somewhat important in allocating work among partners. There were instances in which senior partners denied the existence of partner proprietorship in clients or would not give a figure but nevertheless admitted that a certain percentage of their time was spent on their "own" clients. Only two partners gave consistent partnership answers. These two lawyers were members of a two-man and three-man firm respectively (which was contrary to the expectation that the smaller firms would have strong elements of partner proprietorship in clients), and both were contradicted by their fellow partners.

Despite the uncertainties and ambiguities in the data, the differences in the responses to these questions were marked when the one large firm in which the lawyers handled the receipts and expenses on an office-sharing basis was compared to the two other large firms which handled their money on a partnership basis. In response to the question of what proportion of the clients were clients of a particular partner, the figures for the office-sharing firm averaged 96 per cent; in the other two firms, counting only the estimates of the senior partners, the figures averaged 25 per cent. All of the partners in the office-sharing firm claimed clients on the basis that they brought them in. This was true for only three out of five of the senior partners in the other two firms. In the two firms which were on a percentage basis, the senior partners spent about 25 per cent of their time, on the average, with their own clients. In contrast, the senior partners in the office-sharing firm spent over 90 per cent of their time, on the average, with their own clients. The other two members of the office-sharing firm—a younger brother of one of the partners and a son of another partner—spent 60 per cent and 50 per cent respectively of their time on their own clients. The remainder of their time was spent working for the other lawyers in the firm. The data did not indicate how these two lawyers were compensated for their services. The other two large firms also had junior partners. None of the junior partners in one of these firms identified clients as clients of a particular partner or had his own clients. In the second of these firms, the junior partners, who were farther along than their counterparts in the other firm, had their own clients; one spent half of his time with these clients and the other, one-third.

Client proprietorship was "very important" in allocating the work among the partners in the office-sharing firm, but only one lawyer from each of the other two firms rated client ownership this high as a determinant of allocation. All of the partners in the office-sharing firm set fees on their own except for the two brothers. In the other two firms, all of the lawyers except one junior partner reviewed the fees with their colleagues. Seniority was an important factor in deciding the partnership percentages in the two firms that were organized on this basis.

Of the large firm lawyers who had 10 per cent or more of their work in business practice, each of the office-sharing lawyers did all of the legal work for his principal business clients. In the other two firms, there were tendencies to specialize although specialization was far more the exception than the rule. Two of the senior partners in one of the firms, for example, handled just the personal contacts and let the junior partners do the legal work. In the second firm, two of the senior partners did everything except either the tax work or the labor work. On the other hand, almost all of the lawyers in all three large firms claimed that they reviewed, as a matter of practice, all major issues with their partners.

We should not conclude that the two large firms organized on a percentage basis totally lacked office-sharing characteristics. In this community, differences in practice were relatively slight, and a comparison of these two firms is instructive. All of the senior partners in these firms identified clients in terms of particular partners, and most of these lawyers spent some time on their own clients. The two junior partners in one of these firms gave similar responses; the three juniors in the other firm did not. Why the difference? The two juniors who had their own clients were, on the average, nine years older and had been in practice six years longer than the three juniors in the other firm. The former were simply farther along, while the latter represented a characteristic found in many Prairie City firms—very early partnerships. The age and years in practice of the three juniors were not too dissimilar to the age and years in practice of the *associates* in the other firm. In other words, if we disregard the classification labels—"partners," "juniors," "seniors"—we find that client proprietorship elements were stronger among those lawyers who had been around long enough to work up their own clients. Again, the tendencies to specialize were not of great significance in these two firms. For example, the "tax specialist" in the firm where the others did not do tax work spent only about 20 per cent of his time on his specialty.

The data for small firms organized on a percentage basis also contained a great many contradictions. Among these firms only one firm, composed of two lawyers, gave consistent partnership answers. Both partners, the junior and the senior, said that all the clients were clients of the firm, neither claimed any clients nor said that they spent any time on their own clients, and both said that "whose client it is" was of no importance at all in allocating work. In all of the other firms there were contradictions between the answers of the members of the same firm. The answers nevertheless made clear that the office-sharing features of a small firm, even one organized on a percentage basis, were very strong.

In the small firms organized on a percentage basis, for example, there were twenty-four senior partners, twenty-one of whom reported that client ownership was either very important or somewhat important in allocating work. Again, fourteen of these senior members identified clients as clients of particular partners; the average proportion of such clients was 67 per cent (73 per cent median). Seventeen of these lawyers spent, on the average, 70 per cent of their time on their own clients. Likewise, specialization was of little significance. Taking both junior and senior partners together, of those who had 10 per cent or more of their practice in the business area, over 80 per cent did all the legal work for their business clients.

In sum, even though most of the lawyers in this community were in partnerships, the dominant characteristics of legal practice were those usually associated with individual practitioners. These lawyers were generalists with "proprietorship" interests in their clients.

A PROFESSIONAL COMMUNITY

The practitioners of this bar worked in close physical proximity to each other, to the courthouse, and to other government offices; therefore, a great deal of professional contact was to be expected between the elite, high, middle, and low groups of lawyers. In an effort to determine what degree of professional contact existed and to what extent it crossed socio-economic lines, each lawyer was asked to name other lawyers, outside of his firm if the respondent was a firm lawyer, with whom he had collaborated on a case "involving more or less continual contact," to whom he had turned over a case, from whom he had received a case, whom he had helped by filing a paper or witnessing a document, or with whom he talked over legal problems.

Fewer of the elite lawyers (only 46 per cent) than of the other groups volunteered this information,[8] but all of those who did had worked with lawyers in the other groups. As Table 3.13 indicates, there was

TABLE 3.13—Degree of Professional Contact Between Income-Client Groups

Type of lawyer responding	Number named	Lawyers with whom respondents had collaborated*			
		% by income-client group			
		Elite	High	Middle	Low
Elite	13	15	23	39	23
High	19	21	42	11	26
Middle	24	25	38	8	29
Low	33	6	42	18	33

* These figures exclude firm partners of the respondents.

considerable working contact between the elite, high, and middle groups, and these three groups also reported considerable contact with the low group. The low group, on the other hand, reported substantial professional contact with the high and middle groups but not with the elite. The figures in Table 3.13 do not represent all the contacts between the groups of lawyers; the information asked for dealt only with situations in which lawyers worked together, not with those in which lawyers dealt with each other while representing opposite sides. Nonetheless, 85 per cent (forty-seven) of the lawyers who gave this information had working contact with lawyers in another group, and 62 per cent dealt with lawyers two groups away (*i.e.*, an elite lawyer with a middle or low group lawyer).

That there was also social contact within the profession across economic lines is apparent. When asked to name the lawyers with whom they were most friendly, 95 per cent (sixty-three) of the lawyers named at least one lawyer from another income-client group, and almost half (48 per cent) named a lawyer two groups away (Table 3.14). Evi-

TABLE 3.14—Degree of Social Contact Between Income-Client Groups

Type of lawyer responding	Number named	Lawyers with whom respondents were most friendly			
		% by income-client group			
		Elite	High	Middle	Low
Elite	21	29	38	33	0
High	38	34	42	13	11
Middle	39	18	41	8	33
Low	52	10	35	31	25

dently, the practice of law tended to bring together people who normally would be socially distant. The incomes of the elite and high lawyers differed considerably from those of the middle group, which in turn differed from those of the low group. Furthermore, membership in the Downtown Club and in the most prestigious country club—life-styles in general—was related to the groups to which lawyers belonged. Nevertheless, work brought lawyers of different groups together, and these lawyers named as friends lawyers in other groups. Although only 10 per cent of the middle and low group lawyers belonged to the most prestigious country club, 62 per cent of the lawyers with whom the elite worked were middle and low group lawyers, and 33 per cent of the lawyers named most friendly by the elite were of the middle group. Generally, it was more common for a lawyer in a lower group to list a lawyer in a higher group as most friendly than the reverse. The disparity was small, however, and lower group lawyers did not seem resentful or hostile toward the upper group lawyers. They probably did not feel that class differences were unbridgeable, and they were responsive, perhaps overly so, to expressions of friendliness.

Thus, despite the differences between the lawyers of this bar in terms of clients, practice, and incomes, a genuine professional community seemed to exist; at least as lawyers these people worked together and were friendly towards each other. The data on participation in and attitudes towards the local bar association supported the finding of a professional community, for leadership and committee positions were spread rather evenly throughout the groups, almost all of the lawyers were satisfied with much of the work of the association, and almost all of them thought that the association was representative of all the lawyers. Professional and social contacts across class lines would follow from homogeneity in background, the similarities in general practice, and close physical proximity.

SUMMARY AND COMPARISON WITH THE
NEW YORK CITY BAR

Because practically all Prairie City lawyers, both firm lawyers and individual practitioners, performed a wide range of legal services, there was very little specialization. The principal differences among the Prairie City lawyers related to professional incomes, wealth of clients, and types of practice.

The elite lawyers were wealthy, represented the biggest businesses in town, and had the wealthiest clients, both individual and business. The high group also enjoyed high professional incomes, but had different clients and different types of practice from the elite group. Their clients, both business and individual, were less affluent than those of the elite. These lawyers were successful in personal injury work; they did more defense work than the other groups and probably represented the better plaintiffs' cases as well. The middle group had lower incomes and poorer clients than the elite and high. Many of these lawyers worked in matrimonial cases and personal injury (plaintiff), but trusts and estates was the principal area of practice. The fees from this work, however, were probably small because of the relatively low income levels of the clients. The business clients of the low group were the smallest enterprises in town; their individual clients were drawn from the less well-off classes. Trusts and estates formed an important area of practice, but fees were probably small. More of the low group than of the others worked in the one-shot, trouble areas—in personal injury (plaintiff), matrimonial, and criminal cases.

Contacts with courts, agencies, and officials were, in general, related to practice, and lack of specialization meant that most lawyers appeared in most of the courts. The low group, however, spent more time in the lowest court, while the middle and low groups spent more time in the routine court tasks.

The bar as a whole was very homogeneous in background characteristics. We found evidence to suggest, however, that lawyers from minority religious groups may have been limited in their choice of clients and areas of practice, though not barred from achieving economic success: while there were Catholic and Jewish lawyers in the high group, no Catholic or Jewish lawyers represented the biggest business clients.

All four income-client groups were about equally active in the local bar association. There was a consensus that the bar association was representative of all the lawyers. The elite lawyers, as compared to the other groups, had a higher level of participation in those civic organizations which gave good publicity but which were also politically neutral. The elite lawyers also had a higher level of participation in the more prestigious social clubs than the other lawyers.

The lawyers did not provide much political leadership and were generally inactive in local public issues. The biggest businesses in the area shunned political activity, not concerning themselves with local issues, and their lawyers tended to mirror their clients' positions. In fact, the one large firm which represented most of the biggest businesses was the most politically inactive.

Despite differences in clients, incomes, and practice, lawyers were content with their careers and generally optimistic about their future, even though there was some slight evidence of dissatisfaction on the part of the lower groups. In addition, despite class lines, professional life brought together lawyers from different groups. To a very considerable extent, work and social contacts cut across class lines.

Class differences, then, were blurred in Prairie City. The principal differences among Prairie City lawyers—in wealth of clients, professional incomes, and types of practice—were offset by lack of specialization, mixed clienteles, homogeneous backgrounds, equal participation in the local bar association, and a great deal of professional and social contact between income-client groups.

In contrast, the stratification system was complete in the New York City bar; there were no bridges between groups. In this bar firm size was an important indicator of sharp differences between lawyers.[9] The large firm lawyers (fifteen or more lawyers per firm) formed an elite. They specialized primarily in business law and in estate and trust work. Their business clients were the very large corporations in heavy industry and major finance, while their individual clients were wealthy and Protestant. These lawyers spent less time in court than the other lawyers, and when they went to court, it was mainly to the higher courts (federal and appellate). They enjoyed the highest incomes. The small firm lawyers (two–four lawyers) and individual practitioners were the low group, representing the small, closely held corporations; individual proprietors in retail, personal service, real estate, and light manufacturing; and individual clients from minority groups and the middle to lower income brackets. Their main areas of practice were personal injury, criminal, matrimonial, and workmen's compensation. The lawyers in the low group went to court more than the elite lawyers, but they appeared more frequently in the local city and municipal courts. Although the elite, middle, and low groups spent about the same amount of time with administrative agencies, the former dealt primarily with federal agencies and the latter with state and local agencies.

The very substantial differences among New York City lawyers in practice, clients, and income were strongly related to differences in background. The small firm lawyers and individual practitioners were predominantly first or second generation Americans, of eastern European origin, and Jewish. The large firm lawyers were at least fourth generation Americans, of British, Irish, or northwestern European origin, and Protestant. The large firm lawyers came from a more advantageous background than the individual practitioners and small firm lawyers, their fathers having had more education and higher status occupations than the fathers of the latter.

A selective recruiting process and the patterns of career mobility suggested that there was "a marked degree of continuity and stability among the various status groups" in the New York City bar.[10] Religion, socioeconomic background, type of college and law school, and grades in law school were important factors in recruitment of lawyers into the various strata of the profession. For example, Jewish lawyers were less likely than non-Jewish lawyers to be employed by the large law firms, regardless of type of college and law school attended and socioeconomic background.[11] Career mobility between groups was uncommon, for, generally, New York City lawyers tended to remain in the group in which they started. Very few large firm lawyers came from other groups, although there was some tendency for lawyers in middle-sized and small firms to become individual practitioners. Large firm lawyers, if they moved down, went primarily to middle-sized firms; very few individual practitioners had ever been large firm lawyers. Mobility, too, was correlated with background factors. Carlin pointed out in his study: "Lawyers who begin and remain in a large firm are more likely than those who move 'down' to be Protestant, to come from a family of high socioeconomic status, and to have gone to a prestige college and an Ivy League law school. Moreover, lawyers who move 'up' from individual practice more often have these same characteristics than those who remain at the lower level." [12]

Professional and social differences between New York City lawyers were reinforced by the lack of contacts between elite and low groups, for professional and social contacts were primarily between members of the same group. Bar associations showed the same division along status lines: the Association of the Bar of the City of New York was primarily an elite organization, both in membership and in leadership, while the New York County Lawyers Association was composed primarily of middle and low group lawyers.

In the metropolitan bar, class differences between lawyers were sharp; the groups of lawyers were isolated from each other. This segmentation was a product of size, of specialization, of recruitment practices, and career histories, firm size marking social and professional divisions. In Prairie City, on the other hand, the stratification system seemed more fluid. Several of the elites, for example, had started their own firms; others had been individual practitioners and then joined firms. The types of clients acquired determined status, yet the groups in Prairie City were not isolated from each other. They were linked by a common background and training, by work and social contacts, by participation in the local bar association, and by close physical proximity. In short, then, the New York City bar was segmented; despite its differences, the Prairie City bar was a professional community.

Part II

Ethics and Social Control

CHAPTER 4

THE FORMAL DISCIPLINARY MACHINERY

It is important that the legal profession be both competent and ethical. The profession, in the words of Talcott Parsons, is "one of the very important mechanisms by which a relative balance of stability is maintained in a dynamic and rather precariously balanced society." [1] Important issues of liberty and property are subject to its influence. In addition, clients are dependent upon lawyers for technical solutions to problems which the clients themselves cannot solve. Clients must trust their attorneys, yet it is difficult to judge the quality and honesty of lawyers in advance. The profession is in a position to exploit clients.

Lawyers are obligated to obey the ethical standards of the community —not to steal, cheat, or embezzle. They are, in addition, enjoined to obey standards which are strictly those of "legal ethics"—rules for lawyers alone. These are, or are said to be, geared to specific problems of professional life. For example, clients tell lawyers secret information about their affairs or the affairs of others. These confidences must be protected. A lawyer should not sacrifice the interests of a client for the interests of more important clients or use secret information for personal profit. Pressure from clients to accomplish results can place lawyers in positions in which they are tempted to seek improper advantages from courts or other government officials by gift-giving, by bribery, or by submitting false or misleading evidence. Specific rules cover these. Other rules concern ethical standards in dealings between lawyers. Pressure to engage in unethical conduct, for example, is allegedly liable to increase if lawyers advertise and solicit business. These dealings, too, are proscribed by rules of "legal ethics."

In addition, lawyers are said to have some sort of responsibility for justice and the rule of law beyond the immediate concerns of their clients and their practice. [2] The responsibility of lawyers for public service is vaguely and variously described, but legal authorities are certain that the responsibility exists. Dean Pound defined a profession as "a group of men pursuing a learned art as a common calling in the spirit of public service—no less a public service because it may incidentally be a means of livelihood." [3] Henry Drinker lists as one of the "primary characteristics which distinguish the legal profession from a business," "a duty of public service, of which the emolument is a by-product, and in which one may attain the highest eminence without making much money." [4]

The competency and ethicality of lawyers rest almost exclusively in the hands of the profession. The profession has large powers over the training and recruitment of members and over the discipline of deviant members. Continuing efforts have been made, with some degree of success, to increase the competence of those seeking admission. Applicants for admission to the bar are also required to demonstrate that they are of good moral character, but less than 1 per cent of all applicants fail to gain admission on this ground.[5] How many people with less than the requisite ethical standards are admitted to practice is, of course, not known. Henry Drinker is "confident that the bar is today in sounder and healthier condition than for a century; that year by year it is becoming more so, and more than ever determined to maintain its standards." [6] But recent studies of metropolitan bars present a less sanguine picture.[7]

In Part I of this study we examined the responsibility of Prairie City bar for public service. The data suggested that at least so far as this bar was concerned, this responsibility rested more on hope than on fact: lawyers in this community apparently did not engage in public service and were not influential in community affairs. In Part II, we are concerned with the role of the bar in discharging obligations to clients and colleagues and in the administration of justice. Professional responsibility will be examined in its relation to the social structure and characteristics of this bar. What is the nature and extent of unprofessional conduct and what is the bar doing about it? We will examine the disciplinary efforts of the organized bar, the principal enforcement agency of legal ethics. Since no law enforcement agency can function effectively unless there is widespread agreement on norms, we shall also consider the willingness of the lawyers themselves to accept and adhere to their ethical rules. Finally, we shall compare the extent and nature of the problems of social control of this bar with the New York City bar.

This chapter deals with the formal disciplinary machinery. The materials are based on an examination of the disciplinary files of the state bar association for a fifteen-year period, on state supreme court opinions, on interviews, and on an examination of the files of the Prairie City bar association. We have tried to find out who in the bar is punished and for what and how the disciplinary machinery operates. There are certain gaps in the data: although we have information on the number of lawyers charged, the number of complaints, the number of complaints per lawyer, the types of offenses charged, and the disposition of the cases, we have no information on other factors which may affect the decision to bring a lawyer before a bar association grievance committee or the factors affecting the decisions of the committees. We know the ages and years in practice of the lawyers charged, but we do not know anything about their type of practice, clientele, income, and size of firm. Despite these deficiencies, the data nevertheless tell a great deal about the operation of the formal disciplinary machinery.

STRUCTURE AND PROCEDURE

THE STATE BAR ASSOCIATION

State high courts generally have final authority to discipline lawyers for misconduct. Procedures vary from state to state. Initial complaints against lawyers may be filed before bar associations, trial courts, or even appellate courts; and if filed in court, the complaint may be referred to a master or heard by a judge, or the respondent may be entitled to a jury trial.[8]

In the state in which Prairie City is located, the supreme court had long asserted its power to discipline lawyers.[9] The first rule promulgated by the court, in 1880, vested the authority to initiate disbarment proceedings in the Attorney General or in the local prosecutor by his filing an information containing "clear and specific charges, [and] giving the time, place and acts of misconduct with reasonable certainty." Shortly after the turn of the century, the rule was amended to provide that, in addition, "the president and secretary of a regularly organized Bar Association, either incorporated or unincorporated, or any person aggrieved by the misconduct of the attorney charged" could file the information. In the 1930's the court provided an alternate method of bringing proceedings. It authorized the governing board of the state bar association "to investigate . . . practices of attorneys-at-law which tend to defeat the administration of justice or to bring the courts and the legal profession into disrepute, . . . to receive, entertain, inquire into and take proof concerning complaints against attorneys-at-law . . . and . . . make all necessary rules and regulations concerning the conduct of such inquiries. . . ." The order provided for hearings at the bar association level and for the filing of the reports in the supreme court "for hearing and disposition in this court." In subsequent years the information practice was abandoned, and the authority to initiate disciplinary proceedings rested exclusively in the bar association.

Disciplinary procedures were set forth in a supreme court rule. The complaint against the lawyer had to be signed either by the person or persons aggrieved, by the president and secretary of a "regularly organized bar association," or by the chairman of a "regularly appointed committee" of the state bar association. Hearings were held before committees of the bar association and were private unless the respondent requested that they be public. The committees could obtain subpoenas to compel testimony and the production of documents. If the committee report recommended action "of any kind" by the supreme court, then the board of governors of the bar association reported to the court "its conclusions of fact and law concerning the complaint, answer and proof." The matter was then set down for hearings in the supreme court on briefs and oral argument. The supreme court could adopt, alter, or reject the recommendations of the board of governors. If the charges were sustained, in whole or in part, the lawyer could be censured, suspended, or disbarred. There were provisions for reinstatement.

Under the procedures at the time of the study, the state bar association had two committees to handle disciplinary matters: the committee on inquiry and the committee on grievances. The general counsel of the bar association performed a screening function for the inquiry committee. Complaints were first registered with him. He was responsible for acquainting himself with the facts and deciding whether or not the complaint warranted further consideration. He had the authority to dismiss complaints. If, on the other hand, he decided that the complaint warranted further investigation, he then referred it to the inquiry committee, which was composed of a chairman, a general committee, and district committees for the several judicial districts. The chairman of the inquiry committee, upon receipt of the complaint, notified the chairman of the district committee, who in turn requested the member of the district committee living closest to the respondent to investigate the complaint. A report was sent to the general chairman of the inquiry committee. The investigator or the district chairman amplified the written report at a meeting of the entire inquiry committee. A "no" vote on the part of the inquiry committee ended the matter. If the inquiry committee recommended that some action be taken against the respondent, the case was referred to the hearing division of the grievance committee. There the matter received a full hearing and would be referred to the board of governors.

THE LOCAL BAR ASSOCIATION

The bar association of the county in which Prairie City is located also had a committee on grievances, appointed by the local bar association president with the advice and consent of the executive committee. The by-laws of the association empowered the committee ". . . to take notice of unprofessional and unethical conduct of any member of this Bar, and after investigation, if in its opinion the facts shall so warrant, take appropriate action in conformity with the rules of" the supreme court and the state bar association.

The procedures of the local committee were very informal. All complaints against lawyers were referred to the chairman, and if, in his opinion, there was any hint of unprofessional or unethical conduct, he called a meeting of the committee. Before the meeting, the respondent either appeared or submitted a letter or an affidavit. If the committee thought, as a result of the hearing, that the matter required further investigation, it held a formal hearing. It could decide to dismiss the action or could recommend that the lawyer be censured or expelled from the association. Recommendations were made to the executive committee, and the decision was made by the full association. Finally, the committee could send the whole file and the complaint to the state bar association for further action.[10]

THE NUMBER AND DISPOSITION OF DISCIPLINARY ACTIONS

In 1964 there were about four thousand lawyers within the disciplinary jurisdiction of the state bar association. The general counsel of the state bar association stated that he received either directly or by referral between twenty-five and fifty complaint letters per week, an average of not quite two thousand letters per year. The general counsel considered the vast majority of these letters to be so lacking in merit as not to warrant any consideration by the inquiry committee. A great majority of the complaints which he screened out were from disappointed litigants who were convinced that their loss of the lawsuit was a result of their lawyer's failure to do his job properly. They were complaining about an adverse jury verdict or bench decision. Most of the letter writers, according to the general counsel, were people of low income and education. Another group of complaints was from "professional complaint letter writers," several of whom were inmates of state institutions and periodically wrote the state bar association about their lawyers' conduct. Most of these letters were easily identified and rejected.[11] On many occasions the general counsel wrote or telephoned the attorney involved for further information. Sometimes the attorney then saw his client and straightened out their disagreement. On other occasions clients saw the general counsel in person; in these instances complaints were either screened out conversationally, or, if the general counsel thought that the complaint had merit, the client was asked to submit it in writing. The general counsel, then, did not merely screen out complaints; he also aided in clearing up misunderstandings and smoothing over hurt feelings.

Few complaints ever went beyond the general counsel's office. In an average year, only seventy-four of the two thousand letters received raised charges sufficiently serious to be referred to the inquiry committee. This committee, in turn, screened out sixty-nine of these cases on the average, and only five were referred to the hearing division for a formal hearing (Table B.15, Appendix B).

Because problems of unethical or unprofessional conduct may involve more than one client or because one client may charge his lawyer with more than one infraction, it is important to know not only the number of lawyers charged with unethical or unprofessional conduct but also the number of charges. Table 4.1 shows the distribution of charges in both the inquiry committee and the hearing division. During the fifteen-year period studied, 2,565 charges were referred to the inquiry committee, representing an average of 2.3 charges per case. During the same period, the hearing division heard 70 cases; these cases involved 163 charges, or 2.3 charges per lawyer. The fate of the cases before the hearing division is shown in Table 4.2. In eight of the twenty-two instances of disbarment the respondents consented to having their names stricken from the roll of attorneys, an action equivalent to a guilty plea. In addition, one respondent was serving a prison term when his case was

TABLE 4.1—Distribution of Charges in the Inquiry Committee and Hearing Division of the State Bar Association, 1949–63

Charges	Inquiry Committee		Hearing Division	
	Number	Per Cent	Number*	Per Cent
Offenses Against Client				
Financial				
a. Conversion, misappropriation of money or property	499	20	38	23
b. Fees: overreaching, disputes about fees, attorney's liens	194	8	8	5
Other				
a. Neglect, misinforming, carelessness, failure or refusal to proceed with litigation, giving bad advice, disputes as to how pending litigation should be conducted, collusion or conspiracy against client	822	32	37	23
b. Threats or blackmail tactics to obtain settlements of claims, either against own client or on behalf of client to the complainant	102	4	1	−1
c. Conflict of interest	85	3	4	2
Offenses Against the Administration of Justice				
Bribery, fixing of court officials	30	1	0	0
Fraud on the court: misrepresentation, concealing evidence, actions in bad faith, subornation or perjury, preparation or submission of false or misleading pleadings or affidavits	339	13	22	13
Government agencies: bribery, fixing, submission of false or misleading evidence	48	2	1	−1
Offenses Against Colleagues				
Direct: breaking agreements, deceiving another attorney, etc.	70	3	5	3
Solicitation, directly or through intermediaries	129	5	11	7
Other Professional Misconduct†				
Corruption (lawyer as a public official)	139	5	10	6
Abuses in connection with admission or disciplinary proceedings	0	0	1	−1
Nonprofessional Misconduct				
Failure to pay personal obligations, bad checks, inducing clients to make bad investments, disagreements in personal business transactions	86	3	16	10
Felonies‡				
Larceny, embezzlement	9	−1	7	4
Forgery	6	−1	2	1
Income tax	2	−1	0	0
Other	5	−1	0	0
TOTAL CHARGES	2,565	100%	163	100%

* The charges are not known for one lawyer.

† Misconduct not arising out of regular practice.

‡ Cases in which a lawyer pleads guilty or is convicted of crime involving moral turpitude.

TABLE 4.2—Disposition of Hearing Division Cases, 1949–63

Action taken	Number	Per Cent
Dismissed	24	34
Censured	13	19
Suspended	10	14
Disbarred		
By committee vote	13	19
By consent	8	11
Respondent in prison	1	1
No record	1	1
Total	70	100%

considered by the hearing division.[12] In thirteen cases, disbarment was recommended by the division after a hearing.

The state bar association could only recommend sanctions. If the respondent protested, he could appeal to the state supreme court, which alone had the formal power to impose sanctions. In the cases that we are considering over the fifteen-year period, thirty-six lawyers could have asked the supreme court to review their cases. These were the lawyers who were either censured (thirteen), suspended (ten), or disbarred by committee vote (thirteen).[13] As Table 4.3 indicates, fewer than one out of three lawyers appealed the decision of the hearing division. There was no correlation between severity of sanction and appeal; just as many lawyers who were censured as those who were disbarred either failed to appeal or appealed. Reluctance to use the supreme court might have been due to the fact that at this level the proceedings were no longer secret, for if the case were appealed, it became part of the public record and was likely to be reported in the

TABLE 4.3—Appeal and Disposition of Hearing Division Cases in the State Supreme Court, 1949–63

	Cases by Hearing Division disposition			
	Censured	Suspended	Disbarred	Total
Cases eligible for appeal	13	10	13	36
Cases appealed to Supreme Court	4	2	4	10
Supreme Court disposition	affirmed 4	affirmed 2	affirmed 3; modified 1 to 5-yr. suspension	...

newspapers, particularly in smaller communities. Perhaps only extreme cases received sanctions from the bar, so that appeal seemed futile. Table 4.3 shows that of the ten cases which were appealed to the supreme court, only one hearing division recommendation was modified —from a disbarment to a five-year suspension for a fifty-year-old lawyer. It may also be that the supreme court was not willing to disturb the findings and conclusions of the bar committees.

In Table 4.4 we have summarized the flow and disposition of the disciplinary cases from the state bar association through the state supreme court during the period studied.

TABLE 4.4—Summary: Flow and Disposition of Disciplinary Cases, 1949–63

A. Complaints to the State Bar Association — 30,000 (approx.)
B. Referred to the Inquiry Committee — 1,107
C. Referred to the Hearing Division — 70

Acquitted	24
Censured	13
Suspended	10
Disbarment recommended	13
Disbarred (consent)	8
Prison term	1
No record	1

D. Appealed to the State Supreme Court — 10

Censured	4
Suspended	3
Disbarred	3

Total Sanctions — 45

Censured	13
Suspended	11
Disbarred	21

In addition to the state bar association, the local bar associations also performed disciplinary functions. The flow and disposition of disciplinary cases at the local level is a matter of conjecture; no attempt was made to gather quantitative evidence, and it is doubtful whether sufficiently reliable records were in existence. One of the past chairmen of the grievance committee of the Prairie City bar association pointed out that "many minor things just never find their way into the files."

The past chairman of the Prairie City bar association, however, estimated that, in addition to a "few crackpot letters," between six and eight genuine complaints were filed a year. At least half of these were not considered to be grievance questions at all. A client might complain about a jury verdict or bench decision, for example, a complaint which the chairman usually settled himself by explaining the situation to the client. Even when he thought that the complaint did not state a grievance, the chairman sometimes took action for the sake of good public relations. In one instance, a client complained that a lawyer would not return a file. The chairman called the lawyer and straightened the matter out. In another instance a client charged a lawyer with being negligent in a real estate transaction. Even though the chairman did not consider this a valid grievance, he called the lawyer to see if something could be done. Finally, the chairman, usually in conjunction with the committee on grievances, also handled grievance matters if he thought that they were not too serious. In one case, a lawyer was charged with filing a false affidavit. The committee sent the lawyer a letter, and he subsequently changed the affidavit.

Local bar associations also participated in more serious disciplinary matters. They were involved, for example, in almost 70 per cent of the hearing division cases during the fifteen-year period. Most of the complaints in these cases were made first to the local associations, who then forwarded the complaints and the files to the state bar association and cooperated with that organization in handling the case. In addition, the local associations could apply the sanctions of group censure and expulsion, a strategy employed by the Prairie City bar on at least one occasion. The effect of these informal sanctions should not be minimized. There is a report that on one occasion a local bar association was responsible for causing a lawyer to retire voluntarily from the practice. Consent disbarments—which were unpublicized—could be obtained at the local level.

OFFENDERS AND OFFENSES

The number of cases in the hearing division over the fifteen-year period was too small to determine whether younger lawyers were more likely to be involved in cases at this level than were older lawyers. Once a case reached the hearing division, however, the chances were somewhat greater that younger lawyers and lawyers more recently admitted were less likely to have their cases dismissed than were older lawyers and lawyers in practice longer. There was some evidence that younger lawyers and lawyers more recently admitted received more punitive sanctions than did older lawyers and lawyers in practice longer. The older lawyers tended to receive suspensions rather than censure or disbarment; for these lawyers, however, suspension might have been tantamount to disbarment.

For the overwhelming majority of lawyers (sixty-four out of seventy), the appearance of their case in the hearing division was the first time that they had been formally in trouble with the state bar association disciplinary machinery. Of the six lawyers who did have prior records, only one was able to have his case dismissed by the hearing division. The recommendation for one was suspension, for two disbarment, and two filed motions to have their names stricken from the record.[14]

Table 4.5 shows the distribution of hearing division recommendations by the type of charge. The table totals all of the charges and gives the proportion of charges which resulted in a recommendation of sanction. Over 70 per cent of all the cases involved more than one charge, but the statistical tabulations do not indicate which charge was determinative. Seventy-six per cent of the cases which received sanctions and which involved a conversion charge, however, also involved either a neglect charge or a nonprofessional misconduct charge (such as failure to pay debts). A lawyer who does not pay his debts or who behaves in an unbusinesslike way is likely to be charged with some of these offenses by a client dissatisfied generally. If a client is disturbed at his lawyer's failure to proceed with litigation (neglect) and is repeatedly put off when he demands the return of the retainer, he can charge conversion (appropriating a client's funds to one's own use) and failure to pay personal debts. Thus, clients may be using the disciplinary machinery to prod the lawyer into taking action—either to pursue the litigation or, more likely, to return the money. But the tabulated cases were different. These cases resulted in sanctions more often than any other category other than felonies, where sanctions were practically automatic. Cases which resulted in sanctions probably always arose out of serious misconduct by the lawyer.

For which offenses are lawyers disbarred? Charges appeared in the records for twenty out of the twenty-one disbarments (both consensual and imposed disbarments). All but three of these cases involved more than one charge, and in sixteen of the twenty cases conversion was one of the charges. Ten cases also involved neglect, but nine of these combined the neglect count with a conversion count, the other combining the neglect count with an embezzlement charge. Of the remaining

TABLE 4.5—Distribution of Hearing Division Cases in the State Bar Association by
Type of Charge, 1949–63

Charge	Number	Total % resulting in sanction recommendations
Offenses against client		
Conversion	38	
Overreaching	7	
Neglect	38	
Threats	1	
Conflict of interest	4	
	88	74
Offenses against the administration of justice		
Direct (bribery)	0	
Fraud	23	
Government agencies	1	
	24	63
Offenses against colleagues		
Direct (breaking agreements)	5	
Solicitation	11	
	16	62
Other professional misconduct (not arising out of regular practice)		
Corruption (public official)	10	
Abuses (admission, disciplinary)	2	
	12	42
Nonprofessional misconduct (failure to pay debts)	14	73
Felonies		
Larceny, embezzlement	7	
Forgery	2	
	9	100

three cases not involving conversion, the charges were (1) solicitation, (2) corruption (lawyer as a public official), (3) embezzlement (convicted) and corruption.

Several factors may account for charges' being brought to the attention of the state bar association. Publicity makes it likely that official machinery will be brought to bear on a claimed infraction and unlikely that the case will be screened out at an early stage. When professional misconduct is uncovered by a grand jury investigation, for example, the bar association is under pressure to clean its own house. If a local bar association forwards a case to the state bar association, recommends disciplinary action, and offers to cooperate, it is unlikely that the case will be screened out. In addition, a case is more likely to survive if more than one charge has been filed against a lawyer, if more than one person filed charges, or if large amounts of money are involved; the presence of these factors would indicate that the case might be serious. Over 60 per cent of the hearing division cases involved such publicity or pressure-building factors.[15]

SUMMARY

Although the state supreme court had the responsibility and the authority to require lawyers to adhere to their ethical rules, it had delegated its responsibility to the bar association, retaining final authority to impose sanctions. In practice, the bar association played the major role in enforcing discipline among the lawyers. In the fifteen years preceding the study, the supreme court had decided only ten cases of legal ethics; the two committees of the state bar association had handled 117 times this load of cases during the same period. If the work of handling complaint letters is also considered, the difference in the volume of matters handled was even more striking. As a practical matter, then, most of the control over lawyers was conducted by the lawyers themselves through the organized bar. This has great importance for two reasons. First, a decision to screen out a complaint or dismiss a grievance proceeding by the committees, was, as a practical matter, probably final; as a result, the organized bar had almost unlimited authority to decline to enforce ethical rules. Second, the bar association committees did not operate in the public eye; the effectiveness of discipline over lawyers depended upon the unpublicized work of the various committees.

How effective were these controls? The number of lawyers punished for misconduct was very small. Of the approximately four thousand lawyers in the disciplinary jurisdiction of the state bar association, there were only five formal hearing division cases in any given year, or 1.2 formal hearings per one thousand lawyers; only three such cases resulted in recommendations of sanction, or approximately 0.75 cases per one thousand lawyers. This does not necessarily mean, however, that the disciplinary machinery was ineffective. It may be that the lawyers adhered to the ethical rules of the bar without compulsion. The highest proportion of cases brought up involved offenses against clients —conversion and neglect; these were also the offenses which were more likely to result in the recommendations of sanction. Were these the only rules violated? If other rules were violated, why were these offenders not disciplined? We will examine these questions in later chapters.

Finally, a word should be said about publicity. It might be argued that a small number of disciplinary cases could still have been effective because knowledge of these cases would deter potential violators. Even though the vast majority of disciplinary matters were processed and terminated at the bar association level, this does not mean that lawyers in the local bar were unaware of these matters. An effective and vigilant local bar association may do far more in maintaining standards of ethical behavior than might decisions of the state supreme court.

In sum, the findings of this chapter show that very few lawyers were formally disciplined. It now remains to be seen whether or not this indicated a healthy ethical climate or whether the organized bar was failing to come to grips with serious professional problems.

CHAPTER 5

THE RULE STRUCTURE OF THE BAR

The remaining chapters deal with the attitudes and behavior of Prairie City lawyers towards various ethical rules. The materials are based primarily on responses to thirteen hypothetical situations, each posing an ethical conflict. The questions following the hypotheticals elicited four types of information.

1. *Opportunities.* For twelve of the thirteen hypotheticals the lawyers were asked, "How often in the past five years has a situation like this come up in your practice?" [1] They could respond "never," "sometimes," or "often." For each hypothetical, this answer told us, at least partially, whether or not the lawyer had been presented with an opportunity to violate an ethical rule. The sum of the individual lawyers' responses to this question for the twelve items gave us the *opportunity rate* for each lawyer. The lawyers were then placed on a scale and, in relation to each other, rated in terms of a high, middle, or low opportunity rate. If a lawyer reported four or more situations occurring in his practice "sometimes" or "often," he was scored high; lawyers encountering two to three situations were scored middle; and lawyers encountering none or one were scored low.

It is quite clear that the opportunity responses gave only a rough indication of opportunities. "Sometimes" and "often" are vague and undoubtedly meant different things to different lawyers. In addition, the hypotheticals presented bare-boned factual situations; ethical conflicts in practice usually do not arise in that simple a form. There are variations, with other factors present. We asked whether "a situation like this" had occurred in an effort to avoid this problem, but this phrase was also subject to a wide range of interpretation by the respondents.

It will be shown, however, that the opportunity responses were reliable as a rough indicator or measure of the types of practice that

87

lawyers had and as a predictor of other responses. The opportunity measure—the scale on which the lawyers were placed according to the number of opportunities to violate ethical rules—contrasted "never" with "sometimes" or "often"; it told us broad differences between types of lawyers in this bar. And the opportunity rates were consistent with other responses and with the results of Carlin's New York study.

2. *Behavior.* The lawyers were then asked what they had done when the situation arose, or would do should the situation come up in the future.[2] We used these responses to measure adherence to ethical rules. The standard of adherence was the official standard of the profession as set forth in the Canons of Professional Ethics and the authoritative sources, described below.

Even though these responses were not behavior data in the usual sense—we did not observe what the lawyers did in the past, and part of the data concerns what they said that they would do in the future— we refer to this information as "behavior" data to distinguish it from "attitude" data. There may have been situations in which lawyers did not accept rules but nevertheless adhered to them. The converse is also possible: the lawyer accepted the rule although he personally had not adhered to it in the past or doubted that he would adhere to it in the future. In the latter instance, the lawyer might have believed that extenuating circumstances justified violating a rule which in the normal course of events should not have been violated. In any event, it is important to distinguish between what lawyers thought about rules as applied to others and rules as applied to themselves. Furthermore, statements by a lawyer as to what he has done in the past or what he would do in the future have relevance to future behavior. Of course, situations may change, and the lawyer's prediction as to his future course of action may not be borne out in fact. But at least we know what he thought his future position would be. "Behavior," then, will be used in this special sense: what lawyers told us they have done in the past or thought that they would do in the future. It is hard to obtain more precise data; we cannot directly observe how ethically the lawyers behave in practice.

The lawyers were scored in terms of their behavior responses and rated according to the number of ethical rules which they had violated or would have violated. Those who, in relation to their colleagues, violated few or no rules were called *conformers* and those who, in relation to their colleagues, violated a significant number of rules were called *violators*. It should be kept in mind, however, that violation rates are relative: by definition a third or a half of this bar were called violators, but only because they took or would have taken more unethical actions than their colleagues—"unethical" by official standards. We will discuss in Chapter 7 to what extent the Prairie City violators were acting unprofessionally or antisocially in other senses.

Another problem with the behavior data is that it indicates only the number of violators, actual or potential, not the number of actual violations. A divorce or personal injury lawyer might have violated one or two rules very many times, while the general practitioner, over a period of time, might have violated three, four, or five different rules only one time each. Under our measure the general practitioner would appear to be the higher violator. Perhaps this problem would have been more serious had this bar been more specialized; the bar was not specialized, but nevertheless the number of violations per lawyer for any one rule is concededly unknown. As a result, the behavior data at most can only hint at the levels or rates of actual violations among the members of this bar.

In addition, the number of rules violated was measured, but not the importance of the rules. A lawyer who had violated several trivial rules would score lower than a lawyer who had violated one or two serious rules. This problem will be discussed later, but we should point out now that this generally was not the case. Lawyers who violated many rules (and were consequently violators on the measure) failed to comply with both trivial and serious rules; the conformers, if they violated at all, infringed only trivial rules.

3. *Attitudes.* Lawyers were asked to evaluate the conduct of the lawyer in the hypothetical (called Lawyer A), which was unethical according to official standards.[3] Respondents could answer "approve," "disapprove," or "neither approve nor disapprove." These responses provided what we call "attitude" data. Generally, attitude patterns followed behavior patterns, although there was no one-to-one relationship. If a lawyer failed to disapprove of the unethical conduct on the part of the hypothetical lawyer, even though he himself may or may not have adhered to the rule, we said that the lawyer rejected the rule. The lawyers were scored according to the number of rules that they rejected and then scaled in terms of "strict," "permissive," or "mixed" attitudes. We found that lawyers with permissive attitudes did not reject the trivial rules only: they rejected more important rules as

well. Lawyers with strict attitudes either accepted all of the rules or
rejected only trivial ones.

4. *Sanctions.* Finally, respondents were asked what they would do
about Lawyer A if they disapproved of his conduct. For each hypothetical (except the *Christmas Cards*), the alternative sanctions were
(1) nothing; (2) comment to another lawyer about what A had done;
(3) warn another lawyer who is about to deal with A; (4) avoid
referring matters to A; (5) avoid having lunch or other social engagements with A; (6) say something to A directly; and (7) report
A to the bar association. Since the sanctions were not mutually exclusive, the respondents were asked to select the most appropriate
sanction and were given two choices. We used the first choice only.

These sanction responses were used primarily to measure the quality
or intensity of attitudes towards the professional rules. We assumed that
if a lawyer disapproved of an unethical act, his choice of sanction
would measure how seriously he regarded the infraction. For example,
a lawyer may accept a rule; he may personally adhere to the rule;
and he may disapprove of another lawyer's violation of the rule. But
if the lawyer thinks that the violator's conduct warrants no sanction
whatsoever, then this rule may not be of much importance to him.

There were a number of problems in using this measure. Even if
a lawyer adhered to a rule and disapproved of violations of the rule,
there could be several reasons why he might refuse to take action: the
violator might be a personal friend, or there might be extenuating
circumstances. Again, the lawyer might not want to get involved and
risk personal unpleasantness, or he might be opposed to a system of
regulation requiring fellow lawyers to report on each other. Personal
"costs" to lawyers are inevitable in a system that depends on self-
policing by members of the group, but these costs are absent from
hypotheticals, so that severe sanctions might appear too frequently
in this study, particularly if respondents wanted to display rectitude.
On the other hand, though these costs were absent from the hypotheticals, it does not necessarily follow that respondents eliminated
consideration of cost in answering the questions.

To eliminate some of the difficulties of personal costs, we gave the
respondents a very wide choice of alternative sanctions, some of which
were relatively mild and, in addition, anonymous (*e.g.,* avoid referring
matters to the violator). If a lawyer would not take even the mildest

form of sanction in a hypothetical situation, we thought it reasonable to assume that he did not regard the unethical action as being of much normative significance.

The correlation between sanctions and attitudes will be discussed later in this chapter. For the most part, sanction responses did seem to give some measure of the quality or intensity of attitudes towards the rules. There was evidence that individual, hidden personal costs did not influence decisions very much.

SOURCES OF OFFICIAL RULES

For Prairie City lawyers the state supreme court was the final arbiter in matters of professional ethics. But most of the disciplinary work was conducted at a lower level by state and local bar associations. From what sources did these agencies derive their working rules?

The Canons of Professional Ethics adopted by the American Bar Association and by Prairie City's state bar association (as well as by most of the bar associations in other states) were the principal formal source of ethical standards. Some states had enacted the canons as statutes; in Prairie City's state, however, the canons were viewed not as "binding obligations" but as a "safe guide for professional conduct." Since an attorney could be punished for violating the canons, the net result was the same as if the canons were part of the statute books.

The canons were a set of general guides or rules; they did not solve specific cases or problems. Although judicial interpretations of the canons were comparatively few, ethics committees of the various bar associations gave and published opinions in response to inquiries submitted by attorneys,[4] and these opinions were a very important source of interpretations. In addition to committee opinions, committees and courts looked to written commentaries on professional ethics. Finally, customs and practices of members of the bar were themselves a source of interpretation and affected decisions on ethical questions.

THE ETHICAL HYPOTHETICALS AND THE
OFFICIAL POSITION

The ethical hypotheticals used in this study presented situations which involved the official rules.[5] The hypotheticals concern the three principal areas of legal ethics: duty to clients, to the administration of justice (courts, agencies, and public officials), and to colleagues.

CLIENT

1. *1% Commission*[6]

Lawyer A represents the buyer in a real estate transaction in connection with which he helps obtain a loan for his client. After the transaction is effected, the lender sends A its usual commission of 1% of the amount of the loan.[7]

a. How often in the past five years has a situation like this come up in your practice?

Never ———

Sometimes ———

Often ———

b. Which of the following alternatives comes closest to what you have done (would do) in this situation?

    1) Accept the commission but take it into consideration in setting the client's fee. ———

    2) Accept the commission and inform the client (or with the client's prior approval). ———

    3) Accept the commission but deduct the amount from the fee and indicate it on the client's bill. ———

    4) Accept the commission without informing the client. ———

    5) Refuse the commission. ———

c. Which alternative do you approve of?

d. Which do you disapprove of?

e. If Lawyer A did any of the acts which you disapprove of, which of the following would you do? If more than one, which would you consider the most appropriate? [8] (Rank each action 1, 2, 3, etc.)

    1) Nothing. ———

    2) Comment to another lawyer about what A had done. ———

    3) Warn another lawyer who is about to deal with A. ———

    4) Avoid referring matters to A. ———

    5) Avoid having lunch or other social engagements with A. ———

    6) Say something to A directly. ———

    7) Report A to the Bar Association. ———

3. *Receiver Sale*[9]

Lawyer A, attorney for the receiver of the Doe Corporation, negotiated a sale of all the corporation's property to a group of promoters for a large sum of money. The sale was approved by the court and was at the best price obtainable. The promoters then turned over the property to a new corporation. Before the receiver sale took place the promoters had a general understanding with A that he should receive an interest in the new corporation. Some months later, after the receiver sale, A is given the opportunity, which he exercises, of purchasing stock of the new corporation for which he pays the same proportionate amount as the promoters.

a. How often in the past five years have you been in a position where an offer like this came up?

Never ———
Sometimes ———
Often ———

b. If ever:

What have you done?

If never:

If it came up, what would you do?

c. With respect to A's purchase of stock in the new corporation, do you

Approve ———
Disapprove ———
Neither approve
nor disapprove ———

d. If you disapprove, which of the following would you do? If more than one, which would you consider the most appropriate? (Rank each action 1, 2, 3, etc.)

1) Nothing. ———
2) Comment to another lawyer about what A had done. ———
3) Warn another lawyer who is about to deal with A. ———
4) Avoid referring matters to A. ———
5) Avoid having lunch or other social engagements with A. ———
6) Say something to A directly. ———
7) Report A to the Bar Association. ———

4. Stock Purchase

Lawyer A learns that his client is planning on purchasing a large amount of stock in a small, privately held company which will result in a substantial increase in the value of the stock of that company. Without informing his client, A has a friend purchase stock in the company for him in the friend's name.

6. Package Deal

Lawyer A is negotiating a personal injury claim with an insurance company adjustor. The adjustor, with whom A has had previous dealings, is under pressure from his supervisors to hold down the amount of recovery of this particular claim and indicates this fact to A, saying that if A will cooperate this time, he (the adjustor) will be able to take care of him next time. The offer is in striking distance of a fair amount. (The respondent is asked to approve, disapprove, or "neither" if A decides to go along with the adjustor.)

7. Assault Charge

Lawyer A, who is defending Jones on a criminal assault charge, learns from the district attorney that the latter's case is so weak that he probably will not be able to get a conviction. A withholds this information from Jones, knowing that if Jones finds this out, he will stop paying installments on A's fees.

11. *Conflict of Interest*

Smith and Jones, partners in several business ventures, have been represented by Lawyer A on both business and personal matters. A controversy has arisen between Smith and Jones, and Smith retains another attorney to commence legal action to dissolve the business partnership. Jones asks A to represent him. (The respondent is asked to approve, disapprove, or "neither" if A decides to represent Jones.)

JUSTICE

5. *Client Payoff*

Lawyer A's client, without A's knowledge, failed to report a sizable amount of income on his tax return. The client was subsequently contacted by an agent of the Bureau of Internal Revenue who offered to overlook the matter for a sum of money. The client tells A that he (the client) is determined to make the payment.

Which of these actions comes closest to what you have done (or would do) under these circumstances?

1. Lawyer A tells the client that it would be very risky to make the payment, but if he wants to, that's his business.

2. Lawyer A tells the client that if he pays off the Revenue Agent, he will no longer be able to represent him.

3. Lawyer A strongly urges his client not to make the payment, but continues to represent him on other matters.

4. Lawyer A tells the client that if he wants to make the payment, that is his business, but not to tell A anything about it.

8. *Police Payoff*

A young man at the beginning of a very promising career in public service is picked up by the police for making homosexual advances to another man. The father of the young man comes to Lawyer A and begs him to do what he can to have the charge removed from the books, believing that it would ruin his son's career. Lawyer A knows that the charge can be removed by making a substantial payment to someone in the police department. (The respondent is asked to approve, disapprove, or "neither" if A makes the payment.)

12. *Divorce Fraud* [10]

A woman comes to Lawyer A seeking a divorce. Her husband has agreed to a consent decree on grounds of physical cruelty, although in fact no such act was committed. Lawyer A knows this. The client asks A to take the case.

(The respondent is asked to approve, disapprove, or "neither" if A agrees to take the case.)

COLLEAGUE (Direct)

2. *Oral Contract*

Lawyer A is given authority by his client to sell a certain piece of real estate for a certain sum of money. After negotiating with attorney Jones, representing a prospective buyer, an oral agreement is reached, A giving Jones his word that Jones' client has the deal. Before any documents are signed, A's client has found a purchaser willing to pay a greater amount and, learning that there is no written agreement with Jones, refuses to permit A to go ahead with the deal with Jones. Lawyer A calls Jones and, explaining the situation, asks to be released. Jones refuses. (The respondent is asked to approve, disapprove or "neither" if A proceeds to represent his client on the deal with the new purchaser at the higher price.)

13. *Referral Fee*

Lawyer A refers a matter to Lawyer Jones for which A accepts a ⅓ referral fee. Lawyer A's only connection with the case has been to hear the client's story, phone Jones, and inform him that he is sending over the client on the matter in question. Lawyer A has no further contact with the client or with Lawyer Jones in this matter.[11]

COLLEAGUE (Solicitation)

9. *Client Kickback*

A previous client of Lawyer A refers another client to A and indicates that he expects some small compensation from A for his services.

Which of these actions comes closest to what you have done (or would do) under these circumstances:

1. Lawyer A gives the previous client a small amount of money.

2. Lawyer A gives the previous client a small gift, or takes him out to dinner.

3. Lawyer A gives the previous client free legal advice, or reduces his fee the next time he represents him.

4. Lawyer A refuses to give the previous client any compensation whatsoever for his services.

10. *Christmas Cards*

Lawyer A sends out Christmas cards to all his active clients. (Do you do this? Is this something you approve of? disapprove of? neither approve nor disapprove of?)

For some of the ethical hypotheticals, official sources do not have to be consulted to know the "correct" position. Bribery, deceit, and gross breaches of trust were unethical in the community at large as well as among the legal profession. It was unethical for Lawyer A or any other citizen to bribe the police. Equally clear answers can be given on the *Divorce Fraud, Stock Purchase, Package Deal, Receiver Sale,* and *Assault Charge.*

The other items speak of conduct which might have been tolerated in the wider community but which "official" standards of legal ethics condemned.

1% Commission. Canon 38 states that a lawyer "should accept no compensation, commission, rebates or other advantages from others without the knowledge and consent of his client after full disclosure." In this hypothetical, the commission properly belongs to the client. Thus, alternative 4—"accept the commission without informing the client"—was clearly unethical. Alternative 2—"accept the commission and inform the client (or with the client's prior approval)"—was ethical because there has been disclosure. Alternative 5—"refuse the commission"—has been classified as ethical although some respondents took the position that this course of action loses an advantage to the client which is rightfully his. Alternative 1—"accept the commission but take it into consideration in setting the client's fee"—has been classified as unethical, since it does not call for disclosure and since the client will not necessarily get the full benefit of the rebate.[12]

Conflict of Interest. Canon 6 states that "it is unprofessional to represent conflicting interests, except by express consent of all concerned given after a full disclosure of the facts. Within the meaning of this canon, a lawyer represents conflicting interests when, in behalf of one client, it is his duty to contend for that which duty to another client requires him to oppose." In the hypothetical, Lawyer A represented Smith and Jones "on both business and personal matters." Without the consent of Smith, it would be unethical for Lawyer A to represent Jones. "A lawyer may not ethically act for either of two clients in a controversy arising out of a transaction in which he has advised both because of the impossibility of eliminating from his new relationship the elements of past confidential relationship with the adverse party."[13] The test is whether there is "any possibility, however remote,"[14] that Lawyer A would use information acquired from Smith when A was Smith's lawyer.

Client Payoff. Canon 16 imposes on the lawyer an obligation to use his "best effort to restrain and prevent" a client from taking an illegal course of action. Accordingly, we have classified as unethical alternative 4—"Lawyer A tells the client that if he wants to make the payment, that is his business, but not to tell A anything about it"— and alternative 1—"Lawyer A tells the client that it would be very risky to make the payment, but if he wants to, that's his business."

Oral Contract. This item involves a contract which is legally unenforceable because it is oral. The canons are quite clear that it would be unprofessional for a lawyer to break such a promise to his colleague.[15]

Referral Fee. A referral fee is improper unless it is "based upon a division of service or responsibility."[16]

Client Kickback. Although it is not uncommon for businessmen to give favors in return for bringing in business, such practices are considered improper for lawyers, even when the favor is merely the giving of a small gift or free advice to the client.[17]

Christmas Cards. It is improper for lawyers to send Christmas greetings to regular clients which are not warranted by personal relations.[18]

These, then, are the official positions on the ethical hypotheticals. To what extent were they working rules for this bar?

THE WORKING RULES OF THE BAR

Table 5.1 reports the percentage of lawyers disapproving unethical action in each of the hypotheticals and shows the sanctions the lawyers would be willing to impose for the misconduct. The final column in the table, called "lack of significance," shows the combined percentages of lawyers for each item who either did not disapprove of the unethical action or, if they did disapprove, would impose no sanction whatsoever. For example, in item 1, 36 per cent of the bar did not disapprove if a lawyer accepted the 1 per cent commission, made no disclosure, and simply adjusted the client's fee; an additional 25 per cent registered disapproval, but would impose no sanction whatsoever. We call this "lack of significance" on the assumption that the violated rule is probably not of much importance to a lawyer who would not impose even the mildest sanction.

Some official rules appeared not to be working rules of this bar; less than half of the bar considered unethical sending Christmas cards to regular clients (*Christmas Cards*), taking a client out to dinner or

TABLE 5.1—Percentage of Lawyers Disapproving Unethical Acts and Severity of
            Sanctions

Item	% disapproving unethical action	
		(Rank order)
Client		
1. 1% Commission:		
Take into consideration	64	(11)
Accept without informing	98	(1)
3. Receiver Sale	70	(10)
4. Stock Purchase	89	(7)
6. Package Deal	94	(2)
7. Assault Charge	59	(12)
11. Conflict of Interest	49	(14)
Justice Payoffs		
5. Client (IRS):		
"Don't tell me"	80	(8)
"Risky but your business"	76	(9)
8. Police Payoff	92	(4)
Justice Fraud		
12. Divorce Fraud	90	(6)
Colleague: Direct		
2. Oral Contract	92	(4)
13. Referral Fee	27	(16)
Colleague: Solicitation		
9. Client Kickback:		
Money	94	(2)
Gift, dinner	48	(15)
Legal advice	58	(13)
10. Christmas Cards*	25	(17)

* Item 10 did not call for sanctions.

giving him a small gift in return for bringing in business (*Client Kickback: gift, dinner*), accepting a referral fee (*Referral Fee*), or representing one of two business partners in a conflict of interest situation (*Conflict of Interest*). The sanctions selected by the lawyers who disapproved of such conduct were relatively mild, and the average proportion of lawyers who either did not disapprove or, if they disapproved, would take no action whatsoever, was about 80 per cent of the bar.

TABLE 5.1—(Continued)

% imposing sanctions (first choice)							% for whom rule lacked significance
Nothing	Comment	Warn	Avoid ref.	Avoid soc.	Say dir.	Bar	
							(Rank order)
25	8	1	11	1	15	4	61 (9)
29	6	1	24	1	24	12	31 (3)
22	10	2	16	0	10	12	52 (8)
29	12	5	18	0	12	12	40 (5)
19	16	2	28	0	18	11	25 (1)
34	8	0	5	0	8	4	75 (12)
29	4	2	2	0	8	5	80 (15)
41	5	0	17	0	13	4	61 (9)
41	5	0	18	0	10	2	65 (11)
19	8	1	11	0	10	42	27 (2)
41	16	0	11	0	13	12	51 (7)
24	8	13	17	0	28	1	32 (4)
18	2	0	4	0	2	0	91 (16)
42	7	2	12	0	12	18	46 (6)
24	7	1	5	0	8	2	76 (13)
34	5	2	7	0	8	1	76 (13)

For three-quarters or more of this bar, nine items were of ethical significance. For some of these items, sanctions corresponded closely with the rate of disapproval. In the *Police Payoff,* for example, over 90 per cent of the bar disapproved Lawyer A's bribing the police to drop the charge. Forty-two per cent of the lawyers would report such an infraction to the bar association, 24 per cent more lawyers than were willing to impose this sanction for any other infraction. An additional 22 per cent would either warn another lawyer who was about to deal with A, avoid referring matters to A, or say something directly to A. The bar was also relatively severe about a lawyer's accepting a commission and secretly appropriating it to his own use (*1% Commission: accept without informing*) or selling out his client to the insurance adjustor even if the offer were in "striking distance of a fair amount" (*Package Deal*). The favorite sanction for *Package Deal* (28 per cent) was to avoid referring matters to such a lawyer. Disapproval of a lawyer's paying a client a small sum of money for bringing in business (*Client Kickback: money*) was somewhat less clear-cut. There was a high rate of disapproval and a willingness to report the violator to the bar association, but at the same time a high proportion of the lawyers who disapproved would have taken no action whatsoever, perhaps because only a small amount of money was involved. On the other hand, the bar appeared far more tolerant of a lawyer's giving a client a small gift, taking him out to dinner, or adjusting the legal fee. The lawyers seemed to distinguish between these two situations: the lawyer who gives money for cases referred by a former client might develop a "chasing" or "running" arrangement with the client, but this was not likely to happen if he merely gave the client a necktie, bought his dinner, or presented him with a lower bill for legal services.

The *Divorce Fraud* presented a similar type of ambiguity: a high rate of disapproval but also a high rate of unwillingness to take action. Several lawyers said that there were divorce "specialists" among the bar and that this fact was generally known in the community. They intimated that these specialists handled the fraudulent divorces; other lawyers were content to stay out of this aspect of the divorce business. In addition, several lawyers reported that once it was explained to the client what the grounds of divorce in the state were and that the lawyer could not take the client's case, the client would show up in another lawyer's office with his story changed to conform to the statutory grounds. Lawyers said that they had sent clients away under these circumstances and that they suspected that they had received clients sent away by other lawyers.[19] To the extent that these practices existed, the sanction responses may indicate attitudes more accurately than the disapproval responses. In the "specialist" situation, the lawyer could adhere to the rule but at the same time be sure that the client would get what he wanted. Where clients were referred with the proper story, the lawyer could adhere to the rule by simply not questioning or doubting the client. Though the lawyers were not in favor of blatant frauds, their adherence to this rule smacked of hypocrisy, for the sanction responses and the arrangements for handling fraudulent divorces indicated that they were willing to aid in its violation.

The sanction responses seemed to reveal differing degrees of acceptance of the rules about bribing officials. In the *Client Payoff* to the Internal Revenue agent, almost 60 per cent of the lawyers said that they would drop a client who made such a payment; another 35 per cent said that they would strongly urge the client not to make the payment although they would continue to represent him on other matters. And in Table 5.1 we see that a high percentage did not feel that a lawyer who merely washed his hands of the matter had done enough. Yet, despite this apparent acceptance of the rule, a high proportion would not do anything about unethical conduct. On the other hand, the willingness to impose the most severe sanction if a *lawyer* makes the bribe (*Police Payoff*) was very great. Both situations involved bribing a public official. Obviously, a lawyer's obligation to restrain a client from wrongdoing was not so important as a lawyer's obligation to do no wrong himself.

Of particular interest are the responses to the hypothetical on the *Oral Contract,* for 92 per cent of the Prairie City lawyers disapproved of the unethical conduct here. One would expect that personal relations between lawyers would be of high value. There was a great amount of interaction in this professional community; and if one lawyer broke his promise, the other lawyer would not sit idly by. If we look at the sanction responses, we find a high rate of disapproval and a low proportion of lawyers who would do nothing. On the other hand, we also find that only 1 per cent of the lawyers would report Lawyer A to the bar association, a proportion which contrasts sharply with the sanction response for other items that have high disapproval rates (e.g., *Police Payoff, Client Kickback: money*). The sanctions which the lawyers preferred for the *Oral Contract*—saying something directly to the lawyer (28 per cent, the highest use of this particular sanction), avoiding referring matters to him, warning other lawyers about him, or commenting to other lawyers about what he had done—in the order preferred, had distinct advantages over reporting the lawyer to the bar association. When confronted with this hypothetical, several lawyers at first said that they would not make that kind of oral commitment. But had a lawyer made such a commitment, reporting A to the bar association would have advertised to other lawyers in detail that the reporting lawyer had exposed himself on an oral commitment. When warning another lawyer or commenting to another lawyer, the lawyer who had committed himself could gloss over details; in addition, the lawyers may have thought that private, informal forms of punishment were more appropriate sanctions for breaches of personal relationships. Under either view the sanction responses seemed tailored to the type of infraction.

In Table 5.2 we have arranged the rules in terms of their relative importance as measured by the disapproval responses, the sanctions, and lack of significance. The sanction responses have been weighted. For each item we have given one point for each lawyer who gave a sanc-

TABLE 5.2—The Rule Structure

Item	% disapproving		Sanction scores		% for whom rule lacked significance	
		(Rank)		(Rank)		(Rank)
High						
1(4). 1% Commission: accept without informing	98	(1)	97	(2)	31	(3)
6. Package Deal	94	(2)	86	(3)	25	(1)
9(1). Client Kickback: money	94	(2)	83	(4)	46	(6)
8. Police Payoff	92	(4)	138	(1)	27	(2)
2. Oral Contract	92	(4)	81	(5)	32	(4)
12. Divorce Fraud	90	(6)	74	(7)	51	(7)
4. Stock Purchase	89	(7)	79	(6)	40	(5)
Intermediate						
5(4). Client Payoff: "Don't tell me"	80	(8)	49	(9)	61	(9)
5(1). Client Payoff: "Risky, but your business"	76	(9)	41	(11)	65	(11)
3. Receiver Sale	70	(10)	69	(8)	52	(8)
1(1). 1% Commission: take into consideration	64	(11)	48	(10)	61	(9)
Low						
7. Assault Charge	59	(12)	34	(12)	75	(12)
9(3). Client Kickback: legal advice	58	(13)	29	(15)	76	(13)
11. Conflict of Interest	49	(14)	33	(13)	80	(15)
9(2). Client Kickback: gift, dinner	48	(15)	31	(14)	76	(13)
13. Referral Fee	27	(16)	9	(16)	91	(16)
10. Christmas Cards*	25	(17)	...	...	...	...

* This item did not call for sanctions.

tion; if the sanction was direct confrontation, a second point was added; and still another was added if the lawyer would have reported the violator to the bar association. To the right of each of the measures is the rank order of the items.

Table 5.2 appears to confirm the validity of the sanction responses as a measure of attitudes. For fourteen out of sixteen items, the rank order of the items changed by no more than two positions regardless of which measure was used, and the changes in position for the other two items were not significant. The close connection between the three measures indicates that the individual, hidden personal "costs" of imposing sanctions, suggested earlier, were probably not very serious. If an item had a high disapproval rate, there were generally more lawyers willing to impose the more severe sanctions, and there were fewer disapproving lawyers who would take no action whatsoever. The data tell us, then, not only whether the rules were accepted or rejected on a yes or no basis but also indicate how seriously the bar viewed the various rules. Before deciding what the working rules of this bar were, we must first find out whether or not there was a consensus on the relative importance of the rules.

THE RULE STRUCTURE OF THE BAR

The data in the preceding section dealt with the entire Prairie City bar, and among the bar as a whole there was evidence of consensus on the rules of the highest normative significance and on those of the lowest. For the other rules it was not clear whether there was consensus or not. It may be that certain rules were working rules for one group of lawyers but not for others. We know that certain rules did not meet with universal acceptance among the bar. Was rejection randomly distributed or was acceptance correlated with status? Were some of the rules really the rules of the elite and higher status lawyers? These questions are of concern to those interested in maintaining adherence to official rules.

In Part I we suggested that although there was a great deal of homogeneity among the lawyers, the income-client measure did indicate differences. In Table 5.3 the disapproval rates for each item are distributed by the income-client measure. For twelve out of seventeen items the differences in the disapproval rates between the four groups of lawyers were less than 20 per cent. And we must be cautious in drawing conclusions about the lack of consensus for the others because of the

TABLE 5.3—Percentage of Lawyers Disapproving Unethical Acts by Income-Client
         Measure

Item	% of lawyers				% range
	Elite	High	Middle	Low	
High					
1(4). 1% Commission:					
accept without informing	100	100	95	96	5
6. Package Deal	100	90	100	96	10
9(1). Client Kickback: money	100	95	95	96	5
8. Police Payoff	92	90	95	91	5
2. Oral Contract	100	90	90	87	13
12. Divorce Fraud	92	95	84	96	12
4. Stock Purchase	100	90	95	87	13
Intermediate					
5(4). Client Payoff: "Don't tell me"	85	90	74	78	16
5(1). Client Payoff:					
"Risky, but your business"	85	80	68	74	17
3. Receiver Sale	69	55	79	74	24
1(1). 1% Commission:					
take into consideration	77	70	47	65	30
Low					
7. Assault Charge	46	60	63	65	19
9(3). Client Kickback: legal advice	69	75	42	57	33
11. Conflict of Interest	54	55	37	52	18
9(2). Client Kickback: gift, dinner	62	50	37	52	25
13. Referral Fee	23	25	37	26	14
10. Christmas Cards	31	35	11	22	24
	(13)	(20)	(19)	(23)	

small numbers of lawyers. In item 3, the *Receiver Sale,* there was a
24 per cent difference in the disapproval rate (curiously, more of the
middle and low groups disapproved than the elite and high); yet because
more than half of each group disapproved of the unethical act, this
rule was probably a working rule for all of the groups. There was also
a 24 per cent difference in the disapproval rates for the *Christmas
Cards.* Here, since so few lawyers in any of the groups disapproved of
this practice, it is fair to say that this rule was not a working rule for
any of the groups.

The three remaining items which had differences in disapproval rates
of more than 20 per cent were *1% Commission: take into consideration; Client Kickback: legal advice;* and *Client Kickback: gift, dinner.*
But here again, the differences were more apparent than real. We would

normally think of lower income lawyers as more inclined than high income lawyers to violate these three rules for economic reasons. Yet more middle group than low group lawyers rejected the rules. If we divide the bar in terms of the very sharp income differences between the elite and high groups, on the one hand, and the middle and low groups, on the other (see Table 3.8), then the differences in the disapproval rates become practically insignificant.[20] And the moderate lack of consensus concerning the two *Client Kickback* rules is made even less important by the fact that these items were not of great normative significance anyway; over three-quarters of the bar either did not disapprove of the unethical act in these two hypothetical alternatives or would take no action whatsoever even if they did disapprove. For this bar, then, there was not much evidence that differences in income-client measure affected attitudes towards ethical rules. The general consensus was strong.

The relative significance of ethical rules indicated in Table 5.2 accords with common sense: the ethical rules of the lawyer coincided with the ethical norms in the community at large. Lawyers, like laymen, attached high normative significance to rules against the most blatant forms of bribery, breach of trust, and fraud. For several items, it was the degree of the violation which apparently made the difference in normative significance. Secretly appropriating an entire commission, for example, was viewed more seriously than taking the commission into consideration in setting the fee. The *Stock Purchase,* in which the lawyer secretly had a friend buy stock, was seen as a graver offense than the *Receiver Sale,* in which the lawyer buys in at a court-approved sale "at the best price obtainable." Reactions to other offenses against clients are also instructive. Selling out a client to gain an advantage for another client (*Package Deal*) was viewed far more seriously than deceiving a client to protect a lawyer against client exploitation (*Assault Charge*). The remark of one elite lawyer appeared indicative of the bar's feeling on the *Assault Charge;* he said: "Fortunately, I don't have this type of client, but I know several lawyers who do. If I were in their position, where I would have to depend on fees from such clients, perhaps I would do the same thing." Other offenses against colleagues also illustrated a discriminating attitude. The solicitation items which ranked very low (*Christmas Cards; Client Kickback: legal advice* and *gift, dinner*) could not have developed into significant predatory conduct and were not considered particularly outrageous. *Client Kickback:*

money, on the other hand, did pose this threat, and in the *Oral Contract* situation a highly valued aspect of the actual practice among lawyers was threatened.

ETHICAL BEHAVIOR AND THE RULE STRUCTURE

Were the behavior responses credible? Whenever a lawyer disclaimed experience of a situation but asserted that he would violate the official rule if the situation occurred, we may take him at his word. The hypotheticals, it will be recalled, contained no mitigating or extenuating circumstances; to commit oneself to an unethical act in the future without such circumstances would appear to be fairly strong evidence that the underlying rule had not been accepted. Conversely, however, where the lawyer said that the situation had occurred but that he had taken no unethical action, we are less sure of the truth.[21]

In Table 5.4, we have listed the percentages of lawyers who took or

TABLE 5.4—Opportunities and Violations by Separate Ethical Items

Item	% of lawyers for whom item occurred	% who took (or would take) unethical action
High		
1(4). 1% Commission: accept without informing	7	1
6. Package Deal	16	7
9(1). Client Kickback: money	28	1
8. Police Payoff	3	10
2. Oral Contract	27	11
12. Divorce Fraud	59	8
4. Stock Purchase	8	1
Intermediate		
5(4). Client Payoff: "Don't tell me"	6	5
5(1). Client Payoff: "Risky, but your business"	6	1
3. Receiver Sale	6	17
1(1). 1% Commission: take into consideration	7	6
Low		
7. Assault Charge	20	36
9(3). Client Kickback: legal advice	28	17
11. Conflict of Interest	55	39
9(2). Client Kickback: gift, dinner	28	17
13. Referral Fee	47	58
10. Christmas Cards	...	15

would have taken unethical action for each item. Generally speaking, the lawyers' behavior responses corresponded to their attitude responses. The highest percentages of unethical behavior appeared for those items of the least normative significance. The *Referral Fee* rule, for example, had practically no importance for this bar, and almost 60 per cent of the bar freely admitted violating the rule. In addition, the behavior responses indicated a discriminating power on the part of the lawyers. In the *Receiver Sale,* several lawyers said that they would buy in even though there was a conflict of interest. They pointed out that the price was stated in the hypothetical to be "the best price obtainable" and that it was approved by the court. Apparently, at least some of the respondents thought that the violation was only technical, that the transaction was fair, and that no one would be hurt. Several respondents said that the *Stock Purchase* was a "business" problem and not an "ethics" problem, but, in contrast to behavior responses for the *Receiver Sale,* only one lawyer said that he would commit the unethical act. The element of secrecy was repulsive.

The responses to the *Oral Contract* situation, in which the client insists that Lawyer A break an unenforceable oral agreement with another lawyer, indicate the highest rate of unethical behavior for a norm of high significance, even though the rate of violation was only 11 per cent. Perhaps the desire to retain a client outweighed the costs of violating the rule for this group of lawyers; at any rate, in Chapter 6 we will see that recently admitted lawyers with unstable clients were more likely to violate this rule than older lawyers with stable clients. And this fact would be consistent with the responses that were given in the *Conflict of Interest* situation. Here, it was fairly obvious that lawyers were not going to forsake a client because of a conflict of interest. In fact, several lawyers made this point, one lawyer responding: "I don't see why I should give up an old client [*i.e.,* Jones] just because he gets a partner and later has a falling out."

The reactions to the *Police Payoff* situation were probably affected by a recent occurrence in the community. Just before this study took place, a local doctor, young and popular, committed suicide following news of a morals charge against him. Several respondents commented on this tragedy, and when confronted with the alternatives presented in the hypothetical, said that one had to be "realistic" when charges of this nature were made. Their answers reflected their view of realism, for while practically all of the respondents willing to take unethical action in this situation said that a *lawyer* definitely should not make the payment, they said that they would try in some way to help the father bribe the police to get the charge removed. Some said that action of this sort would be more appropriate if the father was a past client and friend of the lawyer.

Table 5.4 also shows the percentages of lawyers who reported that items had occurred "sometimes" or "often" during the past five years (occurrences, or opportunity rates). The opportunity rates per item varied between 3 per cent of the bar and 59 per cent. Since the behavior data will be used to draw conclusions about the ethicality of the lawyers, it is important to find out whether particular items appeared more frequently for one group of lawyers than for others and whether, because of different rates of opportunities, the former would violate more rules than the latter. When we compared the opportunity rates by the income-client measure, for six out of thirteen items there were differences of more than 20 per cent (Table B.16, Appendix B). The small numbers of lawyers, however, probably exaggerated the differences in opportunity rates of the four groups; when the opportunity rates of the elite and high groups were compared to those of the middle and low groups, most of the differences disappeared (Table B.17). This lack of marked differences was not surprising. In Part I, the bar was characterized as a basically homogeneous group of individual practitioners; differences in practice were not correlated with size of firm. If the lawyers had more or less similar practices regardless of firm size, then the distribution of opportunities for items spread throughout areas of practice should be roughly similar for large-firm, small-firm, and individual lawyers. And this is generally what we found (Table B.18). Finally, even if there were substantial differences in opportunity rates in terms of the four groups on the income-client measure, did the differences result in differences in ethical behavior? We found no important relationship. High opportunity rates of particular items for one group did not result in that group's violating more of those rules than the other groups.[22] The evidence suggested that there was little, if any, correlation between the opportunities of particular items and groups of lawyers.

THE ETHICAL BEHAVIOR MEASURE

Table 5.5 summarizes the ethical scores for all of the lawyers. For each ethical answer (as defined by the official sources), a lawyer received

TABLE 5.5—Distribution of Ethical Scores: The Ethical Behavior Measure

Number of items	% of lawyers taking ethical action	Ethical behavior measure
13	11 ⎫	
12	18 ⎭	High: 29%
11	24 ⎫	
10	23 ⎭	Middle: 47%
9	14 ⎫	
8	5 ⎬	Low: 24%
7	5 ⎭	
	(100%)	(100%)

one point. Lawyers who reported taking or who would take ethical action on twelve or more items were classified as "high" on the measure of ethical behavior; those taking ethical action on ten to eleven items were classified as "middle"; and those taking ethical action on less than ten items were classified as "low." In Table 5.5 all of the ethical items were weighted equally, and the lawyers were ranked in terms of the number of rules violated. In other words, the ethical behavior measure did not take into account the qualitative difference in the rules. As a result, a lawyer violating a few rules of low significance could come out with a lower ethical rating than a lawyer violating only one or two rules of high significance.

For the most part, however, this was not the case. By weighting the ethical scores in terms of the normative significance given to each item by the bar, we found a high correlation between the number of items violated and the qualitative significance attached to the items. If a lawyer reported no unethical action for any item, he was scored zero. A lawyer who either admitted taking unethical action or said that he would in an item of low significance received one point; in an item of middle significance, two points; and in an item of high significance, three points. In Table 5.6 we have compared the weighted behavior scores with the ethical behavior measure. Table 5.7 shows the distribution of the lawyers in the ethical behavior measure by the weighted scores.

The data in these two tables show that lawyers who violated very few rules were not likely to violate rules of either high or middle significance and that lawyers who violated several rules were also likely to violate the more important rules. Eighty-three per cent of the lawyers scoring high on the ethical behavior measure either did not violate any

TABLE 5.6—Ethical Behavior Scores, Weighted and Unweighted

Weighted			Unweighted		
Score	%	Measure	No. of items	%	Measure
0	11 ⎫	High: 24%	13	11 ⎫	High: 29%
1	13 ⎭		12	18 ⎭	
2	16 ⎫	Middle: 49%	11	24 ⎫	Middle: 47%
3	13 ⎬		10	23 ⎭	
4	20 ⎭				
5	6 ⎫	Low: 26%	9	14 ⎫	Low: 24%
6	8 ⎪		8	5 ⎬	
7	5 ⎬		7	5 ⎭	
8	5 ⎪				
9	2 ⎭				
		(83)100%			(83)100%

rules or only one rule of low significance. If we break down the figures for the other groups, we find that 57 per cent of the lawyers scoring middle on the ethical behavior measure violated either a high or a middle rule but that 70 per cent of the lawyers scoring low on the ethical behavior measure violated a high rule and an additional 15 per cent

TABLE 5.7—Distribution of Ethical Behavior Measure by Weighted Behavior Scores

Ethical behavior measure		% of lawyers by weighted scores			
		High	Middle	Low	Total
High	(24)	83	17	0	100%
Middle	(39)	0	87	13	100%
Low	(20)	0	15	85	100%

violated a middle rule. In other words, the violators did not, for the most part, restrict their violations to the rules that "don't matter anyway"; the ethical behavior measure contains both a quantitative and a qualitative measure of violators.

SUMMARY AND COMPARISON WITH THE NEW YORK CITY BAR

In Prairie City, there was, in the main, consensus on the relative normative significance of the ethical rules. Among the New York City lawyers, there was a consensus on all but three of the rules. Stratification in the New York City bar, it will be recalled, was measured by firm size. A large majority of the four groups of lawyers (large, middle, small-firm, and individual practitioners) disapproved of the unethical action in eight items.[23] These rules were called *Bar* norms—rules generally accepted by the bar as a whole. Less than half of each group disapproved of the unethical action in four items; these rules were called *Paper* norms —rules generally not accepted by the bar. For three items, there were differences in the disapproval rates of the groups, more large-firm lawyers disapproving than the other lawyers, and these rules were called *Elite* norms. One item (*Oral Contract*) fell in between the *Bar* and *Paper* norms and was not classified. The lower status lawyers in the New York City bar did not have distinctive rules which the elite lawyers did not accept; they simply accepted fewer rules than the elite lawyers, generally accepting *Bar* norms only. For the most part, more elite lawyers than lawyers of the other groups accepted *Bar* as well as *Elite* norms. Middle-sized firm lawyers fell in between the elite and lower status lawyers.[24]

Table 5.8 shows the occurrence, disapproval, and ethical behavior rates for each hypothetical item for the two bars. The order of the rules reflects the attitudes of the Prairie City lawyers. Whether the rules were *Elite, Bar, Paper,* or unclassified norms among the New York City lawyers is indicated immediately to the right of each item.

Six out of twelve items occurred more frequently for New York City lawyers than for Prairie City lawyers, and rejection rates and violation rates were higher among New York City lawyers for eleven items. For several items, however, the differences between the two bars were relatively small. Both bars strongly disapproved of a lawyer's giving a previous client money in return for bringing in business (*Client Kickback: money*), of a lawyer's bribing an official (*Police Payoff*), or of his secretly purchasing stock on the basis of confidential information supplied by a client (*Stock Purchase*). The lawyers in both bars accepted and adhered to the rules which these situations violated. Fewer New York City lawyers rejected the *Package Deal* (an insurance company adjustor asks the lawyer to compromise a claim in return for a promise to help the lawyer out the next time) than did Prairie City lawyers, but violation rates were very low for both bars. Both bars rejected the two other forms of *Client Kickback* (*legal advice; gift, dinner*); more New York City lawyers engaged in the latter practice than Prairie City

TABLE 5.8—Occurrence, Disapproval, and Violation Rates Per Item: Prairie City and New York City Bars

Item	New York City rank	% occurrences			% disapproving			% violating		
		P.C.	N.Y.C.	Diff.	P.C.	N.Y.C.	Diff.	P.C.	N.Y.C.	Diff.
High										
1% Commission: accept without informing	(Elite)	7	78	+71	98	61	+37	1	15	+14
Package Deal	(Bar)	16	16	0	94	82	+12	7	16	+9
Client Kickback: money	(Bar)	28	43	+15	94	94	0	1	3	+2
Police Payoff	(Bar)	3	7	+4	92	84	+8	10	19	+9
Oral Contract	(Unclass.)	27	14	−13	92	40	+52	11	56	+45
Divorce Fraud	(Bar)	59	36	−23	90	73	+17	8	31	+23
Stock Purchase	(Bar)	8	14	+6	89	94	−5	1	11	+10
Intermediate										
Client Payoff: "Don't tell me"	(Bar)	6	22	+16	80	61	+19	5	12	+7
Client Payoff: "Risky, but your business"	(Elite)	6	22	+16	76	43	+33	1	11	+10
Receiver Sale	(Bar)	6	4	−2	70	75	−5	17	32	+15
1% Commission: take into consideration	(Paper)	7	78	+71	64	9	+55	6	33	+27
Low										
Assault Charge	(Bar)	20	7	−13	59	63	−4	36	30	−6
Client Kickback: legal advice	(Paper)	28	43	+15	58	42	+16	17	17	0
Conflict of Interest	(Paper)	55	44	−11	49	50	−1	39	54	+15
Client Kickback: gift, dinner	(Paper)	28	43	+15	48	42	+6	17	29	+12
Referral Fee	(Elite)	47	55	+8	27	29	−2	58	75	+17
Christmas Cards	(Paper)	...	...	...	25	9	+16	15	56	+41
		(83)	(801)		(83)	(801)		(83)	(801)	

lawyers. Both bars also rejected the *Conflict of Interest* (the partnership lawyer representing one of the partners against the other partner) and the *Christmas Cards,* although violation rates were higher among the New York City lawyers.

The differences in the responses to the ethical items indicated differences between the two bars discussed in Part I of this study. In the smaller community, the *Oral Contract* and the *Conflict of Interest* occurred more than in the large metropolitan center. The *Oral Contract* situation involved a rule of high ethical significance for the Prairie City lawyers, indicating that in the homogeneous professional community found in Prairie City, colleague relationships were highly valued. In the large metropolitan center, with its high proportion of individual practitioners and its very sharp stratification system, on the other hand, this rule fell between being a *Bar* norm and a *Paper* norm; 60 per cent of the New York City lawyers rejected the rule, as compared to only 8 per cent of the Prairie City lawyers, and 56 per cent of the New York City lawyers violated the rule, as compared to 11 per cent of the Prairie City lawyers.

The *Divorce Fraud* occurred for more Prairie City lawyers than for New York City lawyers. This fact probably reflected the lack of specialization among the Prairie City lawyers; in New York City prospective clients would probably be less likely to bring divorce cases to large-firm lawyers. It must be remembered, however, that the occurrence rates dealt with numbers of lawyers, not numbers of times that the opportunity was presented to each lawyer. Even though higher proportions of Prairie City lawyers were presented with this situation than New York City lawyers, it could well have occurred very often for the New York City divorce specialists. Rejection rates and violation rates were higher among New York lawyers. The grounds for divorce in the state where Prairie City is located included "extreme cruelty"; these grounds were less stringent and more susceptible to fabrication than the grounds for divorce in New York State (adultery).[25] One would think, therefore, that violation rates would be higher in Prairie City. That the reverse was true probably indicated both the lack of interest in divorce business among Prairie City lawyers and the effectiveness of the informal mechanism for handling the fraudulent divorce in that community. Most Prairie City lawyers did little divorce work, and they were probably confident of receiving a certain number of clients referred by other lawyers. In the large metropolitan bar, where there were divorce specialists, there was probably much more competition for business than in Prairie City and less inclination to turn away clients for what we characterized as a rather hypocritical adherence anyway.

Differences in the responses to the *1% Commission* were large. A lawyer's retaining the entire commission without informing his client was highly disapproved by the Prairie City lawyers but was only an *Elite* norm among the New York City lawyers. The situation in which the lawyer splits the commission with the client but without disclosure was of intermediate significance among the Prairie City lawyers, but only a *Paper* norm among the New York City lawyers. The item (a 15% commission for a title insurance policy) occurred very often within the metropolitan bar and very infrequently for the Prairie City lawyers, however. It may be, then, that the practice of offering a finder's fees was so widespread in New York City that little significance or awareness of ethical problems was attached to the practice.

TABLE 5.9—Ethical Behavior Scores: Prairie City and New York City Bars

No. of ethical responses	% of lawyers scoring "correct" answers	
	Prairie City	New York City
13	11 ⎫ 29% High	2 ⎫
12	18 ⎬	4 ⎪ 27% High
11	24 ⎫ 47% Middle	7 ⎬
10	23 ⎬	14 ⎭
9	14 ⎫	16 ⎫
8	5 ⎬ 24% Low	16 ⎬ 45% Middle
7	5 ⎭	13 ⎭
6	...	9 ⎫
5	...	7 ⎪
4	...	5 ⎬ 25% Low
3	...	2 ⎪
2	...	1 ⎪
1	...	1 ⎭
0	...	...
No answer	...	3%
	(83) 100%	(801) 100%

The *Assault Charge* (if a client learns that the prosecutor's case is weak, he will stop paying his fee) was the only item for which more Prairie City lawyers both rejected and violated the rule than did New

York City lawyers. There is nothing in the data to suggest or explain this result.

The fact that violation rates per item were higher for New York City lawyers meant, of course, that New York City lawyers scored generally lower than Prairie City lawyers on the ethical behavior measure. As a result, the low group in Prairie City was comparable to the middle group in New York City, for no lawyer in Prairie City violated as many rules as the low group in New York City (Table 5.9).

It must be emphasized that behavior data dealt in numbers of lawyers, not in numbers of violations. One could guess that since the New York City bar was very much more specialized than the Prairie City bar, the rates of violations would have been even higher than what was indicated in the behavior data. The divorce specialists in New York City spent much more of their time in this single area than their counterparts in Prairie City. Therefore, the 31 per cent violators in New York City were probably violating more often per lawyer than the 8 per cent in Prairie City, on the simple assumption that the New York City lawyers who were violating had more of an opportunity to do so. Perhaps this assumption is accurate, but we have no specific data.

As in Prairie City, the ethical behavior measure also reflected the qualitative aspects of the ethical rules. In New York City the lawyers who scored "high" generally conformed not only to the *Bar* norms, but to the *Elite* and/or *Paper* norms as well; the "middle" group conformed to the *Bar* norms only; and the "low" group violated all three sets of norms.

CHAPTER 6

CHARACTERISTICS OF ETHICAL BEHAVIOR

What accounted for differences in the ethical behavior of Prairie City lawyers? Why did some lawyers conform to ethical rules and others violate? A lawyer's ethical behavior is the product of his external situation and his internal disposition. We would expect that differences in type of practice would exert different pressures on lawyers—pressures to violate rules or to resist temptation. Other studies of lawyers have indicated that lawyers with clients of lower incomes, specializing in "one-shot," trouble areas of practice (criminal, personal injury plaintiff, matrimonial), and dealing with the lower levels of courts and government agencies were under great pressure to violate ethical rules.[1] These studies also indicated that wealthy clients, stable practice, and practice in higher levels of courts and agencies serve to encourage lawyers to resist temptation. Did these factors affect the behavior of the lawyers of this bar? We must also examine the internal disposition of the lawyers, insofar as we can measure it.

In this chapter all of the ethical rules are assumed to be of equal value or significance, and behavior is measured in terms of how many rules were violated. In the next chapter we will take into account any distortion that may result from this assumption.

SITUATIONAL PRESSURES: CLIENT CHARACTERISTICS

Situational pressures arise from clients, courts, and agencies. Under certain circumstances, the lawyer will be vulnerable to exploitation by the client; a client may insist on results, and the lawyer may feel that he has to produce these results even at the expense of violating an ethical rule. In other situations, clients are vulnerable to exploitation by lawyers. Clients are encouraged to give the lawyer secret information, and quite often they are incapable of evaluating the lawyer's performance. Lawyers, then, are in positions to take unfair advantage of clients and to sacrifice clients' interests either for the benefit of other clients or for the lawyers' personal gain.

Obviously, too, violations of ethical rules, whether the violation consists of cutting a corner on behalf of a client or of the exploitation of a client, depend on the existence of opportunities to violate. In general, we found that behavior was related to opportunities; lawyers with high opportunity rates were more likely to violate ethical rules than were lawyers with low opportunity rates (Table 6.1). Client characteristics

TABLE 6.1*—Relationship Between Opportunities to Violate and Low Ethical Behavior

Ethical behavior	% of lawyers by opportunities to violate	
	0–2	3+
Low	36% (42)	59% (41)

* Because of the small number of lawyers in this study, the tables in this chapter were dichotomized.

have an important bearing on the relationship between opportunities and behavior in two respects. First, it is important to know what types of clients produced different rates of opportunities. Second, we should know whether or not, given similar rates of opportunities, different types of clients still produced differences in behavior. Did lawyers, for example, who had wealthy clients conform because wealthy clients did not generate opportunities to violate, or did they conform even though there were high rates of opportunities to violate?

Wealth and stability of clients. There was a relationship between wealth of individual clients and ethical behavior: lawyers with poor individual clients were more likely to violate ethical rules than lawyers with wealthy individual clients (Table B.20, Appendix B). Opportunity rates were not related to wealth of individual clients (Table B.21). When opportunity rates were controlled, however, we found a very strong relationship between opportunities and behavior for lawyers with poor individual clients and a weak, but positive relationship for lawyers with wealthy individual clients. That is, when lawyers with wealthy individual clients and low opportunities were compared to lawyers with wealthy individual clients and high opportunities, the percentage of violators increased only 9 per cent; but when lawyers with poor individual clients and low opportunities were compared to lawyers with poor individual clients and high opportunities, the percentage of violators jumped 32 per cent (Table 6.2). This suggests that although opportunity rates were strongly related to behavior, lawyers with poor individual clients were those who tended to take advantage of their opportunities. Lawyers with wealthy individual clients did not. Ethical behavior, then, was related to opportunities when individual clients were poor.

TABLE 6.2—Relationship Between Wealth of Individual
Clients and Low Ethical Behavior, Controlling for Opportunities to Violate

Opportunities	% of lawyers with low ethical behavior having	
	Rich clients	Poor clients
0–2	35% (17)	39% (18)
3+	44% (18)	71% (21)

Wealth of business clients was not related either to opportunity rates or to ethical behavior (Tables B.22 and B.23). But when opportunity rates were controlled, we found the same pattern of relationships as we found with wealth of individual clients: among those lawyers with poor business clients, rates of violation increased very sharply when opportunity rates increased; among lawyers with wealthy business clients, the relationship between opportunities and ethical behavior was quite weak. We are led, then, to the same conclusion: lawyers with poor business clients tended to take advantage of opportunities to violate (Table 6.3).

TABLE 6.3—Relationship Between Wealth of Business
Clients and Low Ethical Behavior, Controlling for Opportunities to Violate

Opportunities	% of lawyers with low ethical behavior having	
	Rich clients	Poor clients
0–2	43% (14)	24% (17)
3+	53% (17)	60% (20)

Stability of clients[2] was related both to opportunities and ethical behavior; lawyers with unstable clients tended to have higher opportunities and were more likely to violate ethical rules (Tables B.24 and B.25). When opportunity rates were controlled, we found a pattern similar to the one we found with wealth of clients. With unstable clients, rates of violations increased as opportunities rose, but the rise was not as sharp for the factor of instability as for the factor of poor individual clients. With stable clients, rates of violation also increased as opportunities rose; although the rise was not as sharp as the rise for lawyers with unstable clients, it was still fairly significant (Tables B.26, 6.2, and 6.3). In any event, the combination of unstable clients and high opportunities produced sharp differences in ethical behavior when compared to stable clients and low opportunity rates.[3]

In general, therefore, lawyers with poor or unstable clients tended to violate ethical rules, and lawyers with wealthy or stable clients tended to conform. Ethical behavior was related to opportunities only for lawyers with poor or unstable clients. Lawyers with wealthy or stable clients did not take advantage of opportunities to violate. Since we are looking at external determinants of ethical behavior only, this suggests that a practice composed of poor and unstable clients tended to encourage lawyers to take advantage of opportunities to violate and that a practice composed of wealthy and stable clients tended to restrain lawyers.

Client pressure. Respondents were asked: "How often have clients exerted pressure on you to engage in practices contrary to your standards?" Seventeen per cent of the bar said "never"; 71 per cent said "rarely"; 12 per cent said "sometimes"; and none said "very often."[4] In general, then, although few lawyers reported no pressure at all, the bar as a whole perceived very little client pressure.

There was, nevertheless, some relationship between client pressure and ethical behavior; lawyers who violated tended to report more client pressure than lawyers who conformed (Table B.28). The relationships between client pressure and the client characteristics of wealth and stability were weak, but they were consistent in direction. Lawyers with wealthy clients (individual and business), low opportunities, and stable clients tended to experience fewer client pressures than did lawyers with poor, unstable clients and high opportunities.

Competition. Despite the fact that the Prairie City bar was generally prosperous and satisfied, 88 per cent of the lawyers thought that there was competition among lawyers for law business, 35 per cent thought that there was a "great deal," and 22 per cent thought that they had been hurt by such competition. Fifty-seven per cent of the bar also thought that there was at least some competition from nonlawyers (*e.g.,* real estate brokers, insurance company agents); an additional 14 per cent reported a "great deal"; and 22 per cent said that they had been hurt by such competition.

One would expect that lawyers with poor or unstable clients would report more competition and feel more of the effects of competition than lawyers with wealthy or stable clients. But in fact, approximately the same proportion of lawyers with rich or poor individual clients reported a "great deal" of competition from lawyers; only slightly more lawyers with poor individual clients said that they were hurt from such competition. Somewhat more lawyers with stable clients admitted to being hurt by competition. With business clients, we found the largest differences, and here, lawyers with wealthy business clients reported more competition; but they reported no more harm from this competition than lawyers with poor business clients. The same overall lack of relationship existed with respect to competition from nonlawyers. In sum, the effects of competition were rather evenly spread among the lawyers when they were viewed in terms of the client characteristics of wealth and stability.

Referral and retainer clients. It is usually thought that a business based on referrals generates high competitive pressures. Lawyers who take cases on referral depend on other lawyers for their business, receiving mostly the one-shot, trouble cases which, for one reason or another, the referring lawyer chooses not to handle. In Prairie City there was little referral business; only 15 per cent of the bar said that 10 per cent or more of their income was drawn from other lawyers on referral. A slight majority of these lawyers had a preponderance of poor or unstable clients.

If the combination of poor or unstable clients and dependence on a referral business is likely to intensify competitive pressures, then the presence of retainer clients should lead to the opposite result, since retainer clients represent the private practitioner's closest approach to a guaranteed income.[5] In Prairie City, few lawyers derived much income from retainer clients, only 5 per cent of the bar reporting more than 40 per cent of their income from this source, 18 per cent reporting 10–39 per cent, 24 per cent reporting 1–9 per cent, and 39 per cent reporting no income at all from retainer clients.[6] But there was some relationship between ethical behavior and income derived from retainer clients; lawyers who had higher proportions of income from this source tended to have lower rates of violation.[7] Lawyers with wealthy (individual and business), stable clients had more of the retainer business than lawyers with other types of clients (Table B.29), and, as has already been pointed out, these lawyers tended not to take advantage of opportunities to violate. Retainer clients, we think, generally implied long-term attorney-client relationships, security for the lawyer, confidence in the lawyer, and more intimacy in professional and personal relations.

Involvement. The more intimately a lawyer knows his client's affairs, the more likely it is that he would be presented with opportunities to violate. He would be in a position to take advantage of secret knowledge and exploit the client. In order to measure the relation between client characteristics and involvement, we obtained data on two types of involvement with business clients—control involvement and financial involvement. The lawyers were asked whether they were officers or members of the boards of directors of client corporations, and if so, of how many (control involvement) and whether they held stock or had other financial holdings in any client corporations or enterprises (financial involvement). Generally speaking, there were no relationships between financial involvement and client characteristics. Approximately the same proportions of lawyers with rich or poor clients and stable or unstable clients had such holdings.

We did, however, find relationships between client characteristics and control involvement. Lawyers with wealthy, stable business clients tended to be officers or members of the boards of directors of client corporations (Table B.30). Was there any relationship between control involvement and behavior? We found a relationship between high involvement and high opportunities—lawyers who had high opportunity rates also had high involvement rates. When wealth of business clients was controlled, lawyers with wealthy business clients had high rates of involvement regardless of opportunities; nevertheless, there were no differences in the ethical behavior of these lawyers. Lawyers with poor business clients and low opportunities had a low rate of involvement, but lawyers with poor business clients and high opportunities had high involvement. And lawyers with poor business clients and high opportunities tended to violate, while lawyers with poor business clients and low opportunities did not (see Tables B.31 and 6.3). This again suggests the restraining influence of a practice characterized by wealthy business clients. The ethical behavior of lawyers with wealthy business clients was not affected by opportunity rates despite high involvement with their business clients. For lawyers with poor business clients, when there was high involvement, there were also high opportunities, and there were high rates of violation.

In sum, although the evidence was not very strong, we found that lawyers with poor or unstable clients experienced somewhat more pressure to engage in practices contrary to standards. Although lawyers with wealthy business clients were more closely involved with their business clients than were lawyers with poor business clients, their violations did not reflect this, despite the fact that high involvement increased opportunities to violate. Among the lawyers with poor business clients, high involvement also increased opportunities to violate, and their violation rates seemed to reflect this fact.

SITUATIONAL PRESSURES: COURTS AND AGENCIES

We turn now to the second potential source of situational pressures— contacts with courts and agencies. In Prairie City, practically all of the lawyers spent time in the courts and many of them had dealings with administrative agencies. The questions arise, Was there any relationship between contacts with courts or agencies and ethical behavior and, if so, did it vary with the level of courts or agencies? Specifically, were violation rates higher in the lower courts and agencies?

In Prairie City, courts and agencies were not corrupting influences, and though there was some relationship between ethical behavior and contacts, the relationships appear explainable more in terms of client characteristics of wealth and stability than in terms of courts and agencies as sources of pressure. We will consider first contacts with courts.

Courts. Table 6.4 compares the average time per week in court with ethical behavior. As this table shows, lawyers who spent the most time in court had the highest violation rates. On the other hand, the lawyers who spent the least time in court had higher violation rates than the lawyers who spent between two and seven hours per week in court. The explanation for these behavior patterns is to be sought in client characteristics. Lawyers who spent the most time in court (eight hours or more per week) tended to have unstable, poor individual clients, while lawyers who spent the least time in court (less than two hours per week) tended to have wealthy, stable individual clients.[8] Ethical be-

TABLE 6.4—Relationship Between Time Spent in
Court and Ethical Behavior

Av. hrs. per wk. in court	% violators	No. of violators
−2	53	(15)
2–4	37	(27)
5–7	39	(23)
8+	67	(18)

havior rates of the two middle groups (two to four and five to seven hours per week) were the same, and client characteristics of these lawyers were also approximately the same (Table B.32). Furthermore, when client characteristics were controlled, ethical behavior rates did not increase with increased time spent in court. For example, among the lawyers with poor and unstable clients, behavior rates were the same regardless of time spent in court (Table B.33).

The effects of client characteristics were also quite clear when contacts with individual courts were examined (Table B.34). In three courts—the Justice of the Peace, the County, and the Federal District —there was a slight relationship between contacts and ethical behavior: violations tended to rise as contacts increased. Lawyers who had the most contact with the Justice of the Peace and the County courts, with jurisdiction over minor civil and criminal matters, had higher proportions of poor clients (individual and business) and unstable clients. In the Federal District Court we found no relationship between contacts and wealth of individual clients. Lawyers, however, who had the most contact with this court (which has bankruptcy jurisdiction) had significantly higher proportions of poor business clients and higher proportions of unstable clients, and violation rates rose for lawyers who had poor business clients and unstable clients. This fact probably explains why behavior patterns for lawyers who appeared in the Federal District Court—a court of high prestige—were similar to the patterns for lawyers who appeared in the Justice of the Peace and County courts— courts of lower prestige.

In the Circuit Court there was no relationship between contacts and violations. This was the trial court of general jurisdiction handling the more important civil and criminal trials, and it enjoyed considerably more prestige than the Justice of the Peace and County courts. On the other hand, this court handled personal injury litigation. Proportions of poor individual and unstable clients rose with the numbers of contacts in this court, as was also true for the Justice of the Peace and County courts, but the relationship between contacts and these client characteristics for the Circuit Court was not nearly as strong as the relationship in the Justice of the Peace and County courts. Furthermore, in the Circuit Court proportions of wealthy business clients increased with numbers of contacts, whereas in the Justice of the Peace and County courts proportions of these clients decreased. In other words, the ethical behavior rates for lawyers who worked in these courts seemed to reflect the characteristics of the clients of these lawyers.

The strongest relationship between ethical behavior and court contacts existed in the Probate Court. But here, rates of violations *decreased* as numbers of contacts increased. The Probate Court handled estate business. In this court there was no relationship between poor individual clients and contacts, whereas in the Justice of the Peace, County, and Circuit courts, proportions of poor individual clients rose with contacts. In the Probate Court, proportions of unstable clients decreased as numbers of contacts increased. In no other court was this true. Proportions of poor business clients increased with contacts in the Probate Court. Violation rates were low for lawyers with stable clients and poor business clients (Table B.34).

The relationship between ethical behavior and contacts with particular courts was complex and perhaps inconclusive. In general, the data reinforced the impression that client characteristics of the lawyers appearing before these courts is a better indicator of lawyers' ethical behavior than numbers and types of court contacts.

Agencies and officials. Most of the lawyers in Prairie City had contact with local government agencies—planning and zoning boards, building departments, taxation and assessments officials. The agency most frequently visited on the state level was the Secretary of State's office (either on corporate or motor vehicle matters) and, on the federal level, the Internal Revenue Service. Professional contacts with state or federal agencies on higher levels than these were relatively limited. The official visited professionally most often was the City Manager; fewer professional contacts were made with the Mayor, council members, or state legislators.

We have no evidence that agencies and officials were corrupting influences. For none of the agencies or officials, regardless of the level, did violation rates increase as contacts increased (and in a few cases, in fact, violation rates declined slightly with increased contacts). The one exception was the City Manager. The group of lawyers who saw this official an average of one or more times per month had higher violation rates than the rest of the bar. Again, however, client characteristics provide an explanation: the higher violation group had more unstable and poor clients than the rest of the bar.

CHARACTER AND BEHAVIOR

We turn now to a consideration of the other determinant of ethical behavior—character or internal disposition. We shall first consider the problem of "measuring" character. We shall then examine the relationship between character and professional behavior.

MEASURING ETHICAL CONCERN

In order to have some scale for measuring character, we asked the Prairie City respondents a series of questions designed to elicit information about their concern with ethics in selecting either office sharers or partners. They were asked to select which of seven characteristics they would most want to know about another lawyer before deciding to share an office with him or to go into a partnership with him— type of practice, personality, loyalty to clients, competence, fairness in dealing with colleagues, honesty in dealing with officials, or business-getting ability. The respondents were given a choice of ranking each characteristic first, second, third, no rank at all, or of indicating that they were not concerned about it at all. The lawyers were then ranked on a scale in terms of the importance given to loyalty to clients and honesty in dealing with officials.[9] Lawyers who scored high on the concern measure tended to mention honesty and integrity as qualities they most admired in other lawyers. They were more likely to agree that "the Canons of Ethics need much more active enforcement by the bar and the courts," and they were more likely to have a strict attitude towards violations of ethical rules compared to lawyers who scored low on the measure (Table B.35).

In addition, the respondents were asked to name three lawyers whom they considered "highly ethical." As Table 6.5 indicates, lawyers who scored high on the concern measure were more likely to have a reputation among their fellow lawyers as highly ethical than were lawyers who scored low. The lawyers were not asked to rate every other lawyer;

TABLE 6.5—Relationship Between Reputation for Being
Highly Ethical and Concern with Ethics

Mentioned as "highly ethical"	% with high concern	No.
By at least 1 lawyer	64	(56)
By 2 lawyers	73	(37)
By 3 or more lawyers	86	(22)

therefore, the respondents were probably not expressing an opinion, one way or the other, on lawyers whom they did not mention. On the other hand, the respondents seemed to be quite sure about the lawyers whom they mentioned, and we found that reputations were related to internal concern. This was not surprising. In a homogeneous bar where most lawyers know each other and where they generally see each other frequently, one would expect that a lawyer's concern with ethics would be known by his colleagues.

Finally, as we shall see later, the concern measure was related to ethical behavior: the lawyers who scored high on this measure tended to violate less than the lawyers who scored low.

One might assume that the higher the professional status, the higher the concern with ethics, that ethics were for those who could afford them. But in Prairie City this was not the case; just as many lawyers with low incomes had high concern as did lawyers with high incomes. Nor was there any relationship between the income-client measure and concern for ethics. One might also assume that lawyers with high concern with ethics would be those with few opportunities and few pressures to violate ethical rules; since lawyers who experienced these pressures in practice tended to violate, they would be less inclined to focus on the ethical qualities of lawyers with whom they would be associated. But, in the main, there was no relationship between concern and opportunities or situational pressures. Just as many lawyers experiencing high opportunity rates had high concern with ethics as did those lawyers with low opportunity rates. Concern with ethics was again not correlated with wealth of individual clients and stability of clients. Also, the poorer the business clients, the higher the concern with ethics. Although violation rates were highest for lawyers with high opportunities and poor and unstable clients, just as many lawyers with poor individual clients and high opportunities scored high on the concern measure as lawyers with wealthy individual clients and low opportunities. The same was true with wealth of business clients and stability of clients. The ethical concern measure, then, tapped a personality characteristic that was not related to professional status or to other aspects of practice.

On the other hand, concern with ethics was related to age and years in practice: younger lawyers or lawyers more recently admitted to the bar (1950 or later) had less concern for ethics than did older lawyers or lawyers who had been in practice longer (Table B.36). It may be that the younger lawyers of this bar had different values from the older lawyers, although our data on background (education, father's occupation, etc.) were not sufficient to explore this possibility. Or it may be that years in practice have a socializing effect on lawyers, that ethical views may change with time and experience on the job. Because we have no information on the attitudes of the older lawyers during their earlier years in practice, we cannot demonstrate directly whether or not such a change did take place. But we do have some indirect evidence that points in this direction.

The more recently admitted lawyers had lower professional incomes, poorer individual clients, and more unstable clients than the lawyers who had been in practice longer. Their type of practice generated more pressures and more opportunities to violate than did the practice of lawyers who had been in practice longer.[10] But for the most part, concern with ethics was not related to the type of practice of these younger lawyers; approximately as many with high opportunities and poor clients had high concern as those with low opportunities and wealthy clients. With incomes there was actually a reverse relationship: rates of high concern *increased* for the younger lawyers with *lower* professional incomes. The one direct relationship was with stability of clients: rates of high concern decreased among younger lawyers as practice became more unstable (Table B.38).

Younger lawyers were nevertheless less concerned with ethics; their lack of concern may have been related to the unstable nature of their practice. The selection of office-sharer and partner characteristics by this group appeared to reflect the economic anxiety produced by youth and unstable clients. We found that this group tended to be more concerned with the type of practice and the business-getting ability of potential colleagues than did lawyers who had been in practice longer (Table B.39). Fewer young lawyers were concerned with a potential office-sharer's loyalty to clients than old lawyers; young and old lawyers were about equally concerned, however, with a potential partner's loyalty to clients. Why this difference in concern? In a partnership members of the firm are responsible for each other's liabilities; this joint responsibility may have influenced lawyers' thinking. Then, too, if an aggrieved client brought suit for damages against a partner or the firm or filed a grievance complaint, other clients might become aware of the situation and cut their ties with the firm. In either event, the economic interests of all the partners would suffer. In an office-sharing arrangement, on the other hand, there is no joint responsibility; each lawyer is concerned only with his personal clients.

The other characteristic which was used to measure concern with ethics was honesty in dealing with officials. Fewer young lawyers were concerned with this characteristic when considering a future partner than when considering a future office-sharer (Table B.39). This finding, however, may have been a mere artifact of the survey methods used. Lawyers were asked to select only what they considered the three most important characteristics, and honesty in dealing with officials was not a significant issue in Prairie City. Young lawyers had some interest in this insofar as selecting an office-sharer was concerned. For partners, they were more anxious to choose characteristics which served their economic interests, stressing business-getting ability and competence— traits which, in a partnership, bring direct economic benefit. Older lawyers were also concerned with business-getting ability in potential partners, but less so than young lawyers.

Finally, one might also assume that firm arrangements would be related to concern with ethics. In a bar where lawyers know each other, lawyers of like inclination would be likely to form partnerships and continue the association; young lawyers would be likely either to adopt the attitudes of the senior partners or to leave the firm. There were seventeen Prairie City firms in which all members including associates were interviewed, accounting for sixty-two lawyers. In four of these firms, all of the lawyers showed high concern; in the remaining thirteen firms, there were divisions between lawyers of high and low concern. In only four firms in Prairie City (not necessarily the same as the four high concern firms) did all of the lawyers display either strict or permissive attitudes towards violations of professional rules. Since "partnerships" were loose associations in Prairie City, this lack of homogeneity in concern and attitudes within firms is not surprising. It is interesting to note, though, that in the largest firm and the one that had more of the characteristics of a firm than did any other, we found almost complete homogeneity; all of the lawyers but one were of the same concern, and all of the young lawyers in that firm followed the dominant view. In another large firm—a firm in name only—there was an equal division between lawyers of high and low concern; young lawyers were also divided. One cannot conclude from this, however, that to the extent that partnership elements were present in a given firm, there will tend to be homogeneity of concern with ethics and that the young lawyers will be selected on the basis of their concern. Because, as we pointed out in Part I of this study, the dominant characteristic of this bar was that the lawyers were engaged in individual practice, whether in firms or not, the evidence from the other firms was inconsistent and conflicting.

CONCERN AND ETHICAL BEHAVIOR

As stated earlier, there was a relationship between concern with ethics and ethical behavior: lawyers who scored high on the ethical concern measure tended to conform and lawyers who scored low tended to violate (Table 6.6).

TABLE 6.6—Relationship Between Ethical Concern
and Ethical Behavior

Rating on ethical concern measure	% violators	No.
High	37	(52)
Low	65	(31)

Generally speaking, concern with ethics was not related to practice characteristics (opportunities to violate, wealth and stability of clients), but practice characteristics were related to behavior. We found that when we introduced concern with ethics, the relationships between practice characteristics and behavior increased; that is to say, ethical behavior was the product of both situational pressures and internal disposition. Unethical behavior decreased when high concern was combined with features of practice which did not generate pressure to violate (low opportunities, wealthy and stable clients), and unethical behavior increased when low concern was combined with features of practice which generated pressures to violate (high opportunities, poor and unstable clients); these relationships are shown in Table 6.7. Young

TABLE 6.7—Relationship Between Ethical Behavior and Practice Characteristics, Controlling for Concern with Ethics

Lawyers with	% violators		Effect of ethical concern on violation rates
Low opportunities	36%	(42)	
Low opportunities, high concern	26	(27)	−10
High opportunities	59	(41)	
High opportunities, low concern	75	(16)	+16
Rich individual clients	40	(35)	
Rich individual clients, high concern	29	(21)	−11
Poor individual clients	56	(39)	
Poor individual clients, low concern	69	(16)	+13
Rich business clients	48	(31)	
Rich business clients, high concern	50	(14)	+2
Poor business clients	43	(37)	
Poor business clients, low concern	80	(10)	+37
Stable clients	40	(43)	
Stable clients, high concern	38	(29)	−2
Unstable clients	55	(40)	
Unstable clients, low concern	77	(17)	+22

lawyers had higher rates of violation than older lawyers (Table B.40). Violation rates increased, too, for young lawyers with practice character- istics that generated pressure (high opportunities, poor and unstable clients; see Table B.41).

Ethical behavior, then, seemed to be affected both by concern with ethics and by situational pressures. Character, and consequently, ethical concern, may be fixed in childhood, so as to be relatively immune to change by training. Nevertheless, it would still be possible to heighten the bar's conformity to legal ethics, either by controlling entry into the profession or by altering conditions under which lawyers work.

SUMMARY AND COMPARISON WITH THE NEW YORK CITY BAR

In Prairie City relationships existed between ethical behavior and situa- tional pressures generated by client characteristics, although in many instances causal connections between practice characteristics, pressures, and ethical behavior were missing. The small size of the Prairie City bar prevented a more refined analysis. But, more importantly, Prairie City lawyers were primarily unspecialized general practitioners and could not readily be separated from each other on the basis of practice characteristics: personal injury or divorce lawyers also did probate and corporate work; very few lawyers had no wealthy or no poor clients. As a result, the practice of each lawyer contained some characteristics which generated pressures to violate and others which encouraged the lawyer to refrain from violating.

The situation was quite different in the highly stratified and specialized New York City bar. Here, lawyers with lower status clients and insecure practices tended to violate "basic standards of ethical conduct"—the *Bar* norms. They were subject to more opportunities and client pressures to violate and were consequently less able to resist temptation to violate than lawyers with high status clients and secure practices. In New York City, in contrast to Prairie City, courts and agencies constituted situational pressures. Lawyers who dealt primarily with lower courts had greater opportunities and were under greater pressure to violate than lawyers who dealt primarily with higher level courts. In that study it was found that different levels of courts had different "normative climate[s]"; "the more lawyers are exposed to a particular court level, the more likely they are to adopt its perspective toward violation and conformity." [11] In New York City, lower courts tended to be corrupting influences; they strengthened pressures to violate.

In Prairie City, where law firms were loose associations of individual practitioners, there seemed to be little relationship between attitudes and behavior and firm membership. The opposite was true in New York City. Firm membership affected ethical behavior. In offices where members were similar in age and had similar types of practice ("peer-group offices"), situational pressures generated by clients and courts and agencies were reinforced. In the newer offices of this type, there was an informal process of "seeking and giving support for violations among lawyers facing similar problems," [12] while in the older peer-group offices, the longer a lawyer stayed, the more his behavior tended to conform to that of his colleagues. In offices that were stratified, or hierarchically organized, the allocation of work rather than office climate or colleague relations tended to affect ethical behavior, rank and status in these offices determining the work that the lawyer did and therefore the situa-

tional pressures that he encountered. For these lawyers adherence to
ethical rules was related to rank and status.[13]

In Prairie City situational pressures were not concentrated in one
group of lawyers. Pressures were related to client characteristics, yet
in this community all lawyers had a mixed bag of clients. Some firms,
and one in particular, had high proportions of the largest business
clients in town. But these firms were not stable institutions with long
histories; they had experienced mergers, splits, and reorganizations.
The basic generality of practice and the distribution of rich and poor
clients indicated that the practice, and therefore the situational pressures,
of Prairie City lawyers would or could change over time. Again, the
New York City bar stood in sharp contrast. In the large metropolitan
bar, there were sharp differences among lawyers in terms of clients,
types of practice, and income. These divisions, as pointed out, were
relatively stable, for they were maintained by recruitment and career
patterns and by the relative isolation of the elite group from the lower
groups. The stratification system (*i.e.,* the lawyer's position in the hierarchy) determined the type of client and the court-agency contacts to
which the lawyer would be exposed, which, in turn, determined situational pressures. Carlin concludes: "As a result, lawyers at the top experience maximum pressure to conform to distinctively professional
standards [*e.g., Elite* norms], as well as the more ordinary, ethical
norms; at the same time they are insulated from pressures to violate.
Conversely, lawyers at the bottom of the status ladder are maximally
exposed to pressures to violate, and least subject to pressures to conform." [14]

The other determinant of ethical behavior was character or the inner
disposition of the lawyers. The same measure of concern with ethics
was used for the two bars, and, in the main, the results were similar.
New York City lawyers who scored high on the ethical concern measure
were more likely than those who scored low "to emphasize moral characteristics rather than personality traits in judging other lawyers, to
oppose liberalizing the canons and to favor their more strict enforcement,
to disapprove of the more distinctively professional norms, and to perceive law as a profession rather than as a business." [15] Concern with
ethics among New York City lawyers was not related to status in the
bar, situational pressures, or age. Concern also appeared not to be
influenced by professional training: "More important is national origin
and generation in the United States, which suggests that early family

influence may be decisive in the development of ethical concern." [16]
But, as in Prairie City, ethical concern was related to ethical behavior,
concern and situational pressures being "about equally influential" in
determining ethical conduct.[17] The New York study was able to go
further. For lawyers with high ethical concern, the rise in violations
was slower as pressure increased than was true of lawyers with low
ethical concern. That is, "high concern lawyers are far less responsive
to an increase in situational pressures than their less ethically concerned
colleagues." [18]

The Prairie City lawyers scored higher on the ethical behavior measure than New York City lawyers; on the other hand, they displayed
significantly less concern for ethics than the New York City lawyers
(Table 6.8). The scoring on the concern measure, it will be recalled,

TABLE 6.8—Ethical Concern Measure: New York City and
Prairie City

Scores	New York City lawyers		Prairie City lawyers	
	%	Measure	%	Measure
8	2	High: 47%	8	High: 11%
7	3		0	
6	22		1	
5	20		2	
4	40	Middle: 40%	50	Middle: 50%
3	8	Low: 13%	7	Low: 39%
2	4		31	
1	0.1		1	
0	0.4		0	
	(801)		(83)	

depended on whether a lawyer selected "loyalty to clients" and "honesty
in dealing with officials" as characteristics that he would rank highest
in selecting an office-sharer or a partner. It could be that in Prairie
City, the ethical climate was such that these characteristics tended to
be assumed as a matter of course. Several lawyers in Prairie City emphasized how clean practice in their community was in contrast to
what they pictured as the sordid corruption of big-city practice. In New
York City many violations of ethical rules occurred; local bar associations and the judiciary were constantly concerned with deviant behavior
of lawyers.[19] The publicity about deviation may have served to increase

a conscious concern for ethics on the part of high conformers in that bar.

Finally, in the New York study it was found that younger lawyers were more likely to violate than older lawyers. They were more likely to have unstable clients and come into contact with lower level courts and agencies, and violation rates increased more for younger lawyers with unstable clients than for older lawyers with the same type of clients. Although contacts with courts and agencies were not related to ethical behavior in Prairie City, in other respects the younger lawyers seemed to behave in the same way as their counterparts in New York City.

CHAPTER 7

ETHICS AND SOCIAL CONTROL

In this chapter we want to review and to shed light on the bar's commitment to professional ethics, the nature and extent of deviation from ethical rules among Prairie City lawyers, and the effectiveness of efforts to control deviant conduct by the bar association.

THE RULES: ATTITUDES AND ETHICAL BEHAVIOR

In Chapter 6 we were concerned with those characteristics of practice and personality which tended to result in violations. Ethical behavior was measured by how many rules were violated, assuming the rules to be of equal value. The question remains whether or not the violation of *particular* rules was related to aspects of practice and character. Did lawyers with poor clients or low ethical concern, for example, violate or reject certain rules but not others?

We examined the rejection and violation rates of specific rules in terms of the following characteristics of lawyers: attitudes and ethical behavior in general, ethical concern, years in practice, status (the income-client measure), professional incomes, and situational pressures (opportunities to violate, wealth, and stability of clients).[1] On the whole, we found that attitudes and behavior towards particular rules did not vary in terms of practice or personality characteristics. For only two rules of high significance—the *Oral Contract* and the *Divorce Fraud*—were violations related to character (youth and low concern) or situational pressures. The *Oral Contract* hypothetical, in which a client asks his lawyer to break a legally unenforceable agreement with another lawyer, pits the desire to retain a client against the obligation of a lawyer to abide by his agreement with a colleague. Younger lawyers with wealthy business clients tended to violate and reject the rule. Since

135

lawyers in this bar started out rather quickly on independent careers,[2] one would expect these new lawyers to be anxious to hold clients, even if it meant risking the ill-will of fellow attorneys. As lawyers become more secure in their practice, on the other hand, the importance of colleague relationships and friendships increases, and a change in attitude and behavior is not surprising. A single client may not seem quite so important to a lawyer at a later, more secure stage in his career.

Of the few lawyers who violated the *Divorce Fraud,* all but one were admitted to practice in 1950 or later. These young lawyers, with more unstable clients than older lawyers and insecure about their practice, might prefer a bird in the hand to the informal Prairie City system of referring clients to other lawyers after advising these clients of the statutory grounds for divorce. Older lawyers, with more stable clients, were better integrated into the informal system of handling divorce clients and more willing to risk the loss of particular clients.

There was little difference in ethical behavior between rules of high and of intermediate significance; the average percentages of the lawyers who conformed to both sets of rules was about 93 per cent. Yet attitudes differed from ethical behavior. For example, between 20 and 36 per cent of the bar did not disapprove of lawyers who violated the intermediate rules, and the lawyers who accepted these rules were willing to impose only mild sanctions. But attitudes towards rules of intermediate significance did not vary in terms of aspects of practice or character; where differences appeared, they were slight.

The average percentage of lawyers who conformed dropped to 70 per cent for rules of low significance. Rejection and violation rates for these rules further demonstrated the overall finding of consensus. For example, although lawyers may not withhold information from clients, the *Assault Charge* presents a situation in which the lawyer withholds information to protect himself from exploitation. This situation tended to occur more for young lawyers who had permissive attitudes, were violators, had a low concern for ethics, and faced situational pressures; and the distribution of occurrences would indicate high rates of violation. Violation rates were in fact high—36 per cent of the bar had taken or would have taken unethical action. Lawyers for whom the situation had occurred admitted violations, but lawyers for whom the situation had *not* occurred also said that they would violate. Although the situation had occurred for only 10 per cent of the high concern lawyers, 33 per cent of this group said that they would violate if the situation came up. The situation had arisen for only 14 per cent of the lawyers with wealthy individual clients and for 9 per cent of the lawyers with stable clients, yet 40 per cent of these lawyers said that they would violate. As was pointed out in Chapter 5, our most reliable behavior data can be taken from a lawyer's assertion that he will violate if given the opportunity; the significant proportion of lawyers who said that they would violate the *Assault Charge* hypothetical and whom we would *least* expect to violate (*e.g.,* those who had strict attitudes, high concern, high status, high incomes, low situational pressures, and were conformers in other respects) strongly indicates the unwillingness of the Prairie City bar to adhere to this rule. Thirty-nine per cent of high concern and high income lawyers, 46 per cent of the high status lawyers, and about 45 per cent of the lawyers with wealthy and stable clients rejected the rule.

The *Conflict of Interest* situation, in which two partners have a falling out and one partner asks the partnership's lawyer to represent him against the other partner, occurred for more lawyers (55 per cent) than any other ethical situation. This rule had the second highest violation rate of any—39 per cent of the bar. Just as many high income as low income lawyers and as many with poor as with wealthy clients violated this rule. Half of the bar (51 per cent) rejected the rule; although lawyers with high opportunities and unstable clients rejected, as was to be anticipated, rejection also occurred with lawyers having wealthy individual clients and with 45 per cent of the lawyers having wealthy business clients. Furthermore, half of the high concern lawyers rejected this rule. The impressive fact about this rule was that violations and rejections were high throughout the whole bar.

Almost half of the lawyers (47 per cent) had been offered referral fees, and violations were high for all groups of lawyers, including over 50 per cent of the high concern lawyers and 53 per cent of the high income lawyers. The overall rejection rate of this rule rose to 73 per cent of the bar, the percentage including three-quarters of the high concern lawyers.

The fact that the relationships between ethical behavior and practice and personality characteristics, discussed in the preceding chapter, did not indicate much difference among the lawyers is not surprising. We have emphasized the basic homogeneity of the Prairie City bar. There were no specialists. The lawyers in this bar were all essentially general practitioners with shared experiences. Some lawyers made a great deal of money; few were poor. The lawyers worked in the same courts; there was a great deal of personal interaction. Opportunity rates illustrate this homogeneity and these shared experiences. The *Divorce Fraud* situation occurred for 61 per cent of the high status lawyers, 64 per cent of the high income lawyers, 52 per cent of the lawyers with wealthy business clients, and 56 per cent of the lawyers with stable clients. The *Referral Fee* problem occurred for 49 per cent of the high status lawyers, 51 per cent of the high income lawyers, 48 per cent of the lawyers with wealthy business clients, and even for 37 per cent of the lawyers with stable clients. And the similarity in opportunity rates was generally the case for the other ethical problems. The bar's homogeneity accounts for the basic uniformity of the lawyers' responses to individual items.

ETHICAL BEHAVIOR AND SOCIAL RESTRAINTS

In Chapter 4 we saw that, quantitatively speaking, few lawyers were ever disciplined by the state bar association and the state supreme court. Did this mean that the disciplinary machinery was ineffective, or was it that few lawyers engaged in unprofessional conduct? Twenty-four per cent of the Prairie City lawyers violated ethical rules in at least four of the hypothetical situations, and half of the bar violated ethical rules in at least three of the hypotheticals. It would be unrealistic, however, to compare the number of "violators" with the number of lawyers for whom the state bar association recommended sanctions (less than one lawyer per thousand) and conclude that the disciplinary machinery of the organized bar was ineffective in controlling deviant behavior. Instead, we shall examine the practical implications of the rules which had the most violations.

The three rules with the highest violation rates were the *Assault Charge* (26 per cent), the *Conflict of Interest* (39 per cent) and the *Referral Fee* (58 per cent). The proportions of lawyers who either did not disapprove of the unethical action, or if they disapproved, would impose no sanction whatsoever were 75 per cent, 70 per cent, and 91 per cent, respectively. We took as our standard in assessing the relative normative significance of the rules the attitudes of the lawyers themselves. There was a sharp conflict between the official position on these rules and the position of the bar. The official position called the conduct in these hypotheticals unethical, but the bar rejected the official position. The professionals themselves did not regard the conduct as unprofessional, and therefore would not discipline lawyers for engaging in this conduct.

Even if those who staffed the disciplinary machinery were disposed to uphold the official position, violations of these rules were not likely to be detected. The *Assault Charge* situation usually involved the low income criminal defendant who was paying his fee in installments. He would not be likely to know that his lawyer was withholding information or to complain about it (perhaps because the reason for withholding may have been true). The hypothetical did not involve overcharging or overreaching. The *Referral Fee* situation involved another lawyer; therefore there was ready access to the disciplinary machinery. But the other lawyer was not likely to complain, since he rejected the rule himself; if he accepted the rule, he would simply not offer the fee. The *Conflict of Interest* situation also involved another lawyer, but this rule did not suit the Prairie City bar. Attorney-client relationships were usually personal in this community, and this situation came up very often. The lawyers knew each other well, and the chances were that this situation would not have resulted in disciplinary action unless there had been abuses or sharp practices by one of the lawyers and his relation with other lawyers had become acrimonious as a consequence.[3]

Other items which had high rates of violations were *Client Kickback: legal advice* and *gift or dinner* and the *Receiver Sale*. The *Client Kickback* is an offense against colleagues; it is considered an improper method of obtaining business. But this unprofessional form of business-getting could result in serious competition only if the lawyer gave the previous client money. Consequently, over three-quarters of the bar did not think it really wrong to adjust legal fees, to give a gift, or to take the previous client out to dinner. And these violations could not have been detected easily. One takes place in the privacy of the office, and in this community, where clients were friends of lawyers, gifts or dinners might have been perfectly innocent. In the *Receiver Sale,* the sale of the corporation's property "was approved by the court and was at the best price obtainable," and the lawyer paid the same amount for his stock as the promoters did. Even though no one might have been hurt by this particular transaction, conflicts of interest of this type can harm creditors and other stockholders. Judges may not be able to supervise these sales very closely; the lawyer and promoters may be able to "chill" the sale. This rule, as distinguished from those previously discussed, was of intermediate significance. On the other hand, it came up very infrequently, and none of the lawyers for whom it occurred had violated the rule.

The only rules of high significance which 10 per cent or more of the bar had violated or would have violated were the *Police Payoff* and the *Oral Contract*. Eight lawyers reported that they would violate the rule under the circumstances of the *Police Payoff* hypothetical; their responses may well have been affected by fresh memories of a local incident involving a sexual deviance charge.[4] But no Prairie City lawyer had actually violated the rule. Although the *Oral Contract* was an offense against a colleague, it was not likely to come to the attention of the bar association. It has already been pointed out that lawyers would not expose themselves in this way and that, if they did, they would prefer to use informal sanctions.

These then were the items where there was at least some appreciable degree of violation. In none of them was disclosure to the bar association very likely. Failure to prosecute these cases, in other words, could have occurred because they were not brought to the attention of the authorities and not necessarily because the authorities excused or condoned the conduct.

But was the profession remiss in not disclosing or detecting these acts? As pointed out, the profession had practically the exclusive responsibility for maintaining proper professional conduct. How important were the rules that were violated? It can be argued that the rules violated were not serious, for the most part. They did not conflict with usual community standards, such as cheating, stealing, and bribery; and they did not threaten more distinctive professional interests, such as loyalty to clients, honesty and candor in dealings with colleagues, and prohibitions against predatory competitive practices. In several instances, the rules were not applicable to the practice of law in Prairie City.

Giving a referral fee is considered to be an offense against clients and colleagues. It is argued that the ultimate fee charged to clients is higher. If a lawyer can split a fee, he could charge less in the absence of the fee. Referral fees usually were made in contingent fee negligence cases; the rate of fees in these cases was generally standardized. The Prairie City bar association rules on fees were similar to many others throughout the country.[5] It is more realistic to assume that the fees charged to the client would be the same regardless of whether the lawyer split the fee with a colleague. It has been argued too that a lawyer ought to refer cases to the lawyer best qualified to handle them rather than to those who will kick back part of the fee, but so many Prairie City lawyers gave referral fees that the referring lawyer's choices were not limited. The lawyers themselves did not regard this practice as an offense. Besides, only a small proportion of lawyers' professional incomes in Prairie City were derived from referrals.

The *Conflict of Interest* situation is considered an offense against the client, in this case, against the partner who will not be represented by the partnership's lawyer. It was suggested that injuries to the former client would probably result only if the lawyers engaged in sharp tactics and the dispute became acrimonious. Several lawyers indicated that they would represent one of the partners only if the other lawyer did not object; they added, however, that such objections would be very unlikely. In all probability, the relations between lawyers would prevent serious harm to the former client. In addition, one wonders which position would have been more contrary to community expectations—the official position or the position of the Prairie City lawyer. Several respondents stated that it was absurd to expect them to give up a client of long standing because of the client's falling out with a business partner; the client, they said, would feel let down. If this feeling was widespread, it may explain the reason for the rejection and violation of this rule.

The *Assault Charge* is also an offense against a client, but the reason for the deception in this situation was to avoid being cheated by a client. The official position in the *Kickback* situations (adjusting *legal fees, gift or dinner*) we would regard as unrealistic in a community of a size where clients were often friends. The lawyers themselves did not regard this as unfair competition.

The official position on the *Receiver Sale,* on the other hand, is justified: double dealing is unethical, and court approval of the price does not justify the conduct. Creditors and stockholders should not have to rely on a court for protection. The court relies on the representations of the parties, and adversary rules are designed to prevent collusion. Fortunately, however, there was no evidence that violations occurred in this bar. Bribing officials (*Police Payoff*) is contrary to the usual community standards, and violations apparently did not occur. The other rule of high significance that did have some degree of violation was the *Oral Contract.* Violations of this rule were offenses against colleagues, but the lawyers themselves dealt with such violators through informal sanctions.

In summary, only two rules—the *Police Payoff* and the *Receiver Sale*—were at the same time important for the public and rejected by the lawyers; both were applicable to situations that rarely, if ever, came up. The other rules likely to be violated were difficult to detect and of questionable harm and importance. In short, most of what we have called "violations" were not violations of any but the *official* bar standards. Lawyers did not regard the acts as violations, nor would the community be likely to condemn infractions. Perhaps the bar merely showed good sense in not enforcing rules which were of so little consequence.

On the basis of the rules that we tested, one could not conclude that serious professional misconduct was widespread or that the profession failed adequately to control deviant behavior. We did not measure such offenses as conversion or misappropriation of a client's money or property; neglect, carelessness, collusion, and conspiracy against clients; fraud on the court; nonprofessional misconduct (*e.g.,* failure to pay personal obligations), and others—the charges most often brought before the bar association disciplinary machinery. What can we infer from our evidence that sheds light on this bar's general ethical approach? Is there any broader or deeper pattern to the responses we have tabulated and discussed? We have seen that there was a certain amount of fracture between the official position on certain ethical issues and the actual beliefs and practices of the Prairie City bar. Why should this be? And where did the standards of the Prairie City bar come from, if not from the official sources of morality?

Some "unethical" practices were very widespread—almost, one might say, customary in the Prairie City bar. Clearly, there was no pressure to conform or to condemn nonconformists in such cases. Thus, for Prairie City lawyers there were no risks of colleague disapproval or of professional discipline incurred in violating these rules. To make this point, of course, is not to explain how the disjuncture between official and working rules developed or even sustained itself; it is simply to describe its size. The basic question remains.

The lawyers of Prairie City seemed instinctively to condemn practices which, had they become general, would have transformed the Prairie City bar from what it was to something more like the big city, highly competitive, cutthroat bar. They identified their own interests with their style of practice. After all, they were comfortable and respected; class lines in the bar were not great, all things considered;

and the economic pressures on the lawyers were relatively mild. As a result, some of the responses on ethical questions seemed to parallel the lawyers' reasonable perception of the relationship between certain types of conduct and their style of practice. In other cases, they seemed to measure conduct by its probable effect on their business, either in the long or short run. Perhaps the most universally condemned practices were those which at the same time (a) would offend the general ethical standards of the community, (b) would be likely to come to light, (c) in that event would injure the lawyer's business, and (d) if generalized, would turn the Prairie City bar into something like the dirty, competitive, no-holds-barred practice in the lower reaches of the profession in New York or Chicago. Stealing money from clients, for example, would fail all four tests. Several rules which were rejected would not affect their business or their style of practice.

The nature of the lawyers' general ethical approach suggests that the offenses frequently brought before the bar association disciplinary machinery but not tested in this study probably did not occur very often among the bar. Most of these offenses were against clients; they included conversion, neglect, and nonprofessional misconduct. Loyalty to clients was important to the lawyers; furthermore, detection, with unfavorable publicity, was a real possibility. In addition, many of the offenses reported to the bar association stemmed from economic problems: a lawyer, pressed in his personal affairs, converted his client's funds or got into a dispute about fees. In this state the formal complaints against lawyers charging conversion, neglect, and nonprofessional misconduct increased significantly during the Depression. The general level of prosperity of Prairie City lawyers at the time of the study would indicate that in the aggregate, the economic basis for many of these violations was absent, even though individual lawyers might have been in financial difficulties from time to time.[6]

We have stressed the nature and control of deviant behavior, the negative aspects of professional responsibilities. There are many statements in the literature on the affirmative obligations of the bar. Justice Frankfurter, for example, has said:

Certainly since the time of Edward I, through all the vicissitudes of seven centuries of Anglo-American history, the legal profession has played a role all of its own. The bar has not enjoyed prerogatives; it has been entrusted with anxious responsibilities. One does not have to inhale the self-adulatory bombast of after-dinner speeches to affirm that all the interests of man that are comprised under the constitutional guarantees given to "life, liberty and property" are in the professional keeping of lawyers. It is a fair characterization of the lawyer's responsibility in our society that he stands "as a shield," to quote Devlin, J., in defense of right and to ward off wrong. From a profession charged with such responsibilities there must be exacted those qualities of truth-speaking, of a high sense of honor, of granite discretion, of the strictest observance of fiduciary responsibility, that have, throughout the centuries, been compendiously described as "moral character." [7]

The previous discussion about the nature of the commitment of the lawyers to professional ethics would cast doubt on how seriously lawyers assumed at least part of the affirmative obligations. Few lawyers expressed willingness to report a lawyer to the bar association for formal proceedings. When lawyers thought that sanctions were called for, they preferred the individual, private sanctions (*e.g.,* no longer referring business to the violator); this was true even for the items involving bribery and fraud. For only one item (the *Police Payoff*) would a substantial number of the bar report the offending lawyer to the bar association, and this number was still less than half (42 per cent). There were probably social constraints operating in favor of a personalized approach. Reporting a lawyer to the bar association is disruptive of the professional community, forcing lawyers to try fellow lawyers. Even in the professionally integrated community there are expectations about minding one's own business. In this community, an individual lawyer might jeopardize colleague relations if he attempted to uphold ethical rules which were not widely supported. The ethical violation would have to be extremely serious or notorious or threaten to disrupt the professional community for a lawyer to be reported. The *Police Payoff* situation was of this character, but the *Conflict of Interest* situation was tolerated so long as colleague relations were maintained. In addition to the *Police Payoff,* the only other item for which a substantial number of lawyers (18 per cent) would report an infraction to the bar association was *Client Kickback: money,* a situation which posed an economic threat to other lawyers. The lawyers' unwillingness to use disciplinary machinery of the bar association, their lack of concern for the infractions of others, and their apparent rejection of ethical rules which did not serve either their business interests or preserve their style of practice indicate that statements of the affirmative obligations of the profession, such as the one quoted above, probably have little basis in fact. And these attitudes parallel the data concerning professional responsibilities for public issues.

SUMMARY AND COMPARISON WITH
THE NEW YORK CITY BAR

We have argued that violations of ethical rules among Prairie City lawyers were probably not very serious: for the most part, only rules which the professionals themselves rejected were violated, and harm to the public from violations was doubtful. In New York City, on the other hand, *Bar* as well as *Elite* norms were violated—that is, rules which the bar as a whole accepted and which also coincided with usual community standards, involving cheating, bribery, and fraud, were broken. The New York study estimated that 22 per cent of the 20,500 active practitioners, or 4,500 lawyers, were violating these rules. The grievance committee of the local bar association investigated or held formal hearings for about eighty-five lawyers per year—less than 2 per cent of the lawyers estimated to be breaking rules that were generally accepted by the bar. Only about two per thousand violators were disbarred, suspended, or censured. The study concluded "that the formal machinery of the bar does not, and probably could not, do an effective job of policing the profession. Too few violators are formally charged and punished to suggest that this activity by itself does much to weed out or discipline unethical lawyers." [8]

The New York study also doubted the deterrent effect of the threat of sanctions. In that bar solicitation and fraud were the most widespread forms of violation, but according to the disciplinary records, these offenses were the least likely to result in disciplinary hearings, and lawyers who were processed for these infractions generally received the mildest sanctions. The largest proportion of disciplinary adjudications and those that received the severest sanctions involved conversion, but this was the most infrequent type of offense. The study argued that the sanctions were, in a sense, wasted. Solicitation and fraud had little ethical significance, and therefore might most effectively have been deterred by the threat of severe penalties. Because rules against conversion had the highest ethical significance for this bar, conformity was likely; a lawyer willing to misappropriate his client's money was unlikely to be deterred by fear of disbarment. In addition, over half of the disbarments in New York City were by consent, which meant that the record of the case was kept secret. This too would tend to minimize the deterrent effect of sanctions.

Carlin's study also found that the visibility of the offense was strongly related to disbarments; in fact, it even had a "somewhat greater impact" than the seriousness of the offense. Visibility was measured by the amount of money involved, the number of acts of misconduct per lawyer, and publicity or notoriety involved. If the bar attached high ethical significance to the rule and if the infraction had been highly visible, the lawyer was almost certain of being disbarred. If, on the other hand, the rule involved little ethical significance and if the violation had attracted little attention, it was most unlikely that the lawyer would be disbarred.[9]

The study interpreted formal disciplinary actions as a "forestalling of public criticism of the legal profession" rather than as policing or deterring violations. This explained why so few violators were caught, why so many who were caught were disbarred by consent, and why the visibility of the offense had such an impact on the level of sanctions: "It is not the punishment of all violations, or even of all serious violations, that is crucial for avoiding public criticism and control; only the *highly visible* violations are really important. If only some violations are highly visible, few violators need be caught and punished." [10]

In Prairie City, and in the state where Prairie City is located, too few lawyers were formally disciplined to enable conclusions to be drawn about the purposes or effectiveness of the formal disciplinary machinery. In that community, however, informal controls and the threats of sanctions, official or otherwise, might have operated quite effectively. A consent disbarment would probably be widely discussed by other lawyers and would probably be well known to much of the general community. Most cases brought before the state or local grievance machinery probably were at least mildly publicized. The small size of the bar and the extensive interaction among the lawyers would help make disciplinary affairs matters of local gossip.

CHAPTER 8

CONCLUDING REMARKS

This study has been concerned with the role of practicing lawyers in a middle-sized community. Since lawyers performed services for people and businesses in the community, the data and findings reflected the characteristics of the community. We may now ask what the study suggests, in its broader terms, about the relationship of the legal profession to its social setting.

GENERAL PRACTICE AND THE ORGANIZATION OF LAWYERS

Lawyers are conventionally classified by size of firms, and in studies of lawyers in the larger urban centers, size of firm was considered an indicator of differences between lawyers. In this study it was found that this classification was not an indicator of differences. Most Prairie City lawyers were members of firms, yet, in many important respects, the practice of these lawyers closely resembled that of individual practitioners.

In several firms the lawyers held themselves out as a partnership and considered themselves as such, yet the internal arrangements were in fact on an office-sharing basis: the lawyers shared the expenses of the firm but separately billed the clients and retained their own profits. In firms based on this arrangement, there was no specialization, and there was a high degree of client proprietorship. In other firms in Prairie City the internal arrangements were on a partnership basis: billings were paid to the firm, the firm paid the expenses, and the partners received a percentage of the net profits. Yet at the same time these firms displayed an almost complete lack of specialization and a significant degree of client proprietorship. Thus the lawyers of Prairie City, whatever

147

the legal arrangements of their firms, behaved like individual general practitioners.

Statistical studies of lawyers generally divide private practitioners into firm and non-firm lawyers or make a further breakdown by size of firm. These studies assume that differences in practice correspond to differences in the organization of the work setting. Frequently we hear that the number of individual practitioners is declining in proportion to the number of firm lawyers and that firms are increasing in size. This is supposed to indicate the bureaucratization of the legal profession. The firm is conceived of as a joint venture; its clients are firm clients; each member of the firm handles only that part of the client's problems for which he is specially trained. The lawyers are specialists working for each other (*i.e.,* the firm) as well as for the clients. An increase in efficiency results from this specialization; the lawyer's professional tasks will be narrower than those of the individual practitioner, who, on the other hand, has his "own" clients and handles all of his clients' problems.

These are, of course, models or ideal types. The data from this study, however, showed that these models were inaccurate for the Prairie City bar and probably for the bars of comparable and smaller communities. Some doubt is cast on the accuracy of the assumptions made about the bar in larger cities as well. For one thing, the classification of lawyers into firm and non-firm lawyers fails to distinguish the office-sharing arrangement from the partnership arrangement; and although the office-sharing arrangement involves differences in work life from individual practice, these differences do not materially affect the amount of specialization and of client proprietorship. The Prairie City data showed that the office sharer, though a "firm" lawyer, behaved like the individual practitioner. In Prairie City, one of the largest firms in town (six lawyers) was an office-sharing arrangement. It may be true that as firms get larger, the office-sharing arrangement tends to disappear, but in the New York study, 24 per cent of the lawyers were in firms of seven or fewer lawyers. How many of the lawyers in these firms in New York City, as well as in other cities, were office-sharers is not known. Nevertheless, the point remains that the classification of these lawyers as firm lawyers, as distinguished from individual practitioners, may be true only in a very limited sense, and it may actually be misleading.

In Prairie City firms organized on a partnership basis (*i.e.,* billings paid to and expenses paid by the partnership), there were sometimes divisions of labor in terms of "client contacts" as opposed to office work or trial work. One or two of the lawyers might concentrate on bringing in clients while the other lawyers did research, drafting, or litigation. This rough division of labor is not the "specialization" assumed for the model firm of lawyers. Unless the firms are specialized in terms of areas of practice—*e.g.,* personal injury, workmen's compensation, tax—both the "business getter" and the "office partner" will be dealing with a wide range of legal problems. Partners will be working for each other, and the division of labor will increase efficiency; nevertheless, each lawyer will work on almost as broad a range of legal problems as does the individual practitioner. There will be little specialization by area of practice.

In Prairie City no lawyer, regardless of the size of his firm, was a rigid specialist. In New York City, on the other hand, there were many specialists. Seventy per cent of the New York City lawyers were either individual practitioners or in firms of not more than seven lawyers; the same percentage of lawyers spent half or more of their time in one area of practice. The fact that individual practitioners and small firm lawyers were specialists suggests that specialization may operate independently of firm organization, that there would be specialization in the larger urban centers even if there were no firms. Specialization is, in fact, the product of structural differentiation and economic diversification in the community, which in turn produce large masses of legal problems by specific areas of practice. Lawyers in communities with these social and economic characteristics can support themselves by concentrating in single areas of practice, and they can do this either in individual practice, in office-sharing arrangements, or in partnerships. They do not have to form partnerships to specialize. If the legal profession is becoming more specialized, this fact is not necessarily to be measured by the decline in the individual practitioner; in the larger cities, the individual practitioner can also be a specialist.

Client proprietorship has not been examined empirically in the smaller firms of the larger cities. There is no reason to assume, however, that it is present to any less extent than was found in Prairie City. Specialization by areas of practice in the smaller firms does not necessarily mean that the lawyers in these firms do not have their own clients—the individual practitioners who are specialists prove this—and there is some affirmative evidence that client proprietorship is present among these smaller firms. Carlin, in his work on lawyers in Chicago and New York, found that the small firm is a very unstable organization. One of the principal reasons for the instability is the change in clients of one or more of the members of the smaller firm. This forces a renegotiation of the internal arrangements for the division of profits and not infrequently results in the dissolution of the firm. The former members seek other arrangements, carrying "their" clients with them.

In communities comparable to Prairie City or smaller, then, the rationale for classifying lawyers in terms of size of firm may be weak. Many firms were organized on an office-sharing arrangement; other firms, even though organized on a partnership basis, showed little or no specialization and a high degree of client proprietorship. In the larger cities, there was specialization by area of practice, but the existence of office-sharing arrangements and high degrees of client proprietorship suggest that in many respects the smaller firm lawyer resembles the model of the individual practitioner. Why then do lawyers form partnerships? No doubt a firm makes for economies and amenities in work. In addition to sharing the expenses of running an office, lawyers can more readily consult each other, cover the office when a member is away, answer court calls, and handle motions. But an office-sharing arrangement will accomplish these objectives and at the same time avoid some of the more troublesome problems of negotiating and renegotiating partnership shares. The firm, however, may symbolize to many a stable, going concern. It is an expression of professional status and advancement, the standard to which lawyers aspire. If this is true, then the individual practitioner may be temperamentally different from his firm-forming colleague. He may be a lawyer who somehow rejects or is unable to cope with one of the means of professional integration. In New York City, for example, individual practice is the terminal position for a large number of lawyers who had previously attempted one or more small partnerships or who had been members of middle-sized firms; considerably fewer individual practitioners had been in large firms. In Prairie City there were proportionately more firm lawyers than in New York City: perhaps the social penalties of rupture were also higher in a community like Prairie City.[1] In communities smaller than Prairie City, however, the proportion of individual practitioners is higher, comparable to the proportions found in the larger cities. Thus, individual practice seems to be the norm in the small town, but not in the middle-sized community. Since no work has been done on the career patterns of lawyers in smaller towns, we can only speculate on why the small town style of practice is not conducive to partnerships.[2]

SMALL TOWN PRACTICE AND THE PROFESSIONAL COMMUNITY

The accuracy with which the practice of law in Prairie City fits the image of practice in the smaller communities is impressive. The lawyers had a wide range of clients and handled a wide range of legal problems. They did office work as well as trial work. On the whole, the atmosphere of practice in Prairie City appeared vastly different from the atmosphere described by Carlin in his studies of individual practitioners in Chicago and of the smaller firms and individual practitioners in New York City. The aggressions, tensions, discontent, and economic insecurities of the big city were almost nonexistent in Prairie City; the Prairie City lawyers liked their community, their work, and their way of life.

In Prairie City, the lawyers formed an integrated professional community. Of course, the lawyers of this bar differed among themselves in incomes and probably in styles of life. But all lawyers (except one) belonged to the local bar association, and officerships were within the reach of all. The general practice meant that *as lawyers* persons who were probably socially distant interacted professionally.

The New York City and Chicago bars were fragmented. There were high walls between the groups of lawyers, lawyers of different groups rarely if ever working on the same matters. There were several local bar associations with distinct memberships that tended to reflect the status hierarchy, and the status differences in the New York and Chicago bars reflected the great diversification in those cities. Although the professional community of Prairie City cut across class lines, class lines in that community were rather indistinct. Further research is needed on cities larger than Prairie City and with more economic diversification before generalizations can be made about the ability of a local bar to maintain a professional community. We suspect that as the community becomes more differentiated, the local bar will begin to fragment; that is, size of the city alone would probably be enough to set such a process in motion. The professional integration of the Prairie City lawyers may simply reflect the lack of significantly distinct strata in the community at large.

In one important respect the lawyers in Prairie City did not fit the usual image of small town practice: the role of lawyers in social and political affairs was limited. Why these lawyers were, by and large, not leaders in their community is not clear, for there is little research on the role of lawyers in local politics. Perhaps part of the answer lies in the fact that Prairie City had for some time had successful city manager government. The lack of political activity on the part of the lawyer could have reflected a withdrawal of the middle and upper middle classes—from which both the lawyers and their principal clients came— under this form of government. But we have no information on the role of the lawyers before the change in government or of the role of lawyers in other communities.

This study draws its data from one year in the very recent past. Little work has been done on the practice of law in earlier times. We can make interesting comparisons, however, between the practice of law in Prairie City in 1963 and the practice of law in a nineteenth-century small town in Illinois; and perhaps we can further explain the inactivity of twentieth-century Prairie City lawyers as social and political leaders in their community. The practice in Clinton, Illinois, between 1851–61 and 1870–80 has been explored in a careful and voluminous doctoral thesis.[3]

Clinton was a small town. In 1849 there was only one resident lawyer; in the 1870's there were twenty-one lawyers, but only about twelve stayed throughout the period studied. Most of the legal business was handled by six lawyers. The lawyers were usually in partnerships and were general practitioners. Land transactions were staple items in their practice; they also dealt with railroad matters, collected debts, defended criminals for both petty and serious offenses, and handled divorces and bankruptcies. This was the style of practice of Abraham Lincoln— livestock, fences, and petty crime on the one hand; banks, railroads, and eastern business interests on the other. The subject of the thesis, Clifton H. Moore, became one of the wealthiest persons in Clinton. Although he was primarily a commercial and railroad lawyer, throughout his career, he collected small debts and was engaged in matrimonial and criminal practice. In this mixture of minor and major matters, the practice of law in Prairie City, 1963, resembles that of Clinton a century before. Prairie City is larger and more diversified and has a larger bar, but the elite lawyers still handle at the same time affairs of large enterprises with international markets, and personal injury cases, small claims, and family matters. The details of the areas of practice have changed, but the generality of the practice has remained.

On the other hand, the lawyers of Clinton were, in the main, important figures in political and social affairs. Moore, along with other lawyers, took prominent part in resolving local issues and in providing leadership in the town, concerning himself with schools, roads, bond issues, county political conventions, civic committees, and committees to promote railroads. Lawyers were active in organizing the community's Civil War efforts. Moreover, the lawyers' importance extended farther than their town. This may have been simply because Clinton was in the region of the state where Abraham Lincoln, David Davis, Leonard Swett, Stephen Douglas, and other important political figures practiced law. At any rate, many Clinton lawyers, including Moore, took active part in Lincoln's campaigns, and they were also active in the Liberal Republican movement in the 1870's. Throughout the period studied, the more successful lawyers in Clinton were prominent in the state legislature and in state constitutional and political party conventions. The lawyers were not always successful in their efforts to lead, particularly in the 1870's, but they played significant roles in almost all local and state political struggles.

In Clinton the lawyers were in a unique position. They, more than any other group, had the knowledge and skill necessary to use the legal tools of nineteenth-century economic and social development— the corporate charters, the banking acts, the land legislation, local government law. In addition, the knowledge of these lawyers extended beyond the horizons of their community. They were, for the most part, educated in other parts of the country. Moreover, they were better educated than the rest of the community, and several had wide reading habits. They represented the eastern financial and business interests that invested and traded in Clinton and its environs. In short, by community standards they were cosmopolitan. They were the chief local experts on economic and political questions.

By the 1960's industrialization had brought to Prairie City a sophisticated class of managers and technicians, and Prairie City industries traded in national and international markets. Most of the lawyers, born, raised, and educated on the local scene, were provincial in comparison with the newer business class. The lawyers, who had been professional generalists, had been largely replaced by other professional specialists —experts in city government and public administration, in land-use controls, banking, and business. Areas once considered under the province of the legal profession had been taken over by technicians of different training—real estate brokers, bank officers (for estate and trust matters), finance companies (for collections), accountants (taxation). The list could be extended. There were no accountants, insurance adjustors, or public administrators in Clinton in the nineteenth century. But in the 1960's, all were flourishing in Prairie City, and the Prairie City lawyer had been almost completely displaced from government and public administration.

This development is only natural. Lawyers serve people in a community; as the social, political, and economic life of the community changes, the structure and functions of the bar will change too. Prairie City lawyers were still general practitioners, but they already felt the impact of size and economic diversification as other professional specialists encroached on tasks that once belonged to the lawyers. Whether the displacement of Prairie City lawyers from certain jobs by nonlawyer specialists will continue as it has in the larger cities will probably depend on forces outside the control of the profession—the growth and economic development of the community. These same forces will probably alter the style of law practice. If Prairie City increases in size and economic diversification, we should expect that the general practitioner would give way increasingly to the specialist, that the distribution of clients would be more fixed, and that the community of lawyers would be more hierarchical.

ETHICS AND SOCIAL CONTROL

Ethics and social control were studied as part of the social structure and characteristics of the Prairie City bar. The bar was homogeneous in background, education, and practice. In the main, the lawyers came from middle and upper middle class families, and they had a fairly high quality of college and professional education. They were integrated professionally, and they were economically prosperous. Competition from other lawyers and the encroachment of lay persons and organizations was not serious. In a very real sense the lawyers were more secure in their roles than at least the lower strata of the bar in the larger metropolitan communities. The hierarchical nature of the metropolitan bar, the economic insecurities, the tensions between the actual practice and the lawyers' professional expectations, the extreme competition for business, the corruption of courts and public officials—all these were absent in Prairie City. Violations of professional ethics can more easily be explained or rationalized in New York or Chicago than in Prairie City.

In Prairie City, then, we found what might be considered optimum conditions for the achievement of one of the important goals of professional ethics, that of placing service and fiduciary obligations to clients, colleagues, and the administration of justice above economic self-interest. The general prosperity, shared experiences, and professional integration of this bar could serve as supports for this goal. In both attitudes and behavior, the lawyers agreed that the rules were in general worthwhile; they agreed too on the relative importance of the rules. Yet ethical rules were sometimes rejected or ignored. In Chapter 6 it was indicated that ethical behavior was related to wealth and stability of clients and to opportunities to violate ethical rules. The same factors that were related to the ethical behavior of Prairie City lawyers were also related to the ethical behavior of the New York City lawyers. In other words, when the lawyers in Prairie City were faced with pressures similar to those faced by the New York City lawyers, they tended to respond in the same way. This was true despite the fact that the Prairie City lawyers differed from the New York City lawyers in terms of social and economic backgrounds and education. The pressures, or conditions of practice, differed both qualitatively and quantitatively, and, we suggest, this accounted for most of the differences in ethical behavior between the two bars.

We interpret this to mean that the ethical commitment of Prairie City lawyers was conditioned by the characteristics of their practice. When or if the social and economic conditions of the community changed, when the bar became more specialized in terms of clients and areas of practice, it would become increasingly stratified, and professional community would disintegrate. The economic conditions of practice would change and so would the commitment of lawyers to their ethical rules. Proportions of poor and unstable clients and rates of opportunities to violate would rise for certain segments of the bar, and this increase would result in higher levels of violations. As the community increased in size and economic diversity, the bar, in its social characteristics, would look more like the New York City bar; so would its commitment to professional ethics.

Reference Matter

NOTES

Chapter 1

1 William J. Goode, "Community Within a Community: The Professions," *American Sociological Review,* XX (1957), 194–200.
2 J. Willard Hurst, *The Growth of American Law: The Law Makers* (Boston, 1950), p. 366.
3 See, for example, Herbert Jacob, *Justice in America: Courts, Lawyers, and the Judicial Process* (Boston, 1965), ch. 4; Jerome E. Carlin, *Lawyers' Ethics: A Survey of the New York City Bar* (New York, 1966); Jerome E. Carlin, *Lawyers on Their Own: A Study of Individual Practitioners in Chicago* (New Brunswick, N.J., 1962); Erwin O. Smigel, *The Wall Street Lawyer: Professional Organization Man?* (New York, 1964); Vern Countryman and Ted Finman, *The Lawyer in Modern Society* (Boston, 1966), ch. 1.
4 Hurst, *The Growth of American Law,* p. 366.
5 In addition to the work of Carlin and Smigel, cited above in n. 3, see Jack Ladinsky, "Careers of Lawyers, Law Practice, and Legal Institutions," *American Sociological Review,* XXVIII (1963), 47; Dan C. Lortie, "Laymen to Lawmen: Law School, Careers, and Professional Socialization," *Harvard Educational Review,* XXIX (1959), 352; unpubl. diss. (Northwestern, 1964) by Kenneth J. Reichstein, "The Professional Ethics of Lawyers." For studies of lawyers in smaller communities, see unpubl. diss. (Iowa, 1963) by Richard S. Wells, "The Legal Profession and Political Ideology—The Case of the Carr Law Firm of Manchester, Iowa"; unpubl. diss. (Illinois, 1960) by Maurice Graham Porter, "Portrait of a Prairie City Lawyer: Clifton H. Moore, 1851–1861 and 1870–1880." See also Walter I. Wardwell and Arthur Lewis Wood, "The Extra-Professional Role of the Lawyer," *American Journal of Sociology,* LXI (1956), 304–7; Arthur Lewis Wood, "Informal Relations in the Practice of Criminal Law," *American Journal of Sociology,* LXII (1956), 48–55.
6 For example, full-time employees of insurance companies are excluded but lawyers who represent insurance companies in personal injury litigation are not. Even though some lawyers may spend all of their time working for one company, the company comes to the lawyer as a client, not as an employer, and retains the lawyer as an independent professional, not as an employee.
7 Chapter 2 contains a breakdown of the job distribution of all of the lawyers.
8 See Appendix C for the interview schedule. The New York schedule is reproduced in Carlin, *Lawyers' Ethics,* Appendix D.
9 Unless otherwise indicated, the data in the remainder of this chapter

rest on an earlier study of Prairie City prepared by an institute of the University of Illinois and on an unpublished essay by Professor Daniel J. Elazar, Department of Political Science, University of Illinois.

10 U.S. Census, *City and County Data Book* (Washington, 1962).

11 Industrial Development Research Council, *Registered Community Audit* (Atlanta, Ga., 1963).

12 *Ibid.*

13 "Foreign stock" is the U.S. Census definition: "The foreign-born population is combined with the native population of foreign or mixed parentage in a single category term 'foreign stock.' This category comprises all first—and second—generation Americans. Third and subsequent generations in the United States are described as 'native of native parentage.' "

14 The foreign stock in Prairie City in 1960 was as follows: from Germany—3,330 (2 per cent of the population); from the United Kingdom—1,028 (1 per cent); from Ireland—343. The rest—3,056—were of scattered national origin (U.S. Census).

15 National Council of the Churches of Christ in the United States of America, Bureau of Research and Survey, *Churches and Church Membership in the United States: An Enumeration and Analysis by Counties, States, and Regions* (New York, 1957).

16 See n. 9, above.

17 Interview with the executive director, July 1964. Other interviews were held with the President of the Downtown Council, the City Planner, and the City Manager.

18 Interview with a high administrative official who is regarded as an accurate observer of the local political scene.

19 See Edward C. Banfield and James Q. Wilson, *City Politics,* Publications of the Joint Center for Urban Studies of the Massachusetts Institute of Technology and Harvard University (Cambridge, Mass., 1963), ch. 13.

20 Banfield and Wilson point out that in El Paso, Texas, the businessmen were powerful and that the most powerful of this group were referred to as the "Kingmakers." But none of the officers of the biggest businesses—Standard Oil, Texaco, American Smelting and Refining, and Phelps-Dodge—were considered to be within this politically powerful group (*ibid.,* p. 264). This hypothesis is supported in a study of downtown problems in three other middle-sized cities; see the unpubl. MS. (Illinois, 1963) by Everett G. Smith, Jr., "Downtown Change in Three Middle-Sized Cities."

21 In order to determine whether or not Prairie City was representative, we compared it with four other midwestern cities with populations ranging from 108,000 to about 132,000. These cities were located in states which had major metropolitan centers, but the cities were outside the large urbanized areas. Thus, like Prairie City, each city was an independent community. All of the cities had very high per-

centages of nativity; the foreign stock ranged from between 3 and 13 per cent, although the origins of the foreign stock differed. All of the cities except one were overwhelmingly Protestant, and the one exception was 60 per cent Protestant. The educational levels (median number of school years completed and proportions of the population completing high school and college) were approximately the same for all the cities. The median incomes, by families, ranged from $4,801 to $6,421 (Prairie City—$5,943). The proportion of families earning $15,000 or more per year varied between 3 and 4 per cent; the proportion earning less than $3,000, between 14 and 26 per cent (Prairie City—14 per cent). The total number of employed persons was between 38,467 and 47,344 (Prairie City—44,125). The proportion of the working population in wholesale and retail ranged between 18 and 24 per cent; in manufacturing (durable and nondurable) between 21 and 40 per cent (Prairie City—29 per cent); white collar, between 36 and 43 per cent. The highest proportion of manufacturing employees per industry ranged from 24 per cent to 48 per cent (Prairie City—31 per cent). In Prairie City and two of the cities, this industry was food and kindred products; in the other two cities, it was transportation and equipment. Finally, the competitive two-party politics of Prairie City was not unusual, for in three of the other four cities, the election results were fairly close. The principal finding was that, in most respects, Prairie City was either comparable to the other cities, or, where differences existed, Prairie City fell within the range of deviation.

CHAPTER 2

1   Carlin, in his New York City study, classifies firms as follows: large—fifteen or more lawyers; medium—five to fourteen; small—two to four (Jerome E. Carlin, *Lawyers' Ethics: A Survey of the New York City Bar* [New York, 1966]). The smallest of Smigel's large firms had fifty lawyers (Erwin O. Smigel, *The Wall Street Lawyer: Professional Organization Man?* [New York, 1964], pp. 34–35).

2   These totals include the eight lawyers who refused interviews. Three of these lawyers were in small firms (five or fewer lawyers), and five were individual practitioners. Unless otherwise indicated, all other percentages in this study will not include these eight lawyers.

3   See Table B.1, Appendix B. (Hereafter, all references to the tables in Appendix B will be included in the text.) The source of the figures for the United States and for the cities of 50,000 to 200,000 and of the figures in Table B.1 is American Bar Foundation, *The 1964 Lawyer Statistical Report* (Chicago, 1965), pp. 32–35. This report is based on the data for 1963 collected in Martindale-Hubbell, *Law Directory* (New Jersey, 1963). The percentages in Table B.1 exclude retired or inactive lawyers; the Prairie City figures include only the lawyers interviewed. See n. 2, above.

Although it is not entirely clear why Prairie City should have differed so markedly from the proportions found in the *Report,* two reasons may account in part for the discrepancy. In checking the Martindale-Hubbell listings for Prairie City, I found that several lawyers who are considered inactive in this study (less than 25 per cent of their income derived from the practice of law) were not listed as inactive in the *Law Directory.* There were other lawyers listed in the *Directory* who could not be located. If these lawyers were included, then the proportion of individual practitioners in Prairie City would rise to 24 per cent of all lawyers and the proportion of firm lawyers would drop to 54 per cent. Secondly, there were probably great variations within the classes of cities in the *Report.* Upon examining the Martindale-Hubbell figures for the four cities compared to Prairie City in Chapter 1, I found that for all four cities the proportion of individual practitioners was far below the national average and below the average in cities between 50,000 and 200,000, the proportions of individual practitioners in these four cities ranging between 29 and 35 per cent. There was also a great deal of disparity between the four cities. For example, the proportions of firm lawyers ranged between 35 and 60 per cent. Yet these cities were comparable to Prairie City in many respects, and the distribution of Prairie City lawyers as between firm and individual practice was also comparable.

4   Local taxation and assessments were important in Prairie City. In 1960, for example, the total general revenue for Prairie City was $2,953,000 with total tax receipts of $1,963,000. Of this amount, $1,444,000 was raised by the property tax alone (U.S. Census, *City Government Finances* [1960]).

5   In an interview in July 1964, the city manager corroborated the data. It was also his impression that lawyers see him on financial matters in which the city might be of some help and whenever the city is planning the revision of any of the ordinances which might affect clients (*e.g.,* the health codes). Furthermore, lawyers try to have him intercede with the mayor or the local prosecutor whenever there are raids and arrests for gambling, prostitution, or alcoholic beverage violations involving clients.

6   This information is contained in the studies cited in n. 9, ch. 1.

7   Heinz Eulau and John D. Sprague, *Lawyers in Politics: A Study in Professional Convergence* (Indianapolis, 1964), pp. 11, 13 (italics omitted). See also the studies summarized in nn. 3, 5, ch. 1.

8   The findings on the political role of Prairie City lawyers were consistent with the results of a study of the officials of two Louisiana parishes bordering New Orleans. One had a population of 208,000; the other 32,000 (1950 figures). Only two out of fifty-nine officials were lawyers; the majority of the officials were independent farmers, merchants and salesmen, and clerical employees. Moreover, the two lawyers were the district attorneys. That is, no lawyers held official

positions which were not reserved for lawyers (Herbert Jacob, "Why Men Seek Political Office," unpublished paper delivered at the 1961 Annual Meeting of the American Political Science Association, p. 8).

It should also be noted that the Prairie City official referred to in n. 18, ch. 1, stated that he could think of only one lawyer in the community (the lawyer on the city council) who was informed and interested in local civic affairs. As far as this official was concerned, none of the other lawyers exercised much, if any, influence in local affairs. However, after the study was completed, one lawyer was on the *ad hoc* citizens' committee in support of the referendum on the retention of the city manager form of government, and another lawyer led the opposition.

9   See *The 1964 Lawyer Statistical Report,* p. 30.

10   It took an average of 11.7 years to become a partner in the elite Wall Street law firms. Many associates, however, left these firms at a much earlier date for other legal (or nonlegal) jobs (Smigel, *The Wall Street Lawyer,* p. 92).

11   In 1964, the state bar association published an economic survey of the legal profession. The median income of non-salaried lawyers practicing in the major city was $18,000 and $17,200 for the rest of the non-salaried lawyers. "Non-salaried" excluded associates. The figures for the survey were based on a mailed questionnaire. There was a 43 per cent return, and 96 per cent of the returned questionnaires were usable.

12   This figure excludes the nine lawyers who gave no information on incomes.

13   This does not include lawyers who had incomes from securities.

14   The comparison to the New York City bar is based on data collected by Carlin, most of which is presented in *Lawyers' Ethics.* From time to time, however, I will rely on data that was not reported in the published volume. Carlin's "New York City bar" did not constitute a cross-section; it was a sample (801 interviews) of the lawyers in the "central business core of the city" (Manhattan and Bronx). Excluded were "most of the neighborhood and sub-center (mainly Brooklyn) lawyers and all of those in the peripheral areas of the city" as well as salaried lawyers in government and private enterprises and associations (*ibid.,* p. 9).

15   *Ibid.,* pp. 18–19.

16   A full-time university law school is one which does not offer part-time (evening) in addition to full-time (day) programs.

17   The point made here is that the differences between an Ivy League college and law school, on the one hand, and two years of night college and a night law school, on the other, were probably greater than the differences between the various full-time colleges and law schools in the Midwest.

18   Carlin, *Lawyers' Ethics,* p. 13.

Chapter 3

1   The construction of the income-client measure is described in Appendix A.
2   The median amount of time spent did not include the lawyers who spent no time at all in the particular areas of practice.
3   One financially successful lawyer, who was first generation and had a minority group background, complained of this kind of discrimination.
4   One of the differences concerned the question of whether or not the bar association should regulate contingent fees. Three-quarters of the high lawyers, who were the most successful personal injury lawyers, thought not, as compared to 37 per cent of the middle group, who practiced more in trusts and estates. There were, however, no differences in the proportions of the elite and low groups for or against the regulation of contingent fees.
5   This includes one elite lawyer who said that he more often than not voted Republican even though he was a registered Democrat.
6   In recent years, some of the principal businessmen had made progress in the employment of Negroes, for in some of the largest industries the work force was integrated, and Negroes were in supervisory positions. On the other hand, at least until a few years before the study was made, very little progress had been made in improving the environment in which Negroes lived. This might explain why the elite lawyers were more liberal with regard to civil rights legislation on employment than in regard to housing.
7   The figures for Prairie City are from the 1960 U.S. Census.
8   This failure to respond was due primarily to the fact that five of the elite lawyers were in the same firm.
9   See Jerome E. Carlin, *Lawyers' Ethics: A Survey of the New York City Bar* (New York, 1966), ch. 2.
10 *Ibid.*, p. 32.
11 The religious composition of law firms could have been due to tacit discrimination by the firms, or by self-selection by the applicants, or by both. See Erwin O. Smigel, *The Wall Street Lawyer: Professional Organization Man?* (New York, 1964), p. 175; Jack Ladinsky, "Careers of Lawyers, Law Practice, and Legal Institutions," *American Sociological Review,* XXVIII (1963), 47, 53.
12 Carlin, *Lawyers' Ethics,* p. 33.

Chapter 4

1   Talcott Parsons, "A Sociologist Looks at the Legal Profession," in *Essays in Sociological Theory,* rev. ed. (Glencoe, 1964), p. 385.
2   Cf. Parsons, *ibid.* See also Vern Countryman and Ted Finman, *The Lawyer in Modern Society* (Boston, 1966), chs. 6, 7.
3   Roscoe Pound, *The Lawyer From Antiquity to Modern Times* (St. Paul, 1953), p. 5.

4   Henry S. Drinker, *Legal Ethics* (New York, 1953), p. 5.

5   See Ralph S. Brown and John D. Fassett, "Loyalty Tests for Admission to the Bar," *University of Chicago Law Review,* XX (1953), 480.

6   Drinker, *Legal Ethics,* p. 7.

7   Jerome E. Carlin, *Lawyers on Their Own: A Study of Individual Practitioners in Chicago* (New Brunswick, N.J., 1962); Jerome E. Carlin, *Lawyers' Ethics: A Survey of the New York City Bar* (New York, 1966).

8   For a description of state disciplinary procedures, see Orie L. Phillips and Philbrick McCoy, *Conduct of Judges and Lawyers: A Study of Professional Ethics, Discipline, and Disbarment* (Los Angeles, 1952), ch. VI.

9   The court insisted that this power to discipline is inherent in it and exists apart from any legislative determination of grounds for disbarment. Thus, the court claimed the right to impose standards more stringent than those imposed by the legislature.

10 The information on the procedures of the committee was based on an interview with a present member of the committee who had once been its chairman.

11 The general counsel's statements were corroborated by a sampling of the letter file over several years.

12 Two other lawyers were also serving prison terms, but they had filed petitions with the hearing division to have their names stricken. They are included in "by consent" category.

13 Not included among the lawyers who could have appealed to the supreme court were those who consented to having their names stricken from the roll (the case is terminated at this point), the lawyer who was serving a prison sentence (presumably his case was hopeless), and, of course, the lawyers who were acquitted by the hearing division.

14 The data did not indicate the prior records, if any, of lawyers who had charges screened out either by the general counsel or by the inquiry committee or who were in difficulty with the local bar associations.

15 This figure excludes felony cases. The presence of these factors did not necessarily result in a greater chance of a recommendation of sanction. In all hearing division cases, whether these factors were present or not, the lawyer stood a two to one chance of receiving a sanction recommendation. The data concerning the amount of money involved (*e.g.,* allegedly converted) were not very clear, but substantial sums were involved in most of the conversion and fee cases that received sanction recommendations.

CHAPTER 5

1   This question was not asked for hypothetical 10: "Lawyer A sends out Christmas cards to all his active clients." Respondents were asked whether or not they did this.

2   For three items the lawyers were presented with several alternatives

and asked, "Which of the following alternatives comes closest to what you have done (or would do) in this situation?"

3 In addition, the lawyers were asked to evaluate the practice of sending out Christmas cards (item 10). See n. 1, above.

4 Henry S. Drinker's *Legal Ethics* (New York, 1953) is largely a summary of the opinions of ethics committees throughout the country.

5 Except where indicated, the hypotheticals in this study were identical with those used in the New York study. See Jerome E. Carlin, *Lawyers' Ethics: A Survey of the New York City Bar* (New York, 1960), pp. 248–54.

6 The number before the hypothetical corresponds to the number in the interview schedule (see Appendix C). The title of the hypothetical is given to provide a shorthand reference for the remainder of the text. Hypotheticals 5 and 9 used the same questions as those given in the text for hypothetical 1; hypotheticals 2, 4, 6–8, and 11–13 used the questions given in the text for hypothetical 3.

7 In the New York study Lawyer A obtained a title insurance policy and was offered the "usual 15% commission." Since title insurance was not widely used in Prairie City, we changed the hypothetical. It was assumed that the loan problem was more common, but it too turned out to be rare; see p. 114 and Table 5.8.

8 The New York lawyers were not asked question "e."

9 In the New York study the "promoters" were a syndicate.

10 The grounds for divorce were changed from adultery in this hypothetical.

11 This hypothetical could be classified as an offense against a client, particularly if Lawyer Jones charges the client for the referral fee that has to be paid to Lawyer A and if referrals are made other than on the basis of merit. We have classified it as an offense against a colleague because there is evidence that the fees would not be reduced if the referral were not given (see text at pp. 140–41) and that as between two lawyers, one has to pay the other in order to get referral business instead of relying on merit.

12 See *Opinions of the Committee on Professional Ethics of the Association of the Bar of the City of New York* (hereinafter cited as N.Y. City) 5, 155, 203, 637, 777, 809, and the *Opinions of the Committee on Professional Ethics of the New York County Lawyers' Association* (hereinafter cited as N.Y. County) 124, 138, 194.

13 N.Y. City, 608.

14 N.Y. City, 807. See Drinker, *Legal Ethics,* p. 104.

15 Canon 25: " . . . it is dishonorable to avoid performance of an agreement fairly made because it is not reduced to writing, as required by rules of Court." See Drinker, *Legal Ethics,* p. 194.

16 Canon 34.

17 Canon 28: "It is disreputable . . . to pay or reward, directly or indirectly, those who bring or influence the bringing of . . . cases. . . ."

18 Canon 27. See Drinker, *Legal Ethics*, p. 247.
19 On the other hand, only one lawyer said that he specifically referred such a client to another lawyer. But this could mean that a system of distributing the business in a bar of this size worked without specific referrals.
20 The differences in the disapproval rates when the elite and high groups are compared to the middle and low are:

> 1% Commission: "Take into consideration" — 16%
> Client Kickback: legal advice   — 23%
> Client Kickback: gift, dinner   — 10%

21 We used the same hypothetical situations that were used in the New York study. One of the criteria for selection in that study was that the hypotheticals "should involve unethical practices to which lawyers are likely to admit—common or borderline practices rather than flagrantly criminal or vicious ones." A large number of hypotheticals were pretested on fifty-one lawyers previously rated "ethical" or "unethical" by colleagues who knew them well. The final thirteen items were selected where there was a "reasonable correspondence" between the ratings of the fifty-one lawyers and their self-reported behavior. Thus, items were eliminated if "unethical" lawyers failed to report taking unethical action more than "ethical" lawyers. An item failed to "discriminate" between ethical and unethical lawyers if the ethical rule involved lacked significance or if the unethical lawyers failed to tell the truth. Carlin, *Lawyers' Ethics,* pp. 42–48.
22 Compare Tables B.16 and B.19, Appendix B.
23 The New York study did not have sanction data to develop a rule structure.
24 Carlin, *Lawyers' Ethics,* pp. 49–52.
25 In Prairie City at this time the court would find that "extreme cruelty" existed if there was one relatively minor act of violence (*e.g.,* a slap in the face) seen by two persons. It would seem that the parties would be more willing to fabricate this somewhat ritualistic ground than an act of adultery.

Chapter 6

1 See Jerome E. Carlin, *Lawyers on Their Own: A Study of Individual Practitioners in Chicago* (New Brunswick, N.J., 1962); Jerome E. Carlin, *Lawyers' Ethics: A Survey of the New York City Bar* (New York, 1966).
2 It will be recalled that stability of clients was measured by the proportion of time spent in wills, business, personal injury defendant, and real estate, as compared to the proportion of time spent in personal injury plaintiff, matrimonial, and criminal. See Chapter 3, pp. 55–56.
3 See Table B.27. Wealth and stability of clients were both important factors affecting ethical behavior, although our numbers were too small

to determine which factor was more important. There was a slight suggestion that stability might have been fairly important for lawyers with wealthy individual clients; that is, violation rates appeared to rise with opportunities for lawyers with unstable but wealthy individual clients, but not if clients were stable. Stability seemed less important when individual clients were poor. With business clients, the evidence slightly suggests the opposite. Violation rates appeared to rise with opportunities for lawyers with unstable and poor business clients, but not if clients were stable. Stability seemed less important when business clients were wealthy.

4   This question is, of course, not a direct measure of client pressure, and we had no way of testing the reliability of the answers. It was, however, the same question asked of the New York lawyers. The author of the New York study concluded that the lawyers' "reports may be used as a meaningful indication of client pressure" because (1) when items which most clearly involved client pressure occurred in the lawyer's practice, he was more likely to perceive pressure, and (2) the higher the ethical significance of the item, the more likely the occurrence of the item will lead to client pressure. For the full discussion, see Carlin, *Lawyers' Ethics,* p. 73, p. 82, n. 6.

5   Retainer clients are to be distinguished from retainer fees. Quite often a lawyer will receive an advance payment, called a "retainer," for work to be done. This arrangement is not necessarily dependent on a stable, long-term attorney-client relationship. It can be done on a single case; a criminal case is fairly typical. The question that was asked, however, was: "Do you have any annual retainer clients? If yes, what proportion of your income during the past year was accounted for by all fees from such clients?" The answers, then, were given in response to the meaning described in the text.

    Arrangements with retainer clients can be quite varied. Usually the client pays the lawyer a fixed sum over a period of time in return for a variety of legal services, the sum being paid on a yearly, quarterly, or even monthly basis. The understanding can be for all legal services performed within the time period or can encompass only certain categories of legal services, such as more routine matters, with additional billings for unusual services.

6   An additional 2 per cent said that they had retainer clients but did not say what proportion of their income came from that source.

7   There were twenty lawyers who reported 10 per cent or more of their income from retainer clients. Sixty per cent of these lawyers were conformers.

8   See Table B.32. The lawyers who spent the most time in court had more wealthy business clients than some of the other groups, but the difference was not great. In addition, these lawyers had a significant proportion of poor business clients, and, as noted earlier, unstable

clients were related to high violation rates when business clients were poor (see n. 3, above).

9   The ethical concern measure was constructed as follows: in the selection of both office sharers and partners as to "loyalty to clients" and "honesty in dealing with officials," respondents were given two points for a ranking of first, second, or third; one point for no rank at all, and zero if respondents marked "not concerned about it at all." The possible scoring range was from zero to eight. For the distribution of scores for the lawyers, see Table 6.8.

10   See Table B.37. There was no relationship between years in practice and wealth of business clients.

11   Carlin, *Lawyers' Ethics*, pp. 87, 91.

12   *Ibid.*, p. 167.

13   *Ibid.*, ch. 6.

14   *Ibid.*, pp. 168–69.

15   *Ibid.*, p. 134.

16   *Ibid.*, p. 170.

17   *Ibid.*, p. 148.

18   *Ibid.*, p. 136.

19   See Cohen v. Hurley, 366 U.S. 117 (1961) for a description of the ambulance-chasing investigation in the New York City bar.

CHAPTER 7

1   Tables B.42 through B.50, Appendix B, show the distribution of occurrences, violations, and rejections of each of the seventeen ethical rules by the following characteristics of lawyers: attitudes, behavior, concern, years in practice, status (income-client measure), professional incomes, opportunities, wealth of individual clients, wealth of business clients, and stability of clients.

2   See ch. 2, pp. 24–28.

3   At the time of the study a conflict of interest case was being processed by the local bar association grievance committee. The lawyer had sought to gain personally by his conduct (self-dealing in trust property), and there were acrimonious relations between the lawyers involved. This was the only time that the members and former members of the grievance committee who were interviewed could remember a grievance proceeding in a conflict of interest situation.

4   See ch. 5, pp. 107–8.

5   See Frederick Benjamin MacKinnon, *Contingent Fees for Legal Services: A Study of Professional Economics and Responsibilities* (Chicago, 1964), pp. 116–17.

6   We have no data on another aspect of professional responsibility—the quality of legal services. Other studies infer low levels of quality of professional work from the training of lawyers. See Jerome E. Carlin, *Lawyers' Ethics: A Survey of the New York City Bar* (New York,

1966), p. 177; Jerome E. Carlin and Jan Howard, "Legal Representation and Class Justice," *UCLA Law Review,* XII (1965), 381, 384–85; Jack Ladinsky, "The Impact of Social Backgrounds of Lawyers on Law Practice and the Law," *Journal of Legal Education,* XVI (1963), 127, 139. The lawyers of this bar had a higher quality of training than the lower echelon lawyers in the above studies. But we do not know how much low quality work (if any) is due to laziness, other distractions, or too much business.

7   Schware v. Board of Bar Examiners of New Mexico, 353 U.S. 232, 247 (1957), concurring opinion.

8   Carlin, *Lawyers' Ethics,* pp. 160–61.

9   *Ibid.,* pp. 155–61.

10   *Ibid.,* p. 170 (author's italics).

CHAPTER 8

1   In ch. 2, n. 3, it was noted that in four midwestern cities comparable to Prairie City in size and economic diversification, there were comparable proportions of individual to firm practitioners.

2   The study of large firms may also have suffered from inadequate attention to the complexity of business arrangements among lawyers. On the basis of scanty, impressionistic, and even contradictory evidence, some have detected a process of "bureaucratization" of large firms. Many lawyers in large firms specialized by areas of practice, and many lawyers who joined these firms were trained as specialists. On the other hand, there were large firms in which the juniors rotated in specialties and the senior men broadened their areas of practice. In many firms there also appeared to be strong elements of client proprietorship, for large firms have been known to split, with members taking "their" clients with them. In many other firms some lawyers had their "own" clients while some partners had none; these clientless partners worked for other partners. Some firms might be more accurately described as associations of sub-firms. The sub-firms differed in terms of specialization and client proprietorship; within one firm the lawyers in the trusts and estates department might function differently and have different relationships with clients than the lawyers in the corporate department. In short, large firms have varied greatly in their structure. Whether large firms are becoming more "bureaucratized" requires much more careful clarification of concepts and reseach than has been the case heretofore.

3   Unpubl. diss. (Illinois, 1960) by Maurice Graham Porter, "Portrait of a Prairie City Lawyer: Clifton H. Moore, 1851–1861 and 1870–1880."

APPENDIX A

THE INCOME-CLIENT MEASURE

The income-client measure was constructed from three sets of data: (1) professional incomes of the lawyers, (2) wealth of business clients, and (3) wealth of individual clients. Of course, all three sets were related; the rich lawyers tended also to have the rich clients. The three sets were combined into one measure to lessen the impact of fluctuations. For example, in this bar as is true in other bars, income fluctuated for many lawyers; the response for a particular period of time—in this case, 1963—might have resulted in misplacing a lawyer in relation to his colleagues.

The lawyers were divided into three income categories: (1) $20,000 or more per year, (2) $19,999–$11,000, and (3) less than $11,000. These categories are as close to one-third divisions of the cases as possible and, except where specific income categories are used (e.g., $50,000 or more per year), will be referred to as "high," "middle," and "low." We divided the rank order of lawyers by thirds (and for later chapters by halves) rather than in terms of *a priori* decisions as to what should constitute, for example, a lawyer with a low income (e.g., with earnings less than $6,000 per year). Our concern was with the allocation of characteristics of practice (clients, specialties, attitudes, ethical behavior, etc.) among these lawyers. It may be that the Prairie City bar as compared to other bars had a disproportionate number of poor lawyers or wealthy lawyers, but we were concerned with comparing the members of this bar with each other.

Respondents were asked to estimate the proportions of business clients by gross incomes. To measure the wealth of business clients, we used the proportion of business clients with gross incomes of $100,000 or more per year, and again divided the bar into as nearly equal groups as possible. The "high" group (31 per cent) reported that 60 per cent or more of their business clients had gross incomes of $100,000 or more per year; the "middle" (35 per cent), between 5 per cent and 59 per cent; and the "low" (34 per cent), less than 5 per cent.

We encountered problems in using this type of data to indicate wealth of business clients. Respondents had trouble answering this question, and some lacked confidence in making the estimates. Also,

171

APPENDIX A

there was some confusion between gross incomes and net incomes (either before or after taxes). More seriously, gross incomes do not necessarily indicate either the wealth of the business client or the amount of legal work required by the client. Both would depend on the nature of the business. One might assume that businesses with very low gross incomes have neither significant profits nor the ability to afford many legal fees, but this is not certain. And the converse, that businesses with larger gross incomes have higher profits and greater need for legal services, may be even more doubtful. The obvious point is that measures of wealth of businesses are quite complicated. Despite these limitations, however, it was found that the higher the measure of wealth of business clients, the more time the lawyers spent in the business, corporate, and commercial area of practice, the higher proportion of professional income they derived from business matters as distinguished from personal matters, and the more they tended to have clients in manufacturing, banking, and insurance, as distinguished from real estate, retail stores and restaurants, farming, and professional services; these relationships are shown in Tables A.1, A.2, A.3, and A.4. In this bar, however, it must be remembered that differences in areas of practice were not exaggerated. Since we were not interested in comparing individuals and since we were using two other measures of stratification, an error in placing a given individual is probably not too significant.

Wealth of individual clients was measured by the same technique. Respondents were asked to estimate the proportions of individual clients who earned (1) less than $5,000 per year, (2) $5,000–$10,000, (3) $10,000–$20,000, and (4) $20,000 or more. The lawyers were then divided into thirds according to the proportion of individual clients who earned more than $10,000 per year. The high group (32 per cent) estimated 70 per cent or more of their individual clients earned this much or more; the middle group (32 per cent), between 40 and 69 per cent; and the low group (36 per cent), less than 40 per cent.

Almost two-thirds of the lawyers in the low income category also had the poorest individual and business clients, as compared to only 15 per cent of the high income lawyers (Tables A.5 and A.6).

The measures of wealth of business and individual clients were then combined with the measure of professional income. A lawyer was given three points if he ranked high in terms of wealthy business clients, two points for middle, and one for low; he received the same scores for his individual clients. Thus, a lawyer who scored high for both types of clients received six points, but only two points if he ranked low for both types of clients. Twenty-two per cent of the bar scored high on the combined measure (five or six points); 19 per cent were middle (four points); and 27 per cent were low (two or three points). All of the low lawyers had either all low income clients or a combination of middle and low; all of the high lawyers had either

172

THE INCOME-CLIENT MEASURE

TABLE A.1 — Relationship Between Wealth of Business Clients Measure and Amount of Time Spent in Business, Corporate, and Commercial Area of Practice

Proportion of time spent in business area	Total number of lawyers	% of lawyers by wealth of business clients measure		
		High	Middle	Low
More than 20%	(29)	57	38	13
10–20%	(23)	29	38	17
Less than 10%	(31)	14	25	70
Cases		(21)	(24)	(23)

TABLE A.2 — Relationship Between Wealth of Business Clients Measure and Proportion of Income Derived From Business Matters

Proportion of income from business matters	% of lawyers by wealth of business clients measure		
	High	Middle	Low
60% or more	67	42	17
30–59%	24	46	26
Less than 30%	10	13	57
Cases	(21)	(24)	(23)

TABLE A.3 — Relationship Between Time Spent in Business, Corporate, and Commercial Area of Practice and Proportion of Income Derived From Business Matters

Proportion of income from business matters	% of lawyers by amount of time spent in business area		
	20%+	10–20%	10%–
60% or more	62	26	29
30–59%	24	39	23
Less than 30%	14	35	48
Cases	(29)	(23)	(31)

173

APPENDIX A

TABLE A.4—Relationship Between Types of Businesses for Which
Lawyers Work and Wealth of Business Clients Measure

Types of businesses	% of lawyers by wealth of business clients measure*		
	High	Middle	Low
Manufacturing	21	15	10
Transportation, communications, utilities	4	4	2
Banks, trust companies, mortgage houses	11	9	6
Loan companies, collection agencies	9	6	2
Insurance	18	2	4
Real estate	9	18	14
Wholesale trade	4	6	2
Retail trade and stores	16	20	26
Restaurants	0	6	12
Farmers	2	4	14
Professional services	2	9	8
Other small businesses	5	4	2

*Percentages do not equal 100 because lawyers listed more than one kind of main business.

TABLE A.5—Relationship Between Wealth of Business Clients and
Professional Incomes of Lawyers

Wealth of business clients	% of lawyers having professional incomes that are		
	High	Middle	Low*
High	46	25	9
Middle	39	36	27
Low	15	39	64
Cases	(26)	(28)	(11)

*As explained earlier in this appendix, the three income categories for lawyers were established as follows: (1) High—$20,000 or more per year; (2) Middle—$11,000–$19,999; (3) Low—less than $11,000.

TABLE A.6—Relationship Between Wealth of Individual Clients and
(a) Professional Incomes of Lawyers

Wealth of individual clients	% of lawyers having professional incomes that are		
	High	Middle	Low
High	50	20	23
Middle	35	37	15
Low	15	43	62
Cases	(26)	(30)	(13)

(cont.)

TABLE A.6 —(continued)

(b)

Income of individual clients	% of lawyers having professional incomes that are		
	High	Middle	Low
Proportion of clients earning $20,000 or more			
40–79%	27	10	15
80–100%	12	0	0
Proportion of clients earning $5,000 or less			
20–39%	12	33	31
40–79%	4	7	23
	(26)	(30)	(13)

TABLE A.7—Relationship Between Wealth of Clients and Professional Incomes[*]

Combined wealth of clients	% of lawyers having professional incomes that are		
	High	Middle	Low
High	48	21	9
Middle	40	29	9
Low	12	50	82
Cases	(25)	(28)	(11)

[*]Percentages do not include lawyers who had no information for any *one* of the three items.

TABLE A.8—The Ranking of Lawyers Answering Two of Three Items

No. of lawyers	Answers to measurement items			Income–client measure ranking
	Wealth business clients	Wealth Individual clients	Lawyer's income	
2	High	High	. . .	High
1	. . .	High	High	High
2	. . .	High	Middle	Middle
1	Low	High	. . .	Middle
2	. . .	Low	Low	Low
1	Low	Low	. . .	Low
—				
9				

all high income clients or a combination of high and middle; and the middle lawyers had either all middle income clients or a combination of high and low.

The same scoring was used for the income-client measure: three points for high on the combined wealth of client measure and three points for high on the income measure. This meant, of course, that the income data received twice the weight of either of the other sets of data. In our judgment, however, the income data were by and large more reliable than estimates as to wealth of clients.

The relationship between the combined wealth of clients and professional incomes is shown in Table A.7.

Excluded from the income-client measure were the five associates; they were all young lawyers in a unique status and are discussed separately. Fourteen lawyers failed to give information for one or more of the items in the measure, but there was sufficient information for eleven of these lawyers to enable us to make reasonably accurate judgments as to their rank. Nine of the eleven gave information on two out of the three items, and judgments were made on this basis (Table A.8). For example, one high income lawyer had high individual clients, but would not estimate the wealth of his business clients. Nevertheless, he did say that he had as business clients some of the largest enterprises in the community (gross incomes of $5,000,000 or more per year). He was therefore placed high on the income-client measure.

One of the other lawyers gave no information as to the three items except that he also represented some of the largest enterprises in town. He was also placed high. The eleventh lawyer presented, perhaps, the most doubtful case. He was placed high because he was one of the senior partners in a firm of five; all of his partners placed high, and he and his firm were spoken of in terms that indicated wealthy clients and high professional incomes. He was frequently referred to in prestigious terms and would appear to have been in at least the upper third of the bar on the income-client measure.

Finally, the high group on the income-client measure was separated into a subgroup called "elite." These were the lawyers, who in addition to having high incomes and wealthy clients, also represented the largest enterprises in the community (businesses with gross incomes of $5,000,000 or more per year), excluding banks and insurance companies. (See the text, Chapter 3.)

APPENDIX B
SUPPLEMENTARY TABLES

TABLE B.1—Job Distribution of Lawyers in the United States, in Cities by Size, and in Prairie City

Locality	% in private practice				% salaried	
	Ind. prac-titioners	Partners	Asso-ciates	Total	Private*	Govern-ment[†]
United States	44	27	7	78	11	15
Cities (in thousands)						
500 or more	41	23	9	73	14	14
500–200	39	30	8	79	15	10
200–50	44	29	6	79	11	14
Less than 50	49	29	3	81	7	19
Prairie City	19	54	4	77	14	9

*"Private" includes private industry, educational institutions, and other private employment.
[†]"Government" combines judicial, executive, and legislative.
Source: American Bar Foundation, *The 1964 Lawyer Statistical Report* (1965), pp. 32-35. The *Report* is based on the data collected in Martindale-Hubbell, *Law Directory* for 1963. Since Martindale-Hubbell multiple lists lawyers (e.g., a part-time government lawyer may be included in "government" and in "private practice"), the percentages often exceed 100. The percentages in Table B.1 exclude retired or inactive lawyers. The Prairie City figures include only the sample.

177

APPENDIX B

TABLE B.2—Per Cent of Prairie City Lawyers Spending Professional Time with Administrative Agencies

Agency	Ave. times per year			per month		
	Never	Less than 6	7–11	1–3	3+	Total
Local						
Planning, zoning	30%	20	5	39	6	100
Housing, building	37%	24	8	24	6	100
Taxation, assessments	17%	22	12	41	9	100
Health, education, and welfare	80%	7	2	10	1	100
State						
Sales tax	78%	17	1	4	0	100
Corporation tax	69%	16	4	12	0	100
Secretary of State	31%	18	7	37	6	100
Occupational licenses	81%	11	2	6	0	100
Financial reg.	75%	12	2	6	4	100
Regulatory agencies, communications	64%	24	1	10	1	100
Health, education, and welfare	77%	12	4	5	2	100
Federal						
Internal Revenue Service	22%	19	12	37	9	100
Regulatory agencies	88%	7	1	4	0	100
Lending agencies	73%	17	0	10	0	100

TABLE B.3—Year of Admission to Practice by Age, Prairie City

Age of lawyer	% of lawyers admitted from							No. of lawyers
	1900–1909	1910–1919	1920–1929	1930–1939	1940–1949	1950–1959	1960–time of study	
60+	9	45	36	9	0	0	0	(15)
50–59	0	0	17	83	0	0	0	(12)
40–49	0	0	0	15	85	0	0	(29)
30–39	0	0	0	0	0	91	9	(24)
–30	0	0	0	0	0	0	100	(3)
All P.C. lawyers	1	6	10	17	28	33	6	(83)

SUPPLEMENTARY TABLES

TABLE B.4 — Median Amount of Time Spent in Areas of Practice by Income-Client Measure

Areas of practice	% of professional time			
	Elite	High	Middle	Low
Business, corporate, commercial	44	10	10	10
Wills, probate, estates, trusts	23	15	19	24
Real estate	8	12	14	14
Collections	4	4	4	7
Personal injury: plaintiff	10	15	13	7
Personal injury: defendant	21	23	7	4
Matrimonial: divorce	4	4	4	4
Criminal	0	4	4	4

TABLE B.5 — Main Area of Practice* by Income-Client Measure

Areas of Practice	% of lawyers			
	Elite	High	Middle	Low
Business, corporate, commercial	69	15	16	13
Wills, probate, estates, trusts	31	20	16	52
Real estate	8	15	21	4
Collections	0	5	11	4
Personal injury: plaintiff	0	10	5	22
Personal injury: defendant	15	30	0	9
Matrimonial: divorce	0	10	11	9
Criminal	0	5	5	4
	(13)	(20)	(19)	(23)

*The area of practice in which the most time was spent.

APPENDIX B

TABLE B.6 — Source of Largest Portion of Income by
Income-Client Measure

Area of practice	% of lawyers			
	Elite	High	Middle	Low
Business, corporate, commercial	54	0	0	9
Wills, probate, estates, trusts	23	20	63	52
Real estate	8	15	5	0
Personal injury	15	50	16	26
Criminal	0	5	0	4
	(13)	(20)	(19)	(23)

TABLE B.7 — Relation Between Wealth of Individual Clients and
Income-Client Measure of Lawyers Deriving the
Largest Portion of Income from Trusts and Estates

Income-client measure	No. of lawyers	Median wealth of individual clients	% of individual clients earning	
			$10,000 or more per yr.	$20,000 or more per yr.
Elite–High	(6)	$14,500	71	35
Middle	(12)	$10,200	44	16
Low	(12)	$ 8,700	34	10

SUPPLEMENTARY TABLES

TABLE B.8—Contacts with Agencies and Officials by the
        Income-Client Measure

Av. no. of contacts per mo. with agency or official	% of lawyers			
	Elite	High	Middle	Low
Local				
Planning, zoning				
0	39	35	21	22
-1	46	20	16	17
1+	15	45	63	61
Housing, building				
0	46	40	26	35
-1	46	15	32	35
1+	8	45	42	30
Taxation, assessments				
0	31	10	11	17
-1	39	20	37	35
1+	31	70	53	48
Mayor				
0	62	58	50	68
Some	39	42	50	32
City manager				
0	39	20	44	41
-1	54	60	22	32
1+	8	20	33	27
Council members				
0	69	63	37	57
Some	31	37	63	43
State				
Secretary of State				
0	23	25	37	26
-1	31	30	16	30
1+	46	45	47	44
State legislators				
0	77	68	72	77
Some	23	32	22	23
Federal				
Internal Revenue Service				
0	31	25	21	13
-1	31	45	32	17
1+	39	30	47	65
Regulatory				
0	69	95	90	87
Some	31	5	11	13

APPENDIX B

TABLE B.9 — Background Characteristics of Prairie City Lawyers

Characteristics	% of lawyers			
	Elite	High	Middle	Low
No. of generations since immigration to U.S.				
Parents and all grandparents born in U.S.	62	50	74	57
All parents and grandparents born abroad	15	10	0	4
Second generation (at least one grandparent				
born abroad)	15	30	26	30
Descent				
British, Northern, or Western Europe	77	55	90	70
Irish	15	25	5	17
Central, Southern, or Eastern European	0	15	5	9
Religious affiliation				
Protestant	92*	70	68	68*
Catholic	0	15	26	23
Jewish	0	15	5	9
Place of birth				
Born in Prairie City	46	40	53	30
Born in Prairie State (but not in Prairie City)	39	40	21	39
Legal affiliations within family				
Son of a lawyer	23	15	21	17
Lawyer in immediate family	23	25	21	39
Father				
A professional	31	25	32	35
A businessman	39	35	42	35
A semiprofessional or higher white				
collar worker	31	20	21	13
A lower white collar worker or manual laborer	0	15	5	13
Attended college	62	45	37	39
An income of $12,000 or more at time				
respondent entered law school†	9	20	32	16
Of less than $7,000	46	60	42	53
Law School				
State law school of Prairie State	39	40	47	44
Private in-state	31	15	11	13
Notre Dame, other Big Ten	8	15	16	9
Ivy League	15	10	5	0
Law School Performance				
Upper third	77	47‡	63	61
Middle third	23	47	32	17
Lower third	0	5	5	17
	(13)	(20)	(19)	(23)

All percentages exclude lawyers who did not answer.
*One elite gave "other" for religion; 1 low did not answer.
†Two elites, 5 high, and 4 low did not answer.
‡ One high did not answer.

182

SUPPLEMENTARY TABLES

TABLE B.10—Wealth of Business Clients by Size of Firms

Gross annual income of business clients	% of lawyers by size of firm		
	Large firm	Small firm	Individual practitioners
$5,000,000 or more	40	21	11
$1,000,000 or more	20	14	21
Proportion of business clients with gross incomes of less than $50,000 per year			
80% or more	0	34	47
60% or more	15	52	58
	(20)	(44)	(19)

TABLE B.11—Wealth of Individual Clients by Size of Firms

Proportion of individual clients by annual income	% of lawyers by size of firm		
	Large firm	Small firm	Individual practitioners
60% or more of clients earning			
—more than $10,000	75	47	26
—more than $20,000	44	21	5
30% or more of clients earning			
less than $5,000	13	36	42
	(20)	(44)	(19)

TABLE B.12—Relationship Between Stability of Clients Measure and Total Number of Clients

"During the past twelve months approximately how many clients have you done some work for—more than just going through a file or turning over a file to another lawyer?"

Stability of clients measure	% of lawyers having			
	up to 99 clients	100—149 clients	150—249 clients	250 or more clients
Stable	56	40	20	15
Mixed	22	45	45	20
Unstable	22	15	35	65
Cases	(18)	(20)	(20)	(20)

Because of the bunching at the cutting points, we used the fourfold table. The results would be the same on a threefold table:

(cont.)

183

TABLE B.12—(continued)

Stability of clients measure	% of lawyers having		
	up to 149 clients	150–249 clients	250 or more clients
Stable	47	20	15
Mixed	34	45	20
Unstable	18	35	65
Cases	(38)	(20)	(20)

TABLE B.13—Relationship Between Stability of Clients Measure and Proportion of Business Clients Represented for More than Five Years

Stability of clients measure	% of lawyers having		
	88–100% bus. cl.	48–87% bus. cl.	0–47% bus. cl.
Stable	59	32	10
Mixed	29	32	43
Unstable	12	36	48
Cases	(17)	(31)	(21)

Here, we have the same problem of bunching at the cutting points. Even if we move the cutting points, however, we still find the same relationships:

Stability of clients measure	% of lawyers having		
	73–100% bus. cl.	48–72% bus. cl.	0–47% bus. cl.
Stable	49	27	10
Mixed	27	40	43
Unstable	24	33	48
Cases	(33)	(15)	(21)

TABLE B.14—Relationship Between Stability of Clients Measure and Time Spent in Court

Hrs. per wk. in court	% of lawyers having		
	Stable clients	Mixed clients	Unstable clients
Less than 2	37	13	4
2–4	41	33	23
5 or more	22	53	73
	100%	100%	100%
	(27)	(30)	(26)

TABLE B.15—Disciplinary Cases Referred to the Inquiry Committee and to the Hearing Division of the State Bar Association

Year	Inquiry committee	Hearing division	Total no. of cases
1949	66	5	71
1950	69	2	71
1951	65	2	67
1952	60	3	63
1953	73	3	76
1954	84	5	89
1955	59	8	67
1956	56	3	59
1957	75	2	77
1958	78	7	85
1959	84	6	90
1960	89	2	91
1961	93	5	98
1962	86	11	97
1963	70	6	76
Total	1,107	70	1,177
Av. per yr.	74	5	79

TABLE B.16—Occurrence of Ethical Items by the Income-Client Measure

Items	% of lawyers				% variation
	Elite	High	Middle	Low	
1. 1% Commission	23	5	0	9	23
2. Oral Contract	23	25	37	30	14
3. Receiver Sale	8	5	11	4	7
4. Stock Purchase	23	5	5	4	19
5. Client Payoff	8	5	0	13	13
6. Package Deal	8	30	21	9	22
7. Assault Charge	8	20	37	22	29
8. Police Payoff	0	0	16	0	16
9. Client Kickback	8	25	42	35	34
11. Conflict of Interest	62	65	68	48	20
12. Divorce Fraud	31	80	74	52	49
13. Referral Fee	31	60	53	39	29
	(13)	(20)	(19)	(23)	

TABLE B.17—Occurrence of Ethical Items by Elite-High and Middle-Low

Items	% of lawyers		% variation
	Elite-High	Middle-Low	
1. 1% Commission	12	5	7
2. Oral Contract	24	33	9
3. Receiver Sale	6	7	1
4. Stock Purchase	12	5	7
5. Client Payoff	6	7	1
6. Package Deal	21	14	7
7. Assault Charge	15	29	14
8. Police Payoff	0	7	7
9. Client Kickback	18	39	21
11. Conflict of Interest	64	57	7
12. Divorce Fraud	61	62	1
13. Referral Fee	49	45	4
	(33)	(42)	

TABLE B.18—Opportunities of Ethical Items by Firm Size

Items	% of lawyers			% variation
	Large firm lawyer	Small firm lawyer	Individual practitioner	
1. 1% Commission	15	5	5	10
2. Oral Contract	10	38	16	28
3. Receiver Sale	10	7	0	10
4. Stock Purchase	20	7	0	20
5. Client Payoff	5	5	11	6
6. Package Deal	10	16	21	11
7. Assault Charge	20	23	16	7
8. Police Payoff	0	5	0	5
9. Client Kickback	20	32	26	12
11. Conflict of Interest	50	64	37	13
12. Divorce Fraud	60	61	53	8
13. Referral Fee	45	50	26	24
	(20)	(44)	(19)	

TABLE B.19—Ethical Violation Per Item by Income-Client Measure

Item	% of lawyers violating rule			
	Elite	High	Middle	Low
1% Commission: Accept without informing	0	0	0	4
1% Commission: Take into consideration	8	5	11	0
Oral Contract	0	5	21	13
Receiver Sale	15	15	5	13
Stock Purchase	0	0	0	4
Client Payoff: "Don't tell me"	0	5	5	9
Client Payoff: "Risky, but your business"	0	0	0	4
Package Deal	8	5	0	4
Assault Charge	46	15	37	26
Police Payoff	8	15	11	4
Client Kickback: money	0	0	5	0
Client Kickback: gift, dinner	31	5	16	22
Client Kickback: legal advice	8	15	21	17
Conflict of Interest	23	30	58	39
Divorce Fraud	0	5	16	9
Referral Fee	39	30	63	70
	(13)	(20)	(19)	(23)

TABLE B.20—Relationship Between Wealth of Individual Clients and Low Ethical Behavior

Ethical behavior	% of lawyers with	
	Wealthy clients	Poor clients
Low	40% (35)	56% (39)

TABLE B.21—Relationship Between Opportunities to Violate and Wealth of Individual Clients

Opportunity rates	% of lawyers with	
	Wealthy clients	Poor clients
0-2	49	46
3+	51	54
Cases	(35)	(39)

APPENDIX B

TABLE B.22—Relationship Between Opportunities to Violate
and Wealth of Business Clients

Opportunity rates	% of lawyers with	
	Wealthy clients	Poor clients
0–2	45	46
3+	55	54
Cases	(31)	(37)

TABLE B.23—Relationship Between Wealth of Business Clients
and Low Ethical Behavior

Ethical Behavior	% of lawyers with	
	Wealthy clients	Poor clients
Low	48% (31)	43% (37)

TABLE B.24—Relationship Between Stability of Clients
and Opportunities to Violate

Opportunity rates	% of lawyers with	
	Stable clients	Unstable clients
0–2	58	43
3+	42	58
Cases	(43)	(40)

SUPPLEMENTARY TABLES

TABLE B.25—Relationship Between Stability of Clients
and Low Ethical Behavior

Ethical Behavior	% of lawyers with	
	Stable clients	Unstable clients
Low	40% (43)	55% (40)

TABLE B.26—Relationship Between Stability of Clients and
Low Ethical Behavior, Controlling Opportunities
to Violate

Ethical behavior	% of lawyers by client stability, controlling for opportunities			
	Stable		Unstable	
	0−2	3+	0−2	3+
Low	32% (25)	50% (18)	41% (17)	65% (23)

TABLE B.27—The Relationship Between Stability of Clients Measure,
Opportunities to Violate, and Low Ethical Behavior

Stability of clients measure	Opportunities	% violators
Stable	. . .	40 (43)
Unstable	. . .	55 (40)
Stable	0−2	32 (25)
Unstable	3+	65 (23)

TABLE B.28—The Relationship Between Ethical Behavior
and Client Pressure

Ethical behavior	Lawyers reporting client pressure	
	Some	None
Low	51% (69)	29% (14)

APPENDIX B

TABLE B.29—The Relationships Between Client Characteristics and
Proportions of Income Derived from
Annual Retainer Clients

Client characteristics	% of lawyers deriving from retainer clients a proportion of income equal to				Cases
	0%	1–9%	10%+		
Individual clients					
Rich	31	29	40	100%	(35)
Poor	51	36	13	100%	(39)
Business clients					
Rich	23	36	42	100%	(31)
Poor	54	32	14	100%	(37)
Stability					
Stable	40	23	38	100%	(40)
Unstable	47	40	13	100%	(38)
Combined					
Ind. rich, stable	33	17	50	100%	(24)
poor, unstable	60	32	8	100%	(25)
Bus. rich, stable	29	24	48	100%	(21)
poor, unstable	54	38	8	100%	(24)

TABLE B.30—The Relationship Between Control Involvement and
Client Characteristics

Client characteristics	% of lawyers who were officers or members of board of directors of				Cases
	No client corp.	1–2	3+		
Rich, business	29	26	45	100%	(31)
Poor, business	60	14	27	100%	(37)
Rich, stable	24	24	52	100%	(21)
Poor, unstable	58	13	29	100%	(24)

190

SUPPLEMENTARY TABLES

TABLE B.31—The Relationship Between Control Involvement and
Client Characteristics, Controlling for Opportunities

Opportunity rates by client characteristics	% of lawyers who were officers or members of board of directors of				Cases
	No client corp.	1—2	3+		
Opportunities					
0—2	48	29	23	100%	(31)
3+	43	11	46	100%	(37)
Rich (business)					
0—2	21	36	43	100%	(14)
3+	35	18	47	100%	(17)
Poor (business)					
0—2	71	24	6	100%	(17)
3+	50	5	45	100%	(20)

TABLE B.32—The Relationship Between Average Number of Hours
per Week Spent in Court and Client Characteristics

Client characteristics	% of lawyers spending			
	-2 hrs.	2—4 hrs.	5—7 hrs.	8+ hrs.
Poor individual clients	15 (13)	61 (23)	48 (21)	77 (17)
Poor business clients	42 (12)	64 (22)	63 (19)	40 (15)
Unstable clients	27 (15)	44 (27)	48 (23)	78 (18)

TABLE B.33—The Relationship Between Behavior and Court Contacts, Controlling for Client Characteristics

Court contacts per week by client characteristics	% of lawyers with low ethical behavior	No. of lawyers
Wealth of individual clients		
Rich		
1–4 hrs.	35	(20)
5–8 hrs.	47	(15)
Poor		
1–4 hrs.	56	(16)
5–8 hrs.	57	(23)
Wealth of business clients		
Rich		
1–4 hrs.	47	(15)
5–8 hrs.	50	(19)
Poor		
1–4 hrs.	42	(16)
5–8 hrs.	44	(18)
Stability of clients		
Rich		
1–4 hrs.	32	(27)
5–8 hrs.	50	(16)
Poor		
1–4 hrs.	60	(15)
5–8 hrs.	52	(25)

TABLE B.34—The Relationship Between Contacts with Individual Courts, Behavior, and Client Characteristics

"On the average, how many times per month have you been in these courts during the past twelve months? "

Lawyer and client characteristics by courts	% of lawyers by frequency of court visits		
Justice of the Peace	0 times/mo.	1–3 times/mo.	4+ times/mo.
Low ethical behavior (lawyers')	46% (22)	43% (40)	57% (21)
Poor individual clients	25 (20)	53 (34)	80 (20)
Poor business clients	50 (16)	44 (32)	75 (20)
Unstable clients	14 (22)	55 (40)	71 (21)
County Court	0–3 times/mo.	4–6 times/mo.	7+ times/mo.
Low ethical behavior (lawyers')	39% (46)	53% (19)	56% (18)
Poor individual clients	36 (39)	72 (18)	71 (17)
Poor business clients	49 (35)	56 (18)	67 (15)
Unstable clients	35 (46)	42 (19)	83 (18)
Probate Court	0–3 times/mo.	4–6 times /mo.	7+ times/mo.
Low ethical behavior (lawyers')	55% (33)	55% (31)	21% (19)
Poor individual clients	43 (30)	65 (26)	50 (18)
Poor business clients	46 (26)	53 (25)	71 (17)
Unstable clients	52 (33)	52 (31)	37 (19)
Circuit Court	0–3 times/mo.	4–9 times/mo.	10+ times/mo.
Low ethical behavior (lawyers')	50% (36)	39% (23)	50% (24)
Poor individual clients	46 (33)	56 (18)	61 (23)
Poor business clients	60 (30)	56 (18)	45 (20)
Unstable clients	39 (36)	48 (23)	63 (24)
Federal District Court	0 times/mo.	–1 times/mo.	1+ times/mo.
Low ethical behavior (lawyers')	43% (40)	46% (22)	57% (21)
Poor individual clients	50 (34)	52 (21)	58 (19)
Poor business clients	50 (30)	48 (21)	71 (17)
Unstable clients	40 (40)	55 (22)	57 (21)

TABLE B.35—The Relationship Between the Ethical Concern Index
and Other Professional Attitudes

Professional attitudes	% of lawyers with	
	High concern	Low concern
Mentions honesty and integrity as quality most admired in other lawyers	59	43
Favors more strict enforcement of Canons of Ethics	71	35
Has strict attitude towards violations of professional norms	56	38
Cases	(52)	(31)

TABLE B.36—The Relationship Between Concern with Ethics
and Age and Years in Practice

Age and years in practice	% of lawyers with			No. of Cases
	High concern	Low concern		
Age				
40+	70	30	100%	(56)
40–	48	52	100%	(27)
Admitted to practice				
Before 1950	71	29	100%	(51)
1950 or later	50	50	100%	(32)

TABLE B.37—The Relationship Between Practice Characteristics
and Years in Practice

Practice characteristics	% of lawyers entering practice			
	Before 1950		1950 or later	
Income from practice of law				
$15,000+	77		38	
to $14,999	23		62	
	(44)		(29)	
Opportunities to violate				
0–2	59		38	
3+	41		63	
	(51)		(32)	
Types of clients				
Poor individual clients	43	(17)	70	(27)
Poor business clients	60	(42)	46	(26)
Unstable clients	39	(51)	63	(32)

TABLE B.38—The Relationship Between Low Concern with Ethics and
Practice Characteristics, Controlling for Years in Practice

Practice characteristics	Lawyers with low concern entering practice	
	Before 1950	1950 or later
Income		
+$15,000	32% (34)	64% (11)
−$15,000	40% (10)	44% (18)
Opportunities to violate		
0−2	30% (30)	50% (12)
3+	29% (21)	45% (20)
Wealth indiv. clients		
Rich	30% (27)	63% (8)
Poor	35% (20)	53% (19)
Wealth business clients		
Rich	53% (17)	57% (14)
Poor	20% (25)	50% (12)
Stability of clients		
Stable	36% (31)	25% (12)
Unstable	25% (20)	65% (20)

TABLE B.39—Characteristics that Lawyers Would Most Want to Know
About Another Lawyer Before Deciding to Share Office
Space with Him or Before Going into Partnership with
Him, by Years in Practice[*]

Characteristics	% of lawyers entering practice	
	Before 1950	1950 or later
Office-Sharer		
Type of practice	6	19
Personality	61	53
Loyalty to clients	41	19
Competence	78	75
Fairness in dealing with colleagues	49	63
Honesty in dealing with officials	51	47
Business-getting ability	8	16
Partner		
Type of practice	2	19
Personality	47	41
Loyalty to clients	39	31
Competence	88	91
Fairness in dealing with colleagues	51	31
Honesty in dealing with officials	45	31
Business-getting ability	24	47
Cases	(51)	(32)

[*]Respondents were asked to select three characteristics.

APPENDIX B

TABLE B.40—The Relationship Between Years in Practice
and Low Ethical Behavior

Ethical Behavior	% of lawyers admitted to practice	
	Before 1950	1950 or later
Low	39% (51)	59% (32)

TABLE B.41—The Relationship Between Behavior and Practice Characteristics,
Controlling for Years in Practice

Lawyers with	% violators	Admitted to practice before/after 1950	% violators	Effect of years in practice
Low opportunities	36% (42)	(Before)	40% (30)	+4
High opportunities	59 (41)	(After)	75 (20)	+16
Rich individual clients	40 (35)	(Before)	33 (27)	−7
Poor individual clients	56 (39)	(After)	68 (19)	+12
Rich business clients	48 (31)	(Before)	41 (17)	−7
Poor business clients	43 (37)	(After)	75 (12)	+32
Stable clients	40 (43)	(Before)	39 (31)	−1
Unstable clients	55 (40)	(After)	75 (20)	+20

SUPPLEMENTARY TABLES

TABLE B.42—Per Cent of Lawyers* for Whom Ethical Situation Occurs by Attitudes, Behavior, and Concern

Ethical situation[†]	Attitudes		Ethical behavior		Ethical concern	
	Strict	Permissive	High	Low	High	Low
High						
1(4). 1% Commission: Accept without informing	10%	5%	11%	3%	6%	10%
6. Package Deal	15	16	9	23	12	23
9(1). Client Kickback: Money	30	26	21	36	29	26
8. Police Payoff	(2)	(1)	(1)	(2)	(2)	(1)
2. Oral Contract	18	38	18	32	20	39
12. Divorce Fraud	63	54	55	62	64	48
4. Stock Purchase	10	9	9	10	14	3
Middle						
5(4). Client Payoff: "Don't tell me"	10	2	5	8	4	10
5(1). Client Payoff: "Risky but your business"	10	2	5	8	4	10
3. Receiver Sale	5	9	7	8	10	3
1(1). 1% Commission: Take into consideration	10	5	11	3	6	10
Low						
7. Assault Charge	10	30	5	39	10	39
9(3). Client Kickback: Legal advice	30	26	21	36	29	26
11. Conflict of Interest	53	56	48	62	54	55
9(2). Client Kickback: Gift, dinner	30	26	21	36	29	26
13. Referral Fee	48	40	36	51	39	52
10. Christmas Cards	...	...	...	...	...	...
Cases	(40)	(43)	(44)	(39)	(52)	(31)

*In this table and in Tables B.43−50, where numbers were too small to translate into valid percentages, the actual number, rather than the percentage, of lawyers is given in parentheses.

†The ethical situations are grouped according to degree of lawyer approval.

APPENDIX B

TABLE B.43 — Per Cent of Lawyers for Whom Ethical Situation Occurs by Years in Practice, Status, and Incomes

Ethical situation	Admitted to practice		Professional status		Income from practice	
	-1950	1950+	El.-High	Mid.-Low	-$15,000	$15,000+
High						
1(4). 1% Commission: Accept without informing	10%	3%	12%	5%	4%	11%
6. Package Deal	18	16	21	14	11	20
9(1). Client Kickback: Money	26	31	18	38	36	27
8. Police Payoff	(2)	(1)	0	8	(2)	0
2. Oral Contract	22	34	24	33	21	33
12. Divorce Fraud	57	63	61	62	54	64
4. Stock Purchase	6	16	12	5	14	7
Middle						
5(4). Client Payoff: "Don't tell me"	6	6	6	7	11	4
5(1). Client Payoff: "Risky, but your business"	6	6	6	7	11	4
3. Receiver Sale	4	13	6	7	11	7
1(1). 1% Commission: Take into consideration	10	3	12	5	4	11
Low						
7. Assault Charge	6	44	15	29	25	22
9(3). Client Kickback: Legal advice	26	31	18	38	36	27
11. Conflict of Interest	49	63	64	57	57	60
9(2). Client Kickback: Gift, dinner	26	31	18	38	36	27
13. Referral Fee	45	41	49	45	32	51
10. Christmas Cards	...	...	...	...	...	...
Cases	(51)	(32)	(33)	(42)	(28)	(45)

SUPPLEMENTARY TABLES

TABLE B.44—Per Cent of Lawyers for Whom Ethical Situation Occurs by Situational Pressure

Ethical situation	Opportunities		Wealth of ind. cl.		Wealth of bus. cl.		Stability of clients	
	High	Low	Rich	Poor	Rich	Poor	Stable	Unstable
High								
1(4). 1% Commission: Accept without informing	7%	7%	9%	8%	13%	5%	9%	5%
6. Package Deal	29	2	11	23	26	14	9	23
9(1). Client Kickback: Money	46	10	23	36	19	41	14	43
8. Police Payoff	(3)	0	(2)	(1)	(1)	(2)	(1)	(2)
2. Oral Contract	42	12	29	31	29	32	14	40
12. Divorce Fraud	85	31	54	64	52	68	56	60
4. Stock Purchase	20	0	9	5	16	3	14	5
Middle								
5(4). Client Payoff: "Don't tell me"	10	2	6	9	7	8	2	9
5(1). Client Payoff: "Risky, but your business"	10	2	6	9	7	8	2	9
3. Receiver Sale	12	2	6	5	10	5	7	8
1(1). 1% Commission: Take into consideration	7	7	9	8	13	5	9	5
Low								
7. Assault Charge	39	2	14	31	26	22	9	33
9(3). Client Kickback: Legal advice	46	10	23	36	19	41	14	43
11. Conflict of Interest	88	21	57	59	61	57	56	49
9(2). Client Kickback: Gift, dinner	46	10	23	36	19	41	14	43
13. Referral Fee	68	19	46	46	48	43	37	50
10. Christmas Cards	...	...	...	...	...	...	...	...
Cases	(41)	(42)	(35)	(39)	(31)	(37)	(43)	(40)

199

TABLE B.45—Per Cent of Lawyers Who Violate Ethical Situations by Attitudes, Behavior, and Concern

Ethical situation	Attitudes		Ethical behavior		Ethical concern	
	Strict	Permissive	High	Low	High	Low
High						
1(4). 1% Commission: Accept without informing	(1)	0%	(1)	0%	(1)	0%
6. Package Deal	(2)	(1)	(2)	(1)	(1)	(2)
9(1). Client Kickback: Money	0	(1)	0	(1)	0	(1)
8. Police Payoff	3	16	5	15	8	13
2. Oral Contract	8	14	5	18	8	16
12. Divorce Fraud	5	12	2	15	4	16
4. Stock Purchase	0	(1)	(1)	0	(1)	0
Middle						
5(4). Client Payoff: "Don't tell me"	5	5	5	5	6	3
5(1). Client Payoff: "Risky, but your business"	(1)	0	0	(1)	(1)	0
3. Receiver Sale	10	23	9	26	14	23
1(1). 1% Commission: Take into consideration	8	5	2	10	8	3
Low						
7. Assault Charge	20	51	14	62	33	42
9(3). Client Kickback: Legal advice	8	26	7	28	14	23
11. Conflict of Interest	30	44	21	56	33	45
9(2). Client Kickback: Gift, dinner	15	19	7	29	15	19
13. Referral Fee	48	63	34	80	52	61
10. Christmas Cards	13	16	9	21	12	19
Cases	(40)	(43)	(44)	(39)	(52)	(31)

TABLE B.46—Per Cent of Lawyers Who Violate Ethical Norms by Years in Practice, Status, and Income

Ethical situation	Admitted to practice		Professional status		Income from practice	
	-1950	1950+	El.-High	Mid.-Low	-$15,000	$15,000+
High						
1(4). 1% Commission: Accept without informing	(1)	0	0	(1)	(1)	0
6. Package Deal	0	(3)	(2)	(1)	0	(3)
9(1). Client Kickback: Money	0	(1)	0	(1)	(1)	0
8. Police Payoff	12	6	12	7	4	11
2. Oral Contract	2	25	3	17	21	7
12. Divorce Fraud	2	19	3	12	11	7
4. Stock Purchase	(1)	0	0	(1)	0	(1)
Middle						
5(4). Client Payoff: "Don't tell me"	4	6	(1)	7	11	2
5(1). Client Payoff: "Risky, but your business"	0	(1)	0	(1)	(1)	0
3. Receiver Sale	16	19	15	10	25	13
1(1). 1% Commission: Take into consideration	10	0	6	5	4	9
Low						
7. Assault Charge	31	44	27	31	36	38
9(3). Client Kickback: Legal advice	14	22	12	19	18	18
11. Conflict of Interest	31	47	27	48	43	40
9(2). Client Kickback: Gift, dinner	14	22	15	19	18	16
13. Referral Fee	53	59	36	69	71	53
10. Christmas Cards	12	19	9	19	25	7
Cases	(51)	(32)	(33)	(42)	(28)	(45)

APPENDIX B

TABLE B.47—Per Cent of Lawyers Who Violate Ethical Situation by Situational Pressures

Ethical situation	Opportunities		Wealth of ind. cl.		Wealth of bus. cl.		Stability of clients	
	High	Low	Rich	Poor	Rich	Poor	Stable	Unstable
High								
1(4). 1% Commission: Accept without informing	0%	(1)	0%	(1)	0%	(1)	0%	(1)
6. Package Deal	(2)	(1)	(2)	(1)	(2)	(1)	(2)	(1)
9(1). Client Kickback: Money	(1)	0	0	(1)	(1)	0	0	(1)
8. Police Payoff	12	7	9	10	19	3	14	5
2. Oral Contract	10	12	3	18	16	5	9	8
12. Divorce Fraud	12	2	11	5	7	8	2	13
4. Stock Purchase	(1)	0	0	(1)	0	(1)	0	(1)
Middle								
5(4). Client Payoff: "Don't tell me"	2	7	3	8	7	5	2	8
5(1). Client Payoff: "Risky, but your business"	(1)	0	0	(1)	0	(1)	0	(1)
3. Receiver Sale	22	12	23	13	16	22	19	15
1(1). 1% Commission: Take into consideration	7	5	9	5	3	5	7	5
Low								
7. Assault Charge	51	21	40	33	42	27	40	33
9(3). Client Kickback: Legal advice	27	7	11	21	16	16	12	23
11. Conflict of Interest	46	29	40	39	39	35	28	44
9(2). Client Kickback: Gift, dinner	17	17	9	23	19	14	16	18
13. Referral Fee	61	48	51	59	45	57	51	60
10. Christmas Cards	7	21	11	18	10	19	14	15
Cases	(41)	(42)	(35)	(39)	(31)	(37)	(43)	(40)

SUPPLEMENTARY TABLES

TABLE B.48—Per Cent of Lawyers Who Reject Ethical Norms by Attitudes, Behavior, and Concern

Ethical situation	Attitudes		Ethical behavior		Ethical concern	
	Strict	Permissive	High	Low	High	Low
High						
1(4). 1% Commission: Accept without informing	(1)	(1)	(1)	(1)	(2)	0
6. Package Deal	3	9	7	5	6	7
9(1). Client Kickback: Money	3	9	7	5	8	3
8. Police Payoff	0	16	7	10	10	6
2. Oral Contract	5	13	2	14	6	13
12. Divorce Fraud	5	14	7	13	8	13
4. Stock Purchase	5	16	9	13	8	16
Middle						
5(4). Client Payoff: "Don't tell me"	13	28	18	21	25	13
5(1). Client Payoff: "Risky, but your business"	10	37	23	26	19	32
3. Receiver Sale	18	42	27	33	25	39
1(1). 1% Commission: Take into consideration	33	49	32	41	37	36
Low						
7. Assault Charge	20	61	27	56	39	45
9(3). Client Kickback: Legal advice	20	61	27	56	40	42
11. Conflict of Interest	40	61	36	67	50	52
9(2). Client Kickback: Gift, dinner	30	70	41	62	46	58
13. Referral Fee	68	79	64	85	75	71
10. Christmas Cards	55	74	64	67	56	81
Cases	(40)	(43)	(44)	(39)	(52)	(31)

TABLE B.49—Per Cent of Lawyers Who Reject Ethical Norms
by Years in Practice, Status, and Income

Ethical situation	Admitted to practice		Professional status		Income from practice	
	-1950	1950+	El.-High	Mid.-Low	-$15,000	$15,000+
High						
1(4). 1% Commission: Accept without informing	(1)	(1)	0	(2)	(1)	(1)
6. Package Deal	4	9	6	(1)	7	7
9(1). Client Kickback: Money	8	3	(1)	(2)	4	2
8. Police Payoff	8	9	9	7	7	7
2. Oral Contract	4	16	6	10	14	7
12. Divorce Fraud	6	16	6	10	14	7
4. Stock Purchase	8	16	6	10	11	7
Middle						
5(4). Client Payoff: "Don't tell me"	18	25	12	24	21	16
5(1). Client Payoff: "Risky, but your business"	20	31	18	29	32	22
3. Receiver Sale	28	34	39	21	36	29
1(1). 1% Commission: Take into consideration	43	25	27	43	36	38
Low						
7. Assault Charge	39	44	46	33	32	49
9(3). Client Kickback: Legal advice	37	47	27	50	43	39
11. Conflict of Interest	49	53	46	55	54	53
9(2). Client Kickback: Gift, dinner	41	66	46	55	57	42
13. Referral Fee	77	69	76	69	71	76
10. Christmas Cards	59	75	67	83	71	62
Cases	(51)	(32)	(33)	(42)	(28)	(48)

TABLE B.50—Per Cent of Lawyers Who Reject Ethical Norms
        by Situational Pressures

Ethical situation	Opportu-nities		Wealth of ind. cl.		Wealth of bus. cl.		Stability of clients	
	High	Low	Rich	Poor	Rich	Poor	Stable	Unstable
High								
1(4). 1% Commission: Accept without informing	(1)	(1)	0	(2)	(1)	(1)	(1)	(1)
6. Package Deal	12	0	3	5	7	3	5	8
9(1). Client Kickback: Money	5	7	9	3	3	3	9	3
8. Police Payoff	12	5	6	10	13	5	9	8
2. Oral Contract	7	10	6	13	23	0	12	10
12. Divorce Fraud	10	10	14	5	7	8	7	13
4. Stock Purchase	7	14	9	8	7	11	5	18
Middle								
5(4). Client Payoff: "Don't tell me"	15	26	14	23	13	22	19	23
5(1). Client Payoff: "Risky, but your business"	29	19	17	34	23	30	28	19
3. Receiver Sale	42	19	37	26	39	24	33	28
1(1). 1% Commission: Take into con-sideration	34	36	34	41	32	43	40	33
Low								
7. Assault Charge	56	26	43	41	45	35	47	35
9(3). Client Kickback: Legal advice	46	36	31	49	39	38	40	43
11. Conflict of Interest	56	45	57	46	45	54	42	56
9(2). Client Kickback: Gift, dinner	51	50	46	54	48	49	44	58
13. Referral Fee	83	64	71	72	71	68	72	75
10. Christmas Cards	54	76	54	77	74	57	67	63
Cases	(41)	(42)	(35)	(39)	(31)	(37)	(43)	(40)

205

THE INTERVIEW SCHEDULE

Note to the reader: Rather than reproduce the entire in-terview schedule, I have included only the changes between the schedule used in this study and the one used in Jerome E. Carlin, *Lawyers' Ethics* (New York: Russell Sage Founda-tion, 1966), pp. 215–60. For ease of reference, the Prairie City interview schedule has been renumbered to conform to the New York schedule. Page numbers in parentheses refer to Carlin. A limited number of copies of the complete Prairie City interview schedule are on file at the University of Wis-consin Law School library and will be furnished upon request.

All Respondents

(p. 215) 2. Add: "In the summer only? _____"

(p. 215) 3. [Instead of being given cards with questions, as in the Carlin study, respondents were given a copy of the com-plete interview schedule at the beginning of the interview and read along with the interviewer.]
    b. Under "Employee" change "c" to "Firm with five or more lawyers" and eliminate category "d."
       Under "Partner in firm with" change "b" to "More than five lawyers" and eliminate "c."

Individual Practitioners

(p. 216) 6. Change "Did you know any of them personally" to "Were any of them relatives?"
       Under *"If yes"* change
       "Did you know them —   very well or_____
                                       only slightly_____"
       to   "Father_____
                                        Uncle_____
                                        Brother_____
                            Other (specify)_____"

206

Change *"If no ..."* to
"If not a relative:
Did you know any of them personally?   Yes_____

                                         No_____ "

(p. 216) 8. Omit.

Partners

(p. 217) P 5. b. Eliminate: *"If no...."*
          Add: "c. Were any of the lawyers in the firm relatives at the
                    time you joined the firm?   Yes_____
                                                 No_____

              If yes, Interviewer check   Father_____
                                                Uncle_____
                                                Brother_____
                                                Other_____ "
                                              (specify)

(p. 217) P 6. Omit.

Associates

(p. 220) A 4. After *"If yes,"* substitute:
                "Were any of them relatives?   Yes_____
                                                No_____

              If yes, Interviewer check   Father_____
                                                Uncle_____
                                                Brother_____
                                                Other_____
                                              (specify)

          If not a relative:
          Did you know any of them personally?   Yes_____
                                                  No_____ "

(p. 220) A 5. Eliminate remainder of item from second *"If yes."*

Firm Interaction and Activities

Replace pp. 222–24 with the following:
"PROFESSIONAL INTERACTION AND ACTIVITIES
I want to ask you some questions about your work activities
with other lawyers.
During the past year, roughly how many times on the average
did the following occur:
a. Talking over a legal problem with another lawyer
   where there is *no sharing of fees*.   _____per
                                             week; month; year

b. Helping or being helped by another lawyer
(filing a paper, witnessing a document, etc.).

_____ per week;
month; year

c. I. Referring or turning over a case more
or less completely to another lawyer.

_____ per year

IF AT ALL:
1. What types of matters?_____
2. What was your share of the fee?_____

II. Another lawyer's referring or turning over
a case more or less completely to you.

_____ per year

IF AT ALL
1. What types of matters?_____
2 What was your share of the fee?_____

d. Collaborating or working together on a case involving
more or less continual contact, where you *share the fees.*

_____ per year

IF AT ALL:
1. What types of matters?_____
2. What fee arrangements?_____
3. What proportion of your time during the past year was
given to such collaborative efforts?_____

e. Would you please name the lawyers with whom you engaged in these activities?_____
_____
_____ "

Partners, Associates and Employees

(p. 225) 13. Change item to read: "Talked over a legal problem in a
case he was handling or you were handling where there
is *no sharing of fees.*"

(p. 226) 16. Add: "involving more or less continuous contact where
you *share the fees.*"
Eliminate: "(1) At whose initiation, usually?"
Add: "Would you please name the lawyers outside the
firm with whom you engaged in these activities.

_____
_____ "

(p. 226) 17. Change "other lawyers in the office" to "other lawyers."

(p. 226) 18. Omit.

(p. 226) 19. Change "other lawyers in the office" to "other lawyers."

(p. 226) 20. Omit.

(p. 227) 21. Change "New York City" to "Prairie City."

(p. 227) 22–24. Omit.

(p. 229) 31. Under:
>"Real Estate," substitute "mortgage closing" for
>"syndication"
>"Personal Injury," add further subdivision:
>>"a. Plaintiff
>>b. Defendant"
>
>"Matrimonial," add further subdivision:
>>"a. Divorce
>>b. Adoption
>>c. Other"
>
>["Federal (individual)" and "Income Tax" is one cate-
>gory reading "Federal (individual) Income Tax."]
>"Municipal," add further subdivision:
>>"a. Zoning; Land Use
>>b. Other"
>
>Substitute "State and Local Tax" for "Patent, Trade-
>mark, Copyright."

(p. 230) 37. In parenthetical heading above item following "trust," add "Patent, Trademark."

(p. 231) 38. a. For individual practitioners, omit category "Conferring with lawyer associates or partners."

(p. 231) 39. Add to "b" "appellate argument."

>Change "c" to: "On the average, how many times
>per month have you been in these courts during the
>past twelve months?"
>Add: "Justice of the Peace Court, Probate Court, and
>Circuit Court."
>Delete: "Magistrates' Court, Municipal and City
>Court, Special Sessions Court, Surrogates' Court,
>and Supreme Court."
>d. Omit.

(p. 232) 40. Replace with:
>"During the past twelve months approximately how
>many times per month on the average have you spent
>professional time with the following agencies or officials:
>a. On the local level: agencies or officials concerned
>with planning and zoning (e.g., the local or county
>zoning board, the Planning Commission, or the Urban
>Renewal Board)

_____ housing and building construction (e.g.,
building inspector, the city engineer, the
Board of Local Improvement)
_____ taxation and assessments (e.g., the
Board of Review, the city treasurer,
the assessor)
_____ health, education, and welfare (e.g.,
county hospitals, boards of education, health inspectors)
_____ others

b. On the state level: the Sales Tax
Commission
_____ the Corporate Tax Division
_____ the Secretary of State's Office
_____ Department of Registration and
Education (occupational licenses)
_____ Department of Financial Institutions
_____ State regulatory commissions (e.g.,
the Commerce Commission)
_____ health, education, and welfare
(public health, mental health,
colleges and universities, welfare agencies)
_____ others

c. On the federal level: the Internal Revenue
Service
_____ regulatory agencies (ICC, SEC,
FCC, etc.)
_____ Federal lending agencies (Housing
and Home Finance Agency, Federal
National Mortgage Authority)
_____ others

Insert:
"During the past twelve months have you spent any
professional time with the following officials:

	Yes	Times
State legislators		
Mayor		
City Manager		
Council members		
Others (specify)		

IF YES:
a. How many times a month on the average?
(CHECK ABOVE FOR EACH OFFICIAL)

b. For what type of business?_____

_____

_____

(PRESS FOR DETAIL)"

(p. 233) 43. Under *"Legal Form of Enterprise"* add "Cooperatives."
Change *"Net Worth of Enterprise ..."* to:
"Gross Income:

Under $50,000	_____%
$50,000 to $100,000	_____%
$100,000 to $500,000	_____%
$500,000 to $1,000,000	_____%
$1,000,000 to $5,000,000	_____%
$5,000,000 and over	_____%
	(100%) "

(p. 235) 53. Omit.

(p. 235) 54. Change to: "Does any ethnic or religious group comprise
a sizeable proportion of your clients?   Yes_____

No_____

IF YES:
What group?_____ "

(p. 235) 56. Omit.

(p. 235) 58. Insert: "Do a relatively small percentage of your
clients account for a relatively large percentage of
your business (e.g., 20% of clients account for
75% of business)?   Yes_____

No_____

IF YES:
What are the approximate percentages?

Clients_____%
Business_____%"

Associates and Employees

(p. 236) A 31. Under "Real Estate," "Personal Injury," "Matrimonial,"
and "Municipal," make the changes indicated in
question 31, above.
Substitute "State and Local Tax" for "Patent, Trademark, Copyright."

(p. 238) A 35. Make the same changes as those indicated in question 39, above.

(p. 239) A 36. Replace with the same replacement question as that
used in question 40, above.

(p. 240)   59.   Change year from "1959" to 1963."
Change income scale to:

"	Law	All
Under $2,000		
$2,000–$3,999		
$4,000–$5,999		
$6,000–$7,999		
$8,000–$10,999		
$11,000–$14,999		
$15,000–$19,999		
$20,000–$34,999		
$35,000–$49,999		
$50,000–$74,999		
$75,000 or more		"

(p. 241)   66.   a.   Change list of Bar Associations to:
"American Bar Association
Prairie State Bar Association
Prairie City Bar
Other (specify)"

(p. 242)   67.   a.   Substitute "Prairie State Bar Association and the
Prairie City Bar Association" for "the Association
of the Bar of the City of New York and the New York
County Lawyers' Association."
c.   Under "Which one?" change   "A.B.C.N.Y.
N.Y.C.L.A."
to   "P.S.B.A.
P.C.B.A."

(p. 242)   68.   b.   Under "In which bar association?" make same
change as in 67 (c) above.

(p. 243)   70.   a.   Change to:
"Do you agree with the Prairie City Bar
Association minimum fee schedules?   Yes____
No____
IF NO, why?_____
Which ones?_____ "
b.   Change "bar associations" to "Prairie State Bar
Association."

(p. 243)   71.   Omit.

(p. 243)   72.   Replace with:
"A.   In which of the following business, religious,
social, and fraternal organization are you presently
active—that is, where you attend meetings more

or less regularly? Specify the number of years
that you have been a member.

	Active	No. Yrs. a Member
Lions		
Rotary		
Kiwanis		
Jaycees		
Assn. of Commerce		
Moose		
Elks		
Eagles		
Masons		
B'nai Brith		
Knights of Columbus		
Y.M.C.A.		
Veterans of Foreign Wars		
American Legion		
Prairie Avenue Club		
Prairie City Club		
Country Club of Prairie City		
Southside Country Club		
Cresthaven Country Club		
Other (specify)		

B. Are you a member of any charitable or civic organizations, such as Community Service, Cancer Society,
American Civil Liberties Union, John Birch Society,
etc.?   Yes____
                                                            No____

IF YES:
What are the names of these organizations?

_____
_____ "

(p. 243) 73. Replace with:
"A. During the past three years have you campaigned
for or against a candidate for local public office?
                                                            Yes____
                                                            No____

IF YES:
a. For what office?_____
b. What did you do?_____

B. During the past three years have you campaigned
for or against local political issues appearing on
the ballot, including bond referendums?   Yes____
                                                            No____

IF YES:
a. For what issue? _____
b. What did you do? _____

C. Did you vote in the last local election?   Yes____
                                              No____

D. Have you ever served on any public boards or
   commissions, such as the planning commission,
   housing authority, public building committee,
   school board, etc.?   Yes____
                                              No____

IF YES:
What were the boards or committees and the dates
served?
1) _____
2) _____
3) _____
4) _____

E. Have you ever been a candidate for an elective
   office including an elective political party office
   (e.g., district committeeman, county chairman,
   etc.)?   Yes____
                                              No____

IF YES:
What were the offices, the dates of the campaigns,
and the outcome of the elections?

	Elected	Defeated
a)		
b)		
c)		
d)		

F. Do you have any interest in being a candidate for
   an elective office?   Yes____
                                              No____

IF YES:
   For what office? _____

G. Have you ever served in local politics in a non-
   elective capacity, such as a member or officer of
   a political club or party or a citizens' group, etc.?
                                              Yes____
                                              No____

IF YES:
In what capacity and what were the dates?
a) _____
b) _____
c) _____
d) _____

H. Have you ever served a governmental body (e.g.,
the county or a district) in a professional capacity,
such as Public Defender, attorney for a fire district
or a school board, and so on?　　　　Yes____
　　　　　　　　　　　　　　　　　　　No____

IF YES:
In what capacity and what were the dates?
a)_____
b)_____
c)_____"
d)_____

(p. 243) 74. Replace with:
"A. Did you favor the change in government in Prairie
City to the city manager form of government?
　　　　　　　　　　　　　　　　　Yes____
　　　　　　　　　　　　　　　　　No____
　　　　　　　　　　　　　No opinion____

IF YES OR NO:
Why?_____
_____

B. Do you now favor the city manager form of govern-
ment in Prairie City?　　　　　　　Yes____
　　　　　　　　　　　　　　　　　No____
　　　　　　　　　　　　　No opinion____

IF YES OR NO:
Why?_____
_____

C. Did you favor the adoption of the new Code of
Criminal Procedure?
　　　　　　　　　　　　　　　　　Yes____
　　　　　　　　　　　　　　　　　No____
　　　　Insufficient time to study the question____
IF YES OR NO:
Why?_____
_____

D. Did you favor the recent bill that all associate
judges of the Circuit Court are to be nominated by
political convention rather than in the county pri-
maries?　　　　　　　　　　　　　Yes____
　　　　　　　　　　　　　　　　　No____
　　　　Insufficient time to study the question____
IF YES OR NO:
Why?_____"
_____

(p. 244) 75. Same except no "other" category.

215

APPENDIX C

(p. 245) 78. Omit.

(p. 245) 82. Add: "e. How he is treated before government officials."

(p. 245) 83. Omit "b. . . ."

(p. 246) 88. Insert:
"A. Why did you decide to practice law in Prairie City?
_____

B. Would you still come to Prairie City if you had to
do it all over again?   Definitely Yes____
(INTERVIEWER CHECK)   Qualified Yes____
(NOTE ALL QUALIFICATIONS   No____
OR COMMENTS)
IF NO OR QUALIFIED YES:
Why?_____
_____"

(p. 247) 89. Change "b" to: "Laws preventing racial discrimination
in employment should be extended and strictly enforced."
Change "d" to: "The bar should take a publicly active
role in supporting civil rights legislation."
Omit "f. . . ."
Under "g" change "New York State" to "Prairie State."
Under "i" eliminate "criminal."

(p. 248) 90. Omit.

(p. 248) 91. Substitute "loan" for "title insurance policy," "lender"
for "title company," "commission of 1% of loan" for
"15% commission on the price charged for client for
services rendered."
Add:
"e. If Lawyer A did any of the acts which you disapprove
of, which of the following would you do? If more
than one, which would you consider the most appropriate? (CHECK BELOW)
1. Nothing
2. Comment to another lawyer about what A had done
3. Warn another lawyer who is about to deal with A
4. Avoid referring matters to A
5. Avoid having lunch or other social engagements
with A
6. Say something to A directly
7. Report A to the Bar Association

216

Items Dis-approved	Nothing	Comment	Warn	Avoid Referring	Avoid Social	Say Direct	Report
1							
2							
3							
4							"

(p. 249) 92. Add:
"d. If you disapprove, which of the following would you do? If more than one, which would you consider the most appropriate?
(Rank each action 1, 2, 3, etc.)
1. Nothing_____
2. Comment to another lawyer about what A had done_____
3. Warn another lawyer who is about to deal with A_____
4. Avoid referring matters to A_____
5. Avoid having lunch or other social engagements with A_____
6. Say something to A directly_____
7. Report A to the Bar Association_____"

(p. 249) 93. Substitute "group of promoters" for "syndicate" throughout the statement of the hypothetical situation.
Add "d"; same as "d" of 92 above.

(p. 250) 94. Add "d"; same as "d" of 92 above.

(p. 250) 95. Add "e"; same as "e" of 91 above.

(p. 251) 96. Add "d"; same as "d" of 92 above.

(p. 251) 97. Add "d"; same as "d" of 92 above.

(p. 251) 98. Add "d"; same as "d" of 92 above.

(p. 252) 99. Add "e"; same as "e" of 91 above.

(p. 253) 101. Add "d"; same as "d" of 92 above.

(p. 253) 102. Substitute "physical cruelty" for "adultery."
Add "d"; same as "d" of 92 above.

(p. 254) 103. Add "d"; same as "d" of 92 above.

(p. 254) 104. Replace the entire item with the following:
"Have you ever reported a lawyer to the bar association for unethical conduct?   Yes____
                                                                                    No____

APPENDIX C

IF YES:
a. To the Prairie City Bar Association or
   the P.S.B.A.?

                                        Prairie City____
                                        Prairie State____
b. For what type of matter?_____

_____
_____ "

(p. 256) 108. Substitute "Prairie City" for "New York City."

(p. 257) 119. a. Substitute for *"Harvard, Yale, or Columbia"*:
              "Prairie State,..., or ...."
           c. After "Did you make Law Review? Yes___No___"
              add: "No Law Review at time_____"

INDEX

Opportunities to violate: definition, 87–88; and behavior, 106, 108, 117, 118, 121, 122, 127; and stability of clients, 119; and ethical concern, 126, 129

Opportunity measure, 88. *See also* Opportunities to violate

Opportunity rates. *See* Opportunities to violate

Oral Contract (hypothetical situation), 95, 97, 101, 107, 111, 113, 135, 140, 141

Organization of lawyers, 5. *See also* American Bar Association; Bar association; Local bar association; State bar association

Package Deal (hypothetical situation), 93, 96, 100, 105, 111

Paper norms, 111, 114, 115

Parsons, Talcott, 73

Partnerships, 24, 25, 26, 35, 128, 147, 148, 149, 150; definition and organization, 58–64

Personal injury, 4, 5, 40, 41, 42, 43, 45, 51, 55

Personality characteristics and ethical behavior, 137

Planning and zoning, 17

Planning Commission, 21

Police Payoff (hypothetical situation), 94, 99, 101, 107, 111, 140, 141, 142, 144

Police pension fund, 21

Political activities, 47, 49–52, 53, 162–63n8. *See also* Elite group lawyers; High group lawyers; Low group lawyers; Middle group lawyers

Pound, Roscoe, 74

Practice characteristics: and behavior, 116–22, 129, 137; and ethical concern, 126–27, 129

Prairie City: location, 6; economic development, 7–8; population and social characteristics, 8–9; religious composition, 8, 161n21; political behavior, 9–10; sources of wealth, 10; size and distribution of firms, 13; library board, 21; party politics, 161n21; median income, 161n21; ethnic composition, 160n14; em-

ployment, 161n21; manufacturing, 161n21; population, 161n21; religion, 161n21; tax receipts, 162n4; Negro employment in, 164n6

Private practitioners. *See* Individual practitioners

Probate Court, 16, 43, 124

Professional associations. *See* American Bar Association; Bar association; Local bar association; State bar association

Professional attitudes, 28, 31–32, 52–54

Professional community, 64–66, 151

Professional contact, 64

Professional ethics. *See* Ethical behavior

Professional income. *See* Income of Prairie City lawyers

Professional problems, 5

Professional values, 3

P.T.A., 50

Public boards, 21, 50

Real estate transactions, 4, 37, 40, 41

Receiver Sale (hypothetical situation), 92, 96, 104, 105, 107, 139, 141, 142

Red Cross, 20, 47, 48

Referral business, 120

Referral Fee (hypothetical situation), 95, 97, 98, 107, 137, 138

Religious affiliation, 49; relation to success in practice, 45, 67; and firm membership, 57

Rent control authority, 21

Republicans, 9, 20, 49, 50, 58

Retainer clients, 37, 120, 121, 168nn5–7

Role of lawyers, 5; in Prairie City, 153–54

Rule of law, 73

Rule structure of the bar. *See* Ethical hypotheticals

Salaried lawyers, 6, 159n6

Sanctions against lawyers, 80, 82–83, 85–86, 90–91, 144, 165n15; in hypothetical situations, 97–103 *passim*, 136, 138, 140, 141

School board, 21, 50

Secretary of State, 17, 124

Selection of judges, 19, 51, 53

Service clubs, 19